DONNA L. LATTA
334-3166

12,13

PRENTICE-HALL SERIES IN SPEECH COMMUNICATION

Larry L. Barker and Robert J. Kibler,
Consulting Editors

Barbara S. Wood

*University of Illinois
at Chicago Circle*

CHILDREN AND COMMUNICATION: VERBAL AND NONVERBAL LANGUAGE DEVELOPMENT

PRENTICE-HALL, INC., ENGLEWOOD CLIFFS, N. J.

Library of Congress Cataloging in Publication Data

WOOD, BARBARA S (date)
  Children and communication.

  (Prentice-Hall series in speech communication)
  Includes bibliographies and index.
  1. Children—Language. 2. Oral communication.
3. Nonverbal communication. I. Title.
P 118.W6   401'.9   75-22452
ISBN 0-13-131896-9

Printed in the United States of America

10 9 8 7 6 5 4 3

Prentice-Hall International, Inc., *London*
Prentice-Hall of Australia, Pty. Ltd., *Sydney*
Prentice-Hall of Canada, Ltd., *Toronto*
Prentice-Hall of India Private Limited, *New Delhi*
Prentice-Hall of Japan, Inc., *Tokyo*
Prentice-Hall of Southeast Asia (Pte.) Ltd., *Singapore*

TO DOUG

contents

CHAPTER 3

communication development:
interpersonal forces *40*

part II

THE CHILD'S COMMUNICATION SYSTEM:
VERBAL DEVELOPMENT *59*

CHAPTER 4

children's language: methods of discovery *63*

CHAPTER 5

the sounds in children's communication *76*

part III

THE CHILD'S COMMUNICATION SYSTEM:
NONVERBAL DEVELOPMENT *175*

CHAPTER 15

participation in communication situations   *301*

APPENDIX

the communication guide   *313*

INDEX   317

preface

Children and Communication: Verbal and Nonverbal Language Development is about children as communicators. While children are acquiring their language, verbal and nonverbal, they are also learning to use that language appropriately in communication situations. This text takes a comprehensive look at children learning to communicate with words, sentences, body language, the voice, and touch (space). To communicate effectively in everyday situations, children must learn to apply their language appropriately—that is, they must select the most appropriate communication strategies.

To understand children as communicators, it is imperative that we know what forces affect their development. We discuss these forces in Part I. Since verbal language plays an important role in communication, Part II examines children's development of words, sentences, and meanings. Most texts stop at this point, but this text explores children's development of nonverbal communication, as well. How children communicate with their bodies, their voices, and "in space" constitutes the subject matter of Part III. Finally, children learn to apply their verbal and nonverbal language to important communication situations. In Part IV we present a model of communication instructions, accompanied by activities, materials, and ideas for classroom use. The aim of communication instruction is this: to increase the repertoire of communication strategies that can be used by children in dealing with critical communication situations.

Because this text assumes no prior knowledge of language study, child development, or communication, its possibilities for application are many. The text is written primarily for those planning to teach children and those who do teach children. Because the book is written with examples and illustrations in a style that is easy to read, anyone with an interest in children's communication can obtain information about aspects of communication development. Parents may find many of the chapters helpful in understanding their children's communication. Undergraduate students in speech, speech pathology, communication, and education will benefit from the comprehensive coverage given to communication and its emergence in children. In fact, anyone concerned about how children learn to communicate (and that includes most of us) will find some important ideas to think about.

Because the subject of children's language development so interests me, I have thoroughly enjoyed the four years I have spent in writing this book. It would not have been possible without the assistance and encouragement given to me by Fred Williams. He convinced me to write about the "big picture." Others helped me with their comments and suggestions on earlier drafts: Mark Knapp, Dorothy Higginbotham, Judy Curry, Robert Kibler, and Larry Barker. My consulting author in Chapter 12, Royce Rodnick Gardner, provided many ideas for Part IV. Credit must also be given to my typist, Curtis Wingert, who encouraged me by saying he enjoyed every page. Dangvole R. Stoncius created many of the illustrations that capture children who are busily communicating. And, finally, a special thanks to my husband, Doug, whose understanding made the whole thing possible.

Barbara Wood

part

I

UNDERSTANDING
THE CHILD
AS A COMMUNICATOR

When we communicate, we share experiences, events, ideas, and feelings with others through verbal and nonverbal channels. We praise a child's drawing by saying, "You did a fine job; your picture of the sun and the apple tree is beautiful." We use words and patterns of words to communicate praise. Our verbal message helps us to share our positive feelings with the child. We also use nonverbal cues to convey our feelings. We move very close to the child to show how much we mean what we say. Our face shows a smile that seems to say, "I like your picture and I like you." And our voice tells the child, "I'm not surprised you have done so well." Because communication involves the sharing of messages through several channels, the study of communication development must include an examination of these channels. Verbal channels include sounds, words, and sentence patterns; nonverbal channels include body motion, the voice, and touch (space).

Children are communicators who must learn to send and understand verbal and nonverbal messages. In this text, we discuss

1

children's development of verbal and nonverbal language in Part II and Part III, respectively. In Part IV we examine how children learn to apply their knowledge of language to important everyday *situations.* In this context, language is viewed as a tool to be used in social relationships. Tools are most effective when they are used appropriately. Children learn rules for *language use* just as they learn the rules of their language, per se. Thus, Part IV of the text examines children's application of their verbal and nonverbal language in critical communication situations. Consequently, our view of children's communication is broad, comprehensive, and functional.

Before we discuss children's communication on the verbal, nonverbal, and situational levels we must consider the bases of communication development. In Part I we examine the role of communication in children's overall development (Chapter 1) and the forces that affect communication development:

1. Intrapersonal forces: factors within the child (Chapter 2).

2. Interpersonal forces: models and children's interaction with these models (Chapter 3).

"HELP ME UNDERSTAND"

Children's communication must be viewed as an integral part of their total development as human beings. As they learn to communicate with words and patterns of words and with their voices and their bodies, they also learn about the world they live in. Children have a wish: they want to understand their world, themselves, and others. They struggle to discover a system of beliefs about reality, self, and others. Their most important tool for discovering beliefs is communication.

To function effectively in their families, their peer groups, and their classroom, children must become aware of the power and assistance that communication offers them. To explain an idea, to ask for help, or to disagree with someone, children must have a repertoire of communication options or strategies for that situation. The instructional aim of this text is to facilitate the selection of appropriate verbal and nonverbal strategies in critical communication situations. In this context, communication allows children to function effectively in their families, their social groups, and their cultures.

FORCES AFFECTING
COMMUNICATION DEVELOPMENT

What forces affect children's communication development? The three-part model below will help us visualize the learning process.

1. *Input (Interpersonal forces):* Children receive "communication data" from important communication models. These models provide children with examples of verbal and nonverbal language they must acquire. Through *interaction* with communication models, children are able to develop meaningful communication.
2. *Children's equipment (Intrapersonal forces):* Children contribute something to their own development of communication. Through the maturation of their brain, body, and vocal apparatus the course of early communication development is affected. Further, children's self-initiated discovery and practice assist them in mastering their language.
3. *Output:* Children's communication is a result of intrapersonal and interpersonal forces. They communicate in a fashion representative of their level of maturation and their communication environment.

CHAPTER

1

"help me understand"

"Children want, more than they want anything else, and even after many years of miseducation, to make sense of the world, themselves, and other human beings."[1] In a matter of years young children must make decisions for themselves, based on their ability to make sense of themselves, others, and the world they live in. It seems unreasonable and unfair to wait until children are eighteen years old and on their own to begin instruction on how they should function in critical situations. Throughout their early years, children must be helped in their struggle to make sense and make decisions. The ability to communicate effectively is at the heart of the process. Without the ability to communicate in a variety of situations that are critical to them, children will find the task of making sense an impossible one. To function in their family, their social groups, their classroom, and their community, children need a kind of *communication power*—the ability to perform effectively in communication encounters.

[1] From the book, *The Underachieving School* by John Holt. Copyright © 1969 by Pitman Publishing Corp. Reprinted by permission of Pitman Publishing Corp.

As parents and teachers of children, we must help children build a repertoire of communication strategies with which they can deal with the critical situations they will encounter. We must help them in their struggle to make sense of themselves, the world they live in, and the persons that are important in their lives. Effective communication is the key to making sense; children must be aware of the options available to them in each situation they encounter.

Parents and teachers have little doubt that children can be effective communicators. Although children's communication may not be adultlike in terms of pronunciation and sentence structure, the effects of their messages are visible. Consider the powerful effect children have on their mother's purchasing of breakfast cereals. An advertiser sells breakfast cereals to six-year-olds who, in turn, convince Mommy to buy Tony the Tiger's Sugar Frosted Flakes or Count Chocula cereal for breakfast the next morning. The television message is simply the necessary stimulus for their sales job. In the case of Count Chocula cereal, a little boy's message may show his excitement about monsters and Dracula-like characters. To sell the cereal to his mother, who is genuinely concerned that he eat breakfast anyway, is not too difficult for the child to accomplish: his repeated suggestions will probably do the trick. The child may also decide to build his sales case on other arguments. The prize in the cereal box, the chocolate flavor of the cereal, or any other bonus item helps to sell the child and, in turn, may help the child sell his mother. The child's success may depend on his ability to use a number of communication strategies, such as repetition, statement of advantages, or even a threat ("I won't eat any other cereal!"). Of course, his mother's readiness to listen has some bearing on the outcome.

The sales job of an infant can also be effective, although it will not be as sophisticated as that of the six-year-old child. Picture a five-month-old girl strapped in her highchair. It's time for her baby food dinner. The menu for the evening sounds exotic: strained beef liver, creamed spinach, and strained beets. Is it any wonder the child wrinkles her nose, turns her head, and grunts every time the spoon approaches her mouth? The child's message is abundantly clear to the mother. (It might interest you to know that spinach, liver, and beets are among Gerber Baby Food's least-popular products.) Apparently, children are capable of influencing their mothers' purchasing of food almost from birth! (Or, maybe the infant is so perceptive that she can read her mother's taste buds.)

The communication strategies employed by our breakfast cereal salesman were more complex and varied than those used by the dining infant. Yet in both cases it could be argued that the child succeeded in accomplishing the desired communication goal. The two instances differ in the number of communication strategies available to the child. Few options are available to a five-month-old infant, but a six-year-old seems to be a never-ending source of reasons and arguments. As adults, we know that our success in communication, particularly when we are selling an idea or product to someone, depends on our ability to choose just the right approach. A wise selection among alternate strategies is essential for continuing success in communication.

Young children are in the process of learning *communication strategies:* verbal and nonverbal language choices appropriate for various communication situations. The instructional goal of this text (which is discussed at length in Part IV) is to build a repertoire of communication strategies for children so that they can function effectively in a variety of communication situations. To reach this goal, we have to understand the nature of children's communication and the course of its development. We have to know the factors affecting communication development (discussed in Part I), the course of verbal language development (Part II), and the process of nonverbal language development (Part III). We need a total view of the child as a communicator. For this reason we must explore every channel of communication available to the child: words, sentences, body movement, the voice, and touch.

On the surface, understanding children's communication seems to be a relatively simple task. Yet researchers become perplexed as they attempt to unscramble the messages of children. The infant's cries, the toddler's first words, and the child's body language present a number of problems to those who study the development of communication in children. Typically, children learn their verbal and nonverbal language without much effort and in a short period of time. To the child, the acquisition process is not a mysterious and complex phenomenon—it just happens. To the language development researcher, on the other hand, the developmental process is both mysterious and complex. There are many aspects of the child's communication development that we simply don't understand.

Probably the most productive period of research in communication development has been the past decade or two. Scientific advances in the study of human behavior have resulted in powerful theories of linguistics, psycholinguistics, and medicine that help to explain the child's acquisition of communication skills. The most perplexing task of these scientists has been not to describe the child's development of skills, but to explain *why* communication learning takes the course it does. Part I offers such an explanation by answering three questions:

1. Why is communication so important to the child's overall development? (discussed in the present chapter)
2. What intrapersonal forces (biological factors) help explain the child's development of communication? (Chapter 2)
3. What interpersonal forces (environmental factors) help explain the child's development of communication? (Chapter 3)

WHY DO CHILDREN COMMUNICATE?

Children communicate in order to build a set of beliefs about their world, themselves, and others. The child's plea, "Help me understand!" explains why children rely on communication as they develop.

making sense of the world

Children want to know how airplanes stay up in the sky, why leaves fall from trees, and why Daddy goes to work. Parents are quite familiar with the abundance of "how" and "why" questions posed by young children. From the point of view of children, their *questions* constitute an attempt to make sense of the world around them. The following parent-child conversation reflects a boy's concern with understanding the world around him.

Child: Daddy, why is that airplane flying in the sky?
Father: Because it's taking people from one place to another. It's carrying passengers.
Child: But why does it go in the sky?
Father: All airplanes go in the sky; they have jet engines to fly very fast.
Child: Why do they have jet engines?
Father: Because they are the fastest engines for making the airplane go.
Child: Dad—why are they the fastest?

The conversation could go on and on because each answer the father gives his child creates for the child a new question about the reality he is trying to understand.

Children also learn about their world through their *sensory experiences*. A young girl may spend ten long minutes watching a leaf carried down a sidewalk by a gentle breeze. She studies the movement of the leaf with her eyes. She may try to catch it with her hands so that she can examine it through touch. But just as she gets close enough to touch the leaf, it may blow away. Now, the child is more curious than ever. Touching, licking, and poking are important means of exploring the world and answering questions about it, especially for young children. When the child's senses do not provide the answer, or when the answer seems a bit odd to the child, she may ask for help. Communication takes over in her quest for information. If she is able to formulate just the right question, she may receive an adequate answer about why her world operates as it does. Rarely do adults have to teach the child *how* to use her senses in exploring the world; rather they must provide the opportunity or the time for the child to engage in such explorations.

Asking questions about the world is different from explaining it: it's not as easy, for well-framed questions do not come naturally to children. The child's basic tool in making sense of his world is his ability to ask all kinds of important questions about reality. Too often, in the home the child's questions are viewed as a nuisance and are answered inadequately. Questions such as "Can't it go like this?" and "How come it works like this?" tend to elicit answers that are short and sweet but say very little. In the school little time is spent on how to ask good questions, but plenty of time is devoted to the proper punctuation and grammatical structure of questions. The child's plea to understand the world is aided little by these kinds of responses. What helps is information about the role of questions in understanding what's around us: when questions can be used, how questions can be posed, and why questions are important in discovery. A functional approach to communication instruction, such as that adopted in Part IV of this text, allows questioning to become a critical communication situation for classroom study. From a functional standpoint, then, communication becomes doubly important: it is the *means* of instruction for dealing with communication situations, as well as the *end* of instruction.

With the help of sensory experience and an ability to question appropriately, the child is able to formulate a set of beliefs about his world. A young boy knows that "it hurts" his sister when he pulls her hair. He also knows that he is a boy and, consequently, is different from his sister in several ways. He may even know that putting a box on his head will not make him invisible (if he's old enough!). These are examples of *primitive beliefs* about physical reality, social reality, and the nature of self. The child acquires such beliefs from direct sensory experience, but also from his interaction with others (typically, older children or adults) who are in a "better position" to know about reality. Primitive beliefs represent reality for the child and help him to make sense of his world.

Our primitive beliefs about reality form the core of our belief system. A visual representation of the human belief system might be

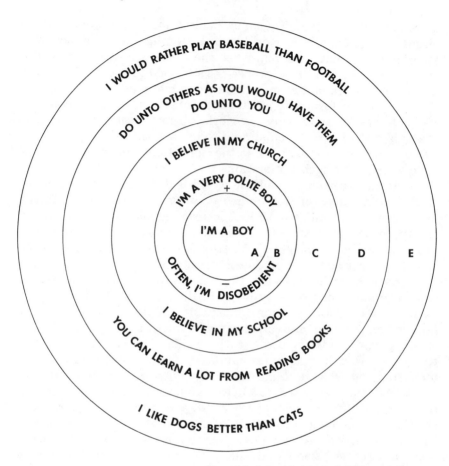

Type A beliefs: primitive beliefs about reality
Type B (+–) beliefs: primitive beliefs about "self"
Type C beliefs: authority beliefs
Type D beliefs: beliefs based on authority
Type E beliefs: inconsequential beliefs

Figure 1.1. *Model of the human belief system. Adapted from Milton Rokeach, "Images of the Consumer's Changing Mind on and Off Madison Avenue," paper delivered at the Eastern Conference of the American Advertising Agencies, November 6, 1963.*

helpful at this point. Figure 1.1, a model constructed by Milton Rokeach,[2] organizes our beliefs into five categories. The model

---

[2] Milton Rokeach, "Images of the Consumer's Changing Mind on and Off Madison Avenue," paper delivered at the Eastern Conference of the American Advertising Agencies (November 6, 1963); a shorter version of this article is contained in *Etc.: A Review of General Semantics*, XXI (September, 1964), 267-73.

visualizes what children must learn as they develop into social beings. The smallest circle in the model—the center of our belief system— contains information on what we know about the world around us. Rokeach calls these primitive beliefs about our world *Type A* beliefs. They are not debatable because we can "see for ourselves" or because they rely on scientific fact. Type A beliefs tell us how airplanes stay up in the sky, why leaves fall from trees, and why Daddy goes to work.

In summary, when children are trying to make sense of the world around them, they are trying to formulate the center of their belief system. They ask adults questions because they want to know what things look like, what makes them "tick," and why things work the way they do. To understand children's communication, parents and teachers must understand *why* children talk. One important reason is their wish to discover their world.

making sense of oneself

Getting to know ourselves is quite different from understanding the world around us. Children who want to understand more about themselves are developing their self-beliefs:

"I am a good girl, most of the time."

"I am a smart girl because I can count to one-hundred."

"I am a pretty girl when I get all dressed up."

Beliefs about self, the *Type B* beliefs in the Rokeach model, are basic to each of us. Their content is derived from our interactions with others. When others let us know what they think of us, through their actions and their words, the content of our self-beliefs is affected. Type B beliefs are slightly more flexible than Type A beliefs because others can disagree with us about their content. Although you may believe you're not very attractive, your friends may think you're quite attractive.

Our beliefs about ourselves can be positive or negative. Essentially, Type B beliefs are our value judgments about ourselves. Studies have shown that adults' Type B beliefs are highly resistant to change. This conclusion cannot be applied to children, however. Throughout their early years, children are in the process of discovering the content of their Type B beliefs. They do this by learning more and more about themselves, based on what others say to them and how others react to them. In this sense, children's self-beliefs "emerge" in their early years. And in contrast with adults' Type B beliefs, those of children are easily affected by the opinions others have of them.

In that Type B beliefs represent value judgments about ourselves, they are based on a *language of morality*. Words such as "good," "bad," "fair," and "just" are key ingredients in self-beliefs. What morality words mean to children constitutes part of their struggle to get to know themselves. For example, a young boy may insist that he has been good because he remembers having done his chores for the day: he did his chores; therefore, he was a good boy. However, his mother might have a different opinion of the matter. She remembers that he was caught cheating in a game at school, that he hit a friend of his, and that he said "I hate you" to her. His excuses—"I didn't like the rules," "My friend took my bike," and "You scolded me, Mommy"—do not alter the mother's judgment.

In this example, the child and his mother have different meanings of "goodness." To the mother, the chores her child performed were a matter of duty, not goodness. She may not realize, however, that the only concept young children have of morality is one of duty. As children grow older, the morality of duty is replaced by the morality of goodness. Often, the differences of opinion adults and children have regarding the child's self-beliefs are based on the different constructs of morality under which they operate.

Children want to understand themselves. They want to know what is right, good, and helpful about their behavior. They also want to know what is wrong, bad, and unhelpful in what they do and say. The tool they use in finding out about themselves is communication. Through their communication with others important to them, children acquire beliefs about themselves. If others communicate to children that they are clumsy, they will probably believe they are clumsy. We hear so much about the importance of a child's self-concept in education courses and textbooks. Experts in education say that a child needs a positive self-concept to get along with others and to learn. Communication is the child's key to the development of a healthy set of self-beliefs.

Children must be given opportunities to communicate their feelings about their own behavior and about others' reactions to that behavior. Children must be allowed to talk about themselves, to ask questions, and to discuss the *morality* of their behavior—as they see it and as others see it. In short, the second reason why children communicate is to make sense of themselves.

making sense of others

Children depend on others in building the remainder of their belief system: beliefs about authorities, beliefs based on authorities, and other, more inconsequential beliefs. *Types C, D,* and *E* beliefs (see the examples in Figure 1.1) are products of children's interaction with important persons in their environment. Children communicate with others in an attempt to formulate which authorities (e.g., institutions, traditions) regulate religion, social behavior, and politics (Type C beliefs); to understand beliefs derived from important authorities (Type D beliefs); and to find preference beliefs (*inconsequential beliefs*) that explain why they like some activities, persons, or things better than others (Type E beliefs). Persons important in the lives of children assist them in discovering a belief system that directs their future behavior in many important ways.

From the child's standpoint, the discovery of others is often a baffling process. Think for a moment how three-year-olds look at adults. First, young children are constantly looking up. Our voices come down from the tops of legs. In the excitement of play with other children they forget about the "big people" and concentrate on the world close to the floor, which is filled with similarly sized friends. Suddenly, out of nowhere may come a pair of adult legs that obstruct their way, and the result is a collision. Our legs got right in their way. It isn't until children are made to stop, look up, and acknowledge the obstruction as a person that they do so. Children see the intrusion as an invasion of their own activities ("Adults are always in the way"), whereas adults may insist that children apologize for "bumping into them" or invading their territory. Young children live in a "three-foot-tall world" and find it difficult to understand the territorial boundaries adults set for themselves. Apologize for that crashing encounter? Definitely not! You were in my way.[3]

Consider a little girl who cries impatiently, asking to be picked up. She might be saying, "Help me—take me into your world, Mommy." Either her world just wasn't right or she needed the assurance and security of the adult world. The wise adult knows that it is sound advice with young children to squat down to their level—to come into their world—in order to show them understanding. To be an active participant in children's activities in the classroom, a teacher knows that it's best to sit in a little chair, too. But the child must also understand the feelings of adults: adults also have space requirements, or territories, that should be cherished. Just as children have their own little territories, adults have adult territories. Sometimes, adult territories are a bit too large for children to understand.

---

[3] The image of the three-foot-tall world was suggested in a paper by an undergraduate student of mine, Jennifer Carter.

Children must learn that people reveal themselves through their verbal and nonverbal communication. If children are to understand the persons around them that are very important in their lives, they must know the value of communication with these persons. Our communication with others helps us to get to know them, and in turn, to better understand ourselves. To make sense of others, children must learn that communication takes place in several channels:

1. The *words* we use give important information to others.
2. The *pattern of words* we employ contains the basis of our message.
3. Our *voice* communicates how we think, what we feel, and what we hope.
4. Our *body language* conveys important information about what we believe, how we feel, and what we know.
5. Our use of *space* in communication, through distance and touch, is an important part of our message.

Our discussion of the child's three-foot-tall world was concerned primarily with the fifth channel of communication: the use of space. Until recently, space was not even considered an important channel of communication. In fact, in planning instructional units for children in the area of communication the continuing emphasis has been on words (the first channel of communication). Children should be aware of all channels of communication if they are to function well in their interpersonal relationships.

Children should see how the channels of communication "go together" to produce a message. Only rarely does one channel operate independently—maybe in a letter, for example. In face-to-face encounters all channels of communication happen at once. A breakdown in communication can occur if a person sends messages through the various channels at the same time. Normally, all messages must be interpreted at once, and the overall message must be determined. But when channels of communication *interact*—that is, when they act together to produce something different from the sum of the messages in each separate channel—understanding is difficult, even for adults.

For example, a sarcastic message communicated to a child, even a twelve-year-old child, is nearly impossible for the child to interpret correctly. If the symbols (for instance, "You really did a fine job!") are coupled with a negative voice, a smile of sorts, and a slightly turned head, they are usually misinterpreted by children. Most adults could decode this kind of message, although they might not enjoy the message. Children do not understand sarcasm properly and react to such messages very negatively.[4] The interaction of all channels of communication to produce the "conflict message," as in joking or sarcasm, presents a difficult challenge to the child. Adults must realize that understanding complex forms of communication takes time in a person's life and that even high school students aren't well equipped to interpret complex conflict messages.

To understand others, the child must become a type of communication expert, able to employ and interpret the several channels of communication in various situations. What makes communication difficult for anyone is that communication is really the sharing of internally experienced events with others. Let's consider an example. A six-year-old girl comes home after school with a story about what happened that day. She "finally" learned how to do a headstand in gym class and she was extremely excited about the event. To share her excitement (internal feelings) with her mother, she had to translate her excitement into verbal and nonverbal language. The child's mother could not experience the original event; she could only experience her daughter's representation of that event through language. So our little six-year-old gives a complete, blow-by-blow account of the moment: "I was in gym class, practicing and practicing, when all of a sudden I did it! I think my teacher was surprised. Wow, was it something." Her eyes opened wide to show her excitement, her smile communicated her pleasure in the accomplishment and her erect posture told how proud she was. The event was clearly a "big deal" that her mother experienced through her child's verbal and nonverbal language.

Children's search to understand others requires them to communicate successfully with the important persons in their lives. To communicate successfully children must take into account the beliefs and ideas of others, as well as their own. Children learn about others by attending to messages conveyed through the verbal and nonverbal communication channels in the sharing process. Although words and patterns of words are certainly a primary means for getting a point across to someone, they are but one way to communicate. One theory suggests that no more than 30 to 35 percent of the "social meaning" of a conversation is conveyed through words.[5] The nonverbal channels thus carry the load.

---

[4] Daphne E. Bugenthal et al., "Perception of Contradictory Meanings Conveyed by Verbal and Nonverbal Channels," *Journal of Personality and Social Psychology*, XVI (1970), 647-55.

[5] Ray L. Birdwhistell, *Kinesics and Context: Essays in Body Motion Communication* (Philadelphia: University of Pennsylvania Press, 1970), p. 158.

Another theory suggests that about 93 percent of the impact of a message is derived from the facial and vocal channels, and a mere 7 percent is attached to the verbal.[6] Both of these estimates of the importance of nonverbal communication are unusually high, but they indicate that the previously neglected nonverbal channels cannot be neglected anymore.

For children to make sense of the important persons in their lives, they must be given information about the critical communication situations they encounter with others. In short, our third answer to the question of why children communicate is this: to understand others.

To summarize, this chapter has suggested that children communicate in order to formulate their belief system. Children interact with others in order to answer three very important questions: (1) What is the nature of my world? (2) How can I understand myself? and (3) How can I understand the important people in my life? Children rely on communication in answering these questions. Communication is what assists children in their struggle:

"Help me understand!"

COMMUNICATION: THE CHILD'S POWER PLAY

As a result of children's pleas to make sense of their world, themselves and other human beings, and given the appropriate assistance from adults in their community, children are on their way to becoming functioning members of their social groups. "Experienced" members of their social groups, such as parents, adult friends, and teachers, must equip children with the communication skills that they need if they are to make sense. A philosophy of elementary education that is consistent with our communication approach is the power philosophy. According to this view, we must "free" the child or "move him from a powerless position in society to one of power."[7] This "power" is not physical strength; rather, it involves an internal feeling about oneself in interaction with others. Preschool-age children have acquired some degree of interpersonal power; it would be foolish to say they have none. But many young children

---

[6] Albert Mehrabian, "Communicating Without Words," in *Communication: Concepts and Processes*, ed. Joseph DeVito (Englewood Cliffs, N. J.: Prentice-Hall, Inc., 1971), pp. 107-13.

[7] Beverly L. Hendricks, "The Move to Power: A Philosophy of Speech Education," *The Speech Teacher*, XIX (1970), 151.

feel powerless because their attempts to exert some influence in the home have been stifled. If communication power is stifled in the home, it is even more critical that it be freed in the school.

Children of all ages often find it difficult to influence the course of their lives. Their suggestions about how things could be done are given relatively little weight. On the other hand, they may feel powerless because they don't know how to ask a teacher for help or their mother for a sympathetic ear. The goal of communication instruction is to provide the opportunities and means for children to develop communication tools that will serve them in their "power move." According to the power philosophy, if children are to escape their powerless position they must understand how others think and feel, and they should be able to communicate with others in a multitude of situations. The potential that children develop in their early years must be expanded in their elementary-school years. Children's ability to communicate with others, to share thoughts and feelings with others, constitutes their power play in their struggle to make sense of their world, themselves, and others.

"During their first few years of life, children—all children— manage perhaps the most complicated bit of learning that humans do: they learn to talk, to use language."[8] In most instances children learn the rules of their language before they enter school. Their elementary education should not provide instruction in the rules of language, per se, but should provide children with instructions in the *use* of language in various situations.

To accomplish this, we must have a total view of the child's development of communication. An even more extreme view has been suggested: children's elementary-school years must equip them with "survival tools."[9] The basic function of education, according to this view, is to increase the survival prospects of children as a group. Education must help children recognize the world they live in and help them master concepts that will allow them to cope with the world and with others. An important tool in their survival kit is the ability to communicate effectively in a variety of situations.

It has been suggested that the ability to communicate is children's most effective tool in their struggle to make sense of their world, themselves, and others. To understand the theory behind any sort of human tool, whether that tool be an electric drill or a native language, one must realize that tools are ineffective unless one

[8] Charles Silberman, *Crisis in the Classroom* (New York: Random House, Inc. 1971), p. 119.

[9] Neil Postman and Charles Weingartner, *Teaching as a Subversive Activity* (New York: Dell Publishing Co., 1969), pp. 207-18.

understands thoroughly the human forces necessary to make them work. Just as an electric drill will not work properly without the human ability to operate such a machine, so will human language function inappropriately without human knowledge of what makes this tool work beneficially. The proper starting point for parents and teachers who realize their important role in the development of children's communication skills is an adequate understanding of the intrapersonal and interpersonal forces affecting this development. Chapters 2 and 3 consider these two kinds of forces.

SUMMARY

Children ask for help in understanding their world, themselves, and others. They require a repertoire of communication strategies with which they can deal with critical communication situations they will face in their lives. To make sense, children build a system of beliefs about reality, self, and others. Their communication about such beliefs is crucial to their total development.

The three basic reasons why children communicate are linked to the three types of beliefs they must build. First, children must learn to understand the nature of the world around them. They must therefore build a set of primitive beliefs about reality. Their communication with others, often in the form of questioning, helps them learn why airplanes fly, why leaves fall from trees, and why Daddy goes to work. Second, children must understand themselves and must therefore have a set of beliefs about themselves. Through their conversations with persons important to them, they discover self-beliefs that help them get to know themselves. Finally, children must understand other persons in their lives. By communicating with others and by attending to all verbal and nonverbal channels of communication, children learn to understand the feelings, beliefs, and ideas of others.

The power philosophy of education is consistent with this text's approach to children's communication. In order to "free" children and to give them a kind of communication power—that is, an ability to communicate effectively in a variety of situations—we need to provide communication instruction that focuses on important communication situations.

SUGGESTED READINGS

HENDRICKS, BEVERLY, "The Move to Power: A Philosophy of Speech Education," *The Speech Teacher*, XIX (1970), 151-60.

HOLT, JOHN, *The Underachieving School.* New York: Pitman Publishing Co., 1969.
POSTMAN, NEIL, and CHARLES WEINGARTNER, *Teaching as a Subversive Activity.* New York: Dell Publishing Co., 1969.
SILBERMAN, CHARLES, *Crisis in the Classroom.* New York: Random House, 1971.

2

communication development: intrapersonal forces

Let's consider a two-year-old girl who is extremely proud of her newly acquired ability to communicate with words. Her language is her most precious possession. That she repeats the words she knows again and again, with delight in each utterance, indicates her feeling of accomplishment. The following dialogue summarizes a five-minute "conversation" that the little girl might have with her mother:

Child: Car, Mommy? (pointing to a little red car she is holding)
Mother: Yes, that's a car.
Child: Car. (pointing to a picture of a car in a magazine)
Mother: Good, that's a fast car, isn't it?
Child: Car! (pointing to a car through their front window)
Mother: Uh-hmmm.
Child: Car. Rum-rum-rum. (crawling on the floor and pretending to be a car with a loud engine)
Mother: Right, honey.

The child's contribution to the conversation is based on one word, "car," and her messages may sound a bit monotonous to an adult.

But the conversation demonstrates the child's delight in her new word. You might think that saying the same words nearly six dozen times a day would be boring for the child; it certainly can be for those listening. But quite the opposite seems to be true: the child doesn't find her repetitions at all boring, and she communicates this in her own special way. The gleam in her eyes, her ear-to-ear smile, and the expectation communicated by her entire body indicate the pleasure she derives from her ability to say the word and say it again. Touch, body movements, and voice have signaled her needs and intentions previously. Now, words are combined with nonverbal channels to produce the total message.

That words are a special treasure to young children is beautifully illustrated by an incident related to me by a friend. Her two-year-old boy, Danny, was waking up every morning at the crack of dawn—about 6 A.M. This was too early for her. In an effort to delay Danny's waking-up time for her own well-being, she decided to disregard Danny's early A.M. cries for "Mommy," hoping he would get the point. One morning she heard a different kind of cry, one that seemed to signal distress. But she was smart by now. Danny had used similar tactics before to make her come running, so she tried to disregard his crying. A few minutes later, and quite reluctantly, she gave up and went to his room. She thought she had heard something different in his voice. She discovered Danny hanging by his two little hands from the railing of his crib. Apparently, he had climbed out of the crib and hung from the edge for some time, just waiting to be rescued. She saved him from potential disaster. He was so happy to have been saved that he squeezed her tightly and gave her his most precious possession in return: he exploded with all the words he knew, one after another—"Mommy, Daddy, Teddy, truck, doggy, milk," and so on. Danny was very happy to be alive, and his response to the possible calamity was revealed in a display of all the words he knew.

Children's pride in their ability to use words, no matter how primitive their attempts may seem to adults, is important in their development of communication. Each new word children learn or each big step they take in mastering sentences is accompanied by an overt display of pleasure. Children know that their attempts please those around them, and in turn they are pleased. Because children's communication attempts are rewarded by others, it is easy to see why they will try again and again. Pleasure and reward are important factors in children's language development, but they are not the only ones to consider. This chapter explores the *children's role* in their communication development. Children are not simply containers into which verbal and nonverbal language abilities are "poured." Rather, children act as if they have some degree of personal commitment to their acquisition of communication. Put another way, there are *intrapersonal forces* that affect the acquisition process:

1. *Biological forces:* children's maturation (both physiological and neurological) accounts for their progress in language development.
2. *Self-initiated forces:* children discover their language and practice what they have learned.

BIOLOGICAL FORCES

Why do most children begin to put words together in sentences sometime between eighteen and twenty-four months of age? Could it be that all mothers start some type of language training at that time? Probably not. In fact, language stimulation by parents probably begins much earlier in the child's life. A more recent and persuasive explanation is based on certain biological theories. According to one view that deserves attention, human beings have the innate capacity to acquire language, and much of the language development process in children is best accounted for by biological factors.[1]

People learn how to stand up and walk without systematic training, and studies suggest, likewise, that people don't have to be taught to use language. Let's explore the walking-talking analogy for a moment. Most scientists agree that the human being's stance and gait are shaped by evolution: man is predisposed to stand upright and walk on two feet. If you have cared for infants during the first six months of life, you know how excited they become when they are stood upright. Infants can be fussy, unhappy, and generally irritable, but if you pull them up into a standing position, they smile, breath faster, and vocalize. Pediatricians believe that if infants show this much eagerness to be stood upright in early months, then there must be an inborn urge to achieve this satisfying position.[2] Their eagerness to be upright is soon followed by their jubilation at being able to walk. Bipedal gait is a characteristic of the human species that has applied to all persons in all cultural groups since the early civilizations. Most important, the emergence of bipedal gait is surprisingly regular among all children.

The development of children's communication proceeds along strikingly similar lines in three crucial areas: (1) emergence of language; (2) readiness for speech; and (3) bodily readiness for

[1] Eric Lenneberg, *Biological Foundations of Language* (New York: John Wiley and Sons, 1969), p. 125.

[2] T. Berry Brazelton, *Infants and Mothers: Differences in Development* (New York: Delacorte Press, 1969), p. 149.

communication. Evidence supporting a biological foundation for communication is discussed in the next section.

the emergence of language in children

Parents pay a great deal of attention to charts that tell how a child's coordination will develop. They become concerned if their little Jennifer isn't sitting alone by six to nine months—after all, the charts say this is the "normal" time for the child to reach this motor milestone—and they conclude that something must be wrong with Jennifer. Language milestones are viewed by parents in a similar manner. By four months of age, for example, a child is usually cooing and chuckling in response to someone or something in her environment. Parents have read that their child "should be" cooing or chuckling at this time. An important point to consider and one that many parents lose sight of in following their child's development, is that milestones are based on averages; they are not criteria for normalcy. In fact, many children develop normally in every respect but do not reach motor milestone and language milestone at the prescribed time.

With this word of caution in mind—that milestones are only averages—let's explore the emergence of language and coordination in children. Figure 2.1 is a chart, accompanied by sketches, of children's early progress in mastering walking and talking. The chart indicates that children progress step by step in developing coordination and language. Mastery in the motor area, such as in being able to sit alone, is often accompanied by mastery in the language area, such as in babbling. Everything seems to happen at once from the parents' point of view. It's hard to keep up with a growing infant.

According to most experts, the most productive step in children's language development is their ability to put words together in sentences (see Figure 2.1, 18 to 21 months). Researchers have tried to teach toddlers younger than eighteen months to join words together, such as "bye-bye" and Daddy," but their attempts usually fail. The utterance of multiple words is physiologically possible for the child; he has acquired the articulation skills necessary to do this. Typically, though, children usually do not string words together before they are eighteen months of age. When they first try to join words together it seems like a lot of work to the adult who is listening and watching. Later, children join words more easily. Consider three illustrations of Johnny trying to say good-bye to his father, who is going to work:

CHILD'S AGE	COORDINATION	LANGUAGE

4 months	Johnny can hold his head up by himself.	Johnny coos and chuckles when people play with him.

6 to 9 months	Johnny can sit alone and can pull himself up into a standing position.	Johnny babbles continually, sounding like this: "gagagag, yayayaya; dadadada."

12 to 18 months	Johnny first stands alone, then he walks along furniture, and, finally, he walks by himself.	Johnny uses a few words, follows simple commands, and knows what "no" means.

Figure 2.1. *Johnny's development of coordination and language. Adapted from Eric Lenneberg, "The Natural History of Language," in* The Genesis of Language, *eds. Frank Smith and George A. Miller (Cambridge, Mass.: M.I.T. Press, 1968), p. 222.*

Figure 2.1. (*continued*)

| 18 to 21 months | Johnny's walking looks stiff and jerky but he does well. He can sit in a chair (his aim is only "fair"), he can crawl down stairs, and he can throw a ball (clumsily). | Johnny understands simple questions and begins to put two or three words together in sentences. |

| 24 to 27 months | Johnny runs well, but falls when making a quick turn. He can also walk up and down stairs. | Johnny uses short sentences composed of words from a 300-400 word vocabularly. |

Figure 2.1. (*continued*)

| 30 to 33 months | Johnny has good hand and finger coordination; he can manipulate objects well. | Johnny's vocabulary increases in size, and three- and four-word sentences are prevalent. His language begins to sound adultlike. |

| 36 to 39 months | Johnny runs smoothly and negotiates sharp turns; he walks stairs by alternating feet; he can ride a tricycle, stand on one foot (briefly), and jump twelve inches in the air. | Johnny talks in well-formed sentences, following rather complex grammatical rules; others can generally understand what he is talking about. |

Johnny (18 months):   Bye-bye. (said slowly)
                       Bye-bye (long pause) *Daddy.* ("Daddy" is said loudly—it
                       is almost exploded—and is followed by a big smile.)

Johnny (21 months):   Bye-bye Daddy. (waves vigorously)
                       Bye-bye Daddy. (said loudly)
                       See you. (turns around and walks away)

Johnny (24+ months):   Bye-bye Daddy.
                       Hurry home.
                       Have a good day.

At first, Johnny seems to have trouble joining two words together in an utterance. When the second word ("Daddy") finally "gets out," Johnny shows his feeling of accomplishment. By twenty-one months of age, Johnny says good-bye with a succession of two-word utterances, although two of them are exactly alike. And finally, after his second birthday, Johnny is able to string words into sentences, and sentences into a little message. Johnny's language is progressing rapidly.

Most children, regardless of culture or language, are able to use two-word sentences at about their second birthday. At first glance, there appears to be something coincidental about the emergence of sentences in children's language at this particular time. However, biologists offer a more reasonable explanation, based on the growth of the human brain.

Brain maturation.   The brain undergoes a very rapid weight increase during the postnatal period: at the end of the first two years of life the brain is roughly 350 percent heavier. In contrast, the increase at the end of the next ten years is only 35 percent. By about age fourteen, the brain has achieved its adult weight and no further increases are registered. According to scientific research, neurons in the cerebral cortex grow in volume, with age. A significant spurt in the growth of the cerebral cortex occurs at about the age of two years. This growth spurt appears to happen at about the same time children join words together in a sentence. The possible relationship is tempting and reasonable. In charting the brain's structural growth, biochemical changes and neurophysiological changes, one notices this trend: a *sharp rise at two years*, a slight leveling off in the remaining preschool years, and a general leveling off at puberty. These biological curves parallel the language acquisition and development curve. Apparently, maturation of the human brain is a prerequisite for language development.

In short, as the brain matures the growing infant successively attains various developmental milestones, such as sitting, walking, and joining words into phrases. The maturation of the brain seems to account for the spurts of growth in both coordination and language.

In fact, if brain maturation is *slowed*, developmental horizons are reached later; the spacing between milestones is prolonged, but the sequence of milestones remains constant. For example, twelve to fourteen months usually elapse between sitting and putting words together, and in general language is fully established within another twenty months. But in the retarded child the lapse between sitting and putting words together may be as much as twenty-four months, and language may not be fully established for another sixty months; The retarded child's early milestones are delayed by a few months, and the delay increases significantly with age. This lag behind norms becomes progressively greater even though the child's condition may not change.

As the human brain develops in the first years of life, the child's language progresses. An examination of growth curves for the brain reveals patterns similar to growth curves for language. It seems reasonable to suggest that an intrapersonal force affecting the child's language development is the maturation of his brain.

Cerebral dominance. A second biological factor that helps explain the emergence of two-word utterances involves one particular phase of the maturation of the human brain—cerebral dominance. In most adults the left hemisphere of the brain is more directly involved in speech and language functions than the right hemisphere, although the right hemisphere is not unimportant in verbal communication. Research has indicated that there is a period in infancy, between birth and two years, when the left and right hemispheres are "equipotential"—that is, either is capable of assuming speech and language functions. Lateralization, or the shift of function to one side of the brain, apparently occurs at about the same time that two-word utterances appear. To most of us, lateralization simply refers to a child becoming right-handed or left-handed. The appearance of "handedness," in other words, is almost simultaneous with the appearance of multiple-word sentences. Let's explore some reasons why "handedness" and language emerge together.

L. S. Basser studied seventy-two infants who had sustained brain lesions in their first two years of life.[3] Over half of these children experienced a normal onset of language. The others developed more slowly, but only five of the infants had language problems of any severity, such as an absence of speech. Children with lesions in the left hemisphere developed speech at the same rate as those with lesions in the right hemisphere. Apparently, in the first two years of life cerebral dominance is not well established. A

[3] L. S. Basser, "Hemiplegia of Early Onset and the Faculty of Speech with Special Reference to the Effects of Hemispherectomy," *Brain*, LXXXV (1962), 427-60.

left-sided lesion is a sufficient condition to confine language functions to the right hemisphere. In the early stages of language development, both hemispheres seem to be equally involved and equally capable of assuming the major responsibility in language development.

By the time the children in the Basser study matured to the stage where language acquisition (in particular, the stringing together of words) is possible, left-sided dominance had manifested itself in a large proportion of them. Left-sided lesions incurred *during* language acquisition resulted in speech disturbances in 85 percent of the children, whereas right-sided lesions created disturbances in only 45 percent. On the other hand, if a child had a lesion during infancy—regardless of its size—such that a hemisphere had to be removed in later life, the surgery caused no aphasia.[4] Individuals who acquired lesions later in life and had a hemisphere removed showed permanent aphasic symptoms if the operation was done on the left side and no aphasia if the operation was performed on the right side.

This study and others indicate a close correspondence between maturation of the brain, in terms of hemisphere dominance, and the emergence of two-word utterances. According to scientists who advocate the biological foundations of language, this close correspondence presents a most convincing argument for a causal relationship between the maturation of the brain and the emergence of language. In short, the child's capacity for language acquisition is intimately related to the maturational history of his brain and to the unique degree of lateralization of brain function.

readiness to acquire speech

Recent evidence suggests that the onset of infants' vocalizations can also be explained biologically.[5] Newborn infants or *neonates*, are physically equipped, to some extent, to hear and produce speech. Although neonates are able to hear rather well, they do not demonstrate an ability to produce speech sounds. Their inability apparently results from initial limitations of the neonatal vocal apparatus. The larynx is positioned relatively high in the neonate, and, consequently, it cannot vary to produce the different sounds of a language. In addition, infants have large tongues that virtually fill their oral cavities. It is nearly impossible for infants to modify their

---

[4] The vast majority of aphasia patients have speech and language disturbances resulting from the internal brain disease that is commonly known as a stroke; brain tissue is destroyed or function is temporarily disrupted because of insufficient blood supply caused by a clot or ruptured vessel.

[5] Paula Menyuk, *The Development of Speech* (New York. The Bobbs-Merrill Company, Inc., 1972), pp. 11-13.

breath stream with their tongues, which are much too cumbersome for such activity. Apparently, neonates fail to reproduce the range of speech sounds not because they have not learned to produce them but because the structure of their vocal mechanism at birth renders them incapable of doing this. The configuration and size of the vocal mechanism changes during early physical maturation; by one or two months of age the child can produce vowel-like sounds.

In contrast, the child's ability to hear adult speech sounds seems to exist from birth. Apparently, no changes occur in the peripheral auditory mechanisms during early maturation. In fact, the infant can discriminate among acoustic signals during this early period. For example, neonates respond differently to different pitch levels, intensities, and durations of speech. Interestingly, infants respond to frequencies in the speech frequency band in a quiet and attentive fashion, but they respond to frequencies above or below speech frequencies with alerting and startling responses.

The results of studies of neonates and infants suggest that human children are programmed for speech in these ways:

1. They are able to distinguish speech from other acoustic signals.
2. They are able to produce speech after their vocal mechanism matures to a certain degree.

So far then, the emergence of language has been explained by the process of brain maturation, while early speech can be linked to physiological and auditory readiness.

bodily readiness to communicate

When we communicate, our messages consist of more than sounds and words. We communicate with our bodies as well. Since this text embodies a total view of children's communication development, we must consider a biological basis for nonverbal language. We must view the intrapersonal forces affecting the emergency of "body messages" as well as those affecting verbal messages. Just as we have cited support for the biological foundations of verbal language, we can also find support for the biological basis of bodily communication.

Let's consider the emergence of nonverbal communication of gender in infants and children. Are there biological factors that help explain our ability to send nonverbal cues which signal our masculinity or feminity to others? Medical studies conducted by Dr. John Money and his associates at Johns Hopkins University say yes—there are biological roots to gender display. The child's gender role appears to be well established about the time he exhibits a command of language: between eighteen months and two years.[6] Surprisingly, the child's capacity for communicating gender non-verbally and his capacity for language (at the two-word utterance stage) seem to emerge *simultaneously*.

The normal two-year-old exhibits a great deal of impersonation of and identification with the parent of the same sex. By four years of age a child's gender role is firmly established. Dr. Money speculated that the child's gender role is "imprinted" in the second year of life and that such an imprint culminates in gender-role determination by two years of age. Imprinting is a kind of learning that requires very specific stimuli; from these stimuli behavior is formed permanently: once the imprint is established, it is indelible. Dr. Money based his speculations on studies of adult hermaphrodites[7] who had been switched from the sex of early rearing to the opposite sex, or to the sex determined by physiological and genetic factors. Prior to eighteen months—again, that magic age in the child's development—an infant's sex can be reassigned: the child is able to adapt and unable to recall the change. After eighteen months, it is too late to make such a reassignment with impunity, and such changes are avoided.

Communication experts, as well, have examined the gender display of infants. Using a set of nonverbal indices typical of adult gender display as the basis for comparison, one researcher analyzed films of infants during their second year of life. His results indicated that infants begin to communicate their gender during this period.[8] A fifteen-month-old female, for example, had become, "bodily speaking," a Southern upper-middle-class female. She held her pelvis in an anterior roll (characteristic of adult females) and kept her arms alongside her trunk (also characteristic of females). A twenty-two-month-old boy in the study was filmed in a spread-legged position (males tend to keep arms and legs at a fifteen-degree angle from the trunk) and rolled his pelvis posteriorly (a male characteristic). On the basis of filmed studies such as this one,

[6] John Money, "Hermaphroditism," *The Encyclopedia of Sexual Behavior* (1961), I, 477.

[7] A hermaphrodite is a person possessing both ovarian and testicular tissue. Complex hermaphroditism involves a person having internal and external organs of both sexes. In transverse hermaphroditism the outward organs indicate one sex and the internal organs the other. Other forms of hermaphroditism exist, as well.

[8] Ray L. Birdwhistell, *Kinesics and Context: Essays in Body Motion Communication* (Philadelphia: University of Pennsylvania Press, 1970), pp. 49-50.

experts can locate the emergence of nonverbal gender communication in the later part of the child's second year.

Our discussion of children's "bodily readiness" to communicate has focused rather specifically on children's gender messages. Medical evidence has helped explain why our gender messages (masculinity, feminity) emerge by about two years of age. In other areas of nonverbal communication, such as the child's acquisition of prosody (the intonation and stress patterns in speech), biological factors are often employed to help explain the particular course of development. The point we must consider in our discussion of intrapersonal forces affecting the development of communication is this:

> *Biological factors are extremely helpful in explaining the emergency and development of children's nonverbal messages.*

It appears that children's development of communication behaviors, verbal and nonverbal, are surprisingly well explained by the maturation of the human brain and the human body. In the future we may be able to outline communication milestones that children achieve in their language development; such milestones may have a strong biological foundation.

children's communication equipment: is it unique?

The thrust of our discussion so far has been that children are specially equipped—neurologically, biologically, and physically—to develop communication in the way they do. The biological approach to communication development maintains that because children are of the species *homo sapiens*, they will acquire language. No other species is equipped in quite the same way, so no other species is capable of communicating in quite the same way. The capacity for language is what sets children apart from apes, cats, and other "intelligent" animals. However, recent studies with animals, particularly chimpanzees, have begun to challenge the notion that only children can learn to talk. Let's get to know three chimps who were given communication instruction.

Gua tries to speak.   The first idea was to train a chimp to speak, using a vocal form of communication typical of infants. Winthrop and Luella Kellogg raised Gua the Chimp in their home, along with their own child.[9] They treated Gua and their child alike: they diapered them, dressed them, placed bonnets on their heads, gave

[9]W. N. Kellogg and L. A. Kellogg, *The Ape and the Child: A Study of Environmental Influence Upon Early Behavior* (New York: McGraw-Hill, 1933).

them toys and so forth. They provided a human atmosphere for both the chimp and the child. By using such treatment the Kelloggs hoped to establish optimal conditions for developing, among other behaviors, speech and language in the chimp. They reasoned that previous attempts to teach chimps to talk had failed because of the "non-human" treatment of the animal.

During the early months of their lives, Gua was better at responding to oral commands than the child was. The chimp's motor skills were also superior to the child's during this early stage (prior to one year of age). But after their first birthdays, the trend reversed. In spite of his surroundings and the continual stimulation from the Kelloggs, Gua could only bark, screech, scream, and make an "oooo" cry. He couldn't even babble! But he was a master at nonverbal communication. For example, when he was tired and wanted to go to bed, he faced his "parents" and fell backward, hitting the floor with a gigantic thud. His message was clearly "articulated."

Gua's failure to develop speech has been related to the chimp's neurological deficiencies and to the inadequacy of his pharyngeal region, which is necessary for the production of speech sounds. Remember that changes in the brain and vocal apparatus seem to precipitate children's language learning. But for Gua, such changes did not take place. Maturational curves for chimps reveal a sharp growth until the end of their first year, with a leveling off after twelve months. The child, on the other hand, continues to develop more complicated brain and physiological mechanisms for communication.

Sarah has a language. Next, let's get to know Sarah the Chimp. Sarah was not given lessons on how to speak because scientists had convinced her teacher that chimpanzees do not have the necessary equipment for speech.[10] Instead, Sarah was given instruction in another channel of communication. She received her language lessons from a piece of machinery called a language board, which holds magnetic forms varying in shape, size, and color. Plastic forms constituted Sarah's 120-item vocabulary. She was given instruction in four functions of language: words, sentences, questions, and metalanguage. Sarah was able to perform these functions:

1. *Word:* If a banana were placed on the table by Mary, a trainer, Sarah could place the banana form on the language board, her reward being a real banana to eat.
2. *Sentence:* Sarah was able to describe on her language board a situation in

[10] David Premack, "The Education of Sarah," *Psychology Today,* IV (1970), 55-58.

which Randy gave an apple to Mary. The forms would record, *Randy give apple Mary.* (Note: Sarah didn't like it if someone got "her food"—the apple, in this case—so the trainer had to reward Sarah's success with something better than the apple—for instance, a cookie; otherwise Sarah might have gotten upset.)

3. *Questions:* Sarah could answer yes-no questions. If shown an apple and a banana and asked on the language board, "same or different?" Sarah could reply accordingly. (Note: Sometimes, Sarah would select two forms and reply "no same" instead of "different," indicating her potential capability of joining words together.)

4. *Metalanguage:* Sarah was able to respond "name of" or "no name of" when an object and a symbol (form) were placed in front of her.

Sarah learned these language functions following two years of extensive training. She demonstrated that chimpanzees have far more language capability than scientists had ever thought.

But there is a real *difference* between Sarah the Chimp and a child acquiring language:

Chimpanzees must be conditioned for every language response, whereas human children seem to learn their language in the absence of intensified conditioning.

Children have unique communication equipment in one important sense: it seems to be self-activated.

Washoe has a sign language. A more recent study of chimpanzees goes one step further in challenging the idea that children are uniquely equipped for communication. Washoe the Chimp was instructed in the sign language often employed by deaf human beings.[11] Washoe acquired a sign language of about thirty words by twenty-five months of age, a vocabulary comparable to that of a human child (eighteen to twenty-four months). The most important thing about Washoe's language is that she can use it spontaneously and inventively. There is even some evidence that Washoe can teach the sign language to her friends and that her fellow chimps pick it up rather well. But when linguists review Washoe's accomplishments, they find that she lacks syntactic ability. Although she can use words to refer to events, she is inconsistent in her ordering of words into sentences. Many of Washoe's multiple-word sentences have been explained as unintegrated series of words, ordered not on the basis of grammatical relations but on their importance to Washoe.

Our brief introductions to Gua, Sarah, and Washoe reveal that chimpanzees are far more capable in communication than we had

[11] R. A. Gardner and B. Gardner, "Teaching Sign Language to a Chimpanzee," *Science,* CLXV (1969), 664-72.

previously thought. Chimps can be taught, through conditioning procedures, to use words in nonverbal ways. It is important to remember, however, that children appear to be better equipped, neurologically and physiologically, to use verbal language. Until we discover the limits to the chimp's ability to communicate, an adequate comparison cannot be made. Children are well equipped to learn to communicate and to use language creatively, but chimpanzees are not. Further studies with chimps and children should help us decide just how unique language is to our species.

SELF-INITIATED FORCES

Child psychologists often suggest that children are excellent investigators of their world. Children behave like little scientists, trying to discover the rules that make things "tick." According to child psychologist Jean Piaget, the child *acts on things to understand them.* This account vividly describes the scientific capacities of the young child.

> Almost from birth, he touches objects, manipulates them, turns them around, looks at them, and in these ways he develops an increasing understanding of their properties It is through manipulation that he develops schemes relating to objects. When new objects are presented, the child may at first try to apply them to already existing schemes. If not successful, he attempts, again through manipulation, to develop new schemes; that is, new ways of acting on and thereby comprehending the world.[12]

Equipped with a sort of scientific ability to investigate, the child appears to be well qualified to discover the patterns of language. Linguists say that a very powerful intrapersonal force explaining children's communication development is their *creativity* in learning what the principles of language are. Children demonstrate their creative ability by using the intricate "tools" of the scientist at work in a laboratory. The child's laboratory is the world of language, and he discovers the rules of his language rapidly and in an amazingly scientific manner. The child is a busy little scientist, *practicing* and *discovering* the schemes of language.

practicing language

Many children practice their language—that is, they go through a kind of linguistic drill—before falling asleep at night. Others do the

[12] H. Ginsburg and O. Opper, *Piaget's Theory of Intellectual Development: An Introduction* (Englewood Cliffs, N.J.: Prentice-Hall, Inc., 1969), p. 221.

same thing upon waking up or when playing by themselves. If parents stood near the bedside of their child who is in the two-word stage of development, they might hear him practicing his new-found language schemes. The first systematic study of this process was reported by Ruth Weir, who analyzed the presleep monologues of her two-and-a-half-year-old son Anthony.[13] She was able to describe the fascinating practice procedures that are potentially important in a child's development of language.

Many of Anthony's drills focused on the pronunciation of words; he said a word and then corrected his pronunciation over and over again. Other exercises involved practice with grammatical skills. One exercise was the "build up": "The block," "The yellow block," "Look at the yellow block." Another was the "breakdown": "Another big bottle," "Big bottle." Both exercises portray a child working at the intricate operations of his language, able to analyze sentences into component parts. Other drills performed by Anthony showed his ability to substitute nouns in sentence frames: "What color," "What color blanket," "What color map," "What color glass." His practicing covered many realms of linguistic knowledge, such as syntactic negation, verb tense, declarative sentences, and questions.

The accounts of Anthony's practice sessions with language show that he enjoyed his drills. He was playing a game with language. Linguistic form always appeared to be paramount in his drills; the content of his utterances was subordinate to the form. Children's bedtime monologues, or any of their "private" monologues during the day, may constitute an important activity in their development of language. Although the precise role of practice drills in children's development of communication has not been clearly established, the existence of this behavior suggests strongly that it is an important contributor.

discovery: children's creativity with language

Just as a linguist working in a university setting attempts to discover the rules of an exotic African language, so does a child analyze a corpus of speech to discover its underlying rules. The child formulates hypotheses about the way language works, tests them out to see how they work, and, if they are confirmed, "obeys" the rules contained in the hypotheses. Upon discovering a hypothesis that doesn't account for the language the child hears, our little scientist will search for a new hypothesis that might work better.

[13] Ruth Weir, *Language in the Crib* (The Hague: Mouton, 1962).

To illustrate the discovery process, one need only survey reports of how children acquire the grammar of their language. We will cite two examples of children's supreme creativity in language learning. One is related to verb tense and the other to adding inflections to words.

Picture a child searching for schemes to account for verb tense in the speech of her environment. A two-year-old girl may first refer to a past event by saying something like this:

"Daddy went to office."

The sentence appears to reflect some degree of sophistication in past-tense formulation. However, because the second stage of development typically involves a kind of regression, the child probably did not attach meaning to the linguistic change necessary for the creation of the past-tense form of "go." Instead, she may have been imitating the entire form, "went." The second stage might sound something like this:

"Daddy goed to office."

This stage probably reflects the child's first concern with the rules of her language. She knows that walking, talking, and playing done yesterday are said as *walked*, *talked*, and *played*. It seems reasonable to assume that going done yesterday is said as *goed*. The child has discovered a rule of language that accounts for much of the language to which she is exposed—yet, that rule doesn't always work. People may tell her that, as well. Later in her development, maybe as late as four years of age, the child may search for a new set of rules that account for all verbs, including the past irregular verbs. This attempt may result in:

"Daddy wented to the office."

Makes sense, doesn't it? Yet most parents cringe when a child says something such as this; they may not allow such an utterance to go uncorrected. Once the child is able to understand how to apply the rules of past tense to irregular verbs, she is able to perform like this:

"Daddy went to the office."

And the child is back where she started from. She may have said something similar to this at age two, but without any understanding of the rules behind its utterance.

Children in the process of learning verb tense are extremely creative in their use of language schemes. They discover rules according to a kind of scientific procedure. They find rules to account for relationships and they employ these rules to portray such relationships. And even though the rules don't always fit adult language schemes, children's creativity in language cannot be stressed too much.

A second example of children's creativity is their ability to learn a nonsense language composed of made-up words for which they must add appropriate inflectional endings.[14] For example, if children are given the words "wug," "gutch," and "bick," accompanied by imaginary pictures of such phenomena, they can talk creatively about them. If children are shown a picture of a "wug," a birdlike creature, and are then shown two of them, they can pluralize "wug" to "wugz" quite appropriately. Such studies have supported the notion that children approach their language creatively. Children can form plurals, past-tense forms, possessives, and agentive forms for all sorts of nonsense words, illustrating that they work with rules to discover language schemes.

Intrapersonal forces within children direct their acquisition of communication. Through practice and discovery procedures, children demonstrate an amazingly creative ability to learn. Intrapersonal forces are crucial to an explanation of how children learn to communicate.

SUMMARY

Children are innately capable of acquiring language. Their predisposition to communicate is shaped by the maturation of their brain, vocal apparatus, and body. Just as children's development of stance and bipedal gait follows a predictable and "natural" course, and just as children's development of coordination can be characterized by their attainment of motor milestones, their language development can be described in terms of biological milestones.

All children develop language, speech, and bodily communication according to a similar development schedule. For example, at about two years of age children are able to join words together in sentences and communicate gender through bodily means. The co-occurrence of these milestones at this particular stage of development can be explained by advocates of the biological forces position.

The child's language equipment distinguishes him from other animals. Biological theories suggest that language is a species-specific

[14]See for example, Jean Berko, "The Child's Learning of English Morphology," *Word*, XIV (1958), 150-77.

characteristic, although chimpanzees have been taught to use forms of language. There is no clear-cut evidence that children have a strong competitor in terms of language capacity, however.

In addition to the biological forces affecting the child's development of communication, it is important to consider a second set of intrapersonal forces affecting development. First, when children are at work discovering the schemes of their language, they are like busy little scientists. Once they find the rules or schemes for explaining the speech they hear, they *practice* these schemes in certain situations—for instance, before they go to sleep or when they wake up. Further, this process of discovering rules that account for language schemes shows that children are extremely *creative* in their acquisition of a language. In short, children learn to communicate partly because of an intrapersonal force that compels them to discover the rules that make a language work.

SUGGESTED READINGS

DALE, PHILLIP, *Language Development: Structure and Function*, Chap. 3. Hinsdale, Ill.: The Dryden Press, 1972.

LENNEBERG, ERIC, "The Capacity for Language Acquisition," *The Structure of Language: Readings in the Philosophy of Language*, ed. J. A. Fodor and J.J. Katz. Englewood Cliffs, N.J.: Prentice-Hall, Inc., 1964, pp. 579-603.

MENYUK, PAULA, *The Development of Speech*. New York: The Bobbs-Merrill Company, Inc., pp. 3-23.

3

communication
development:
interpersonal forces

A child abandoned on an island will not acquire a language. Clearly, he must be exposed to at least one speaker of a language in order to acquire a language on his own. There is a story that King James VI of Scotland wished to discover the "natural" language of the world—the language that Adam and Eve spoke. His idea was to place two babies, a boy and a girl, in the care of a deaf and mute nursemaid on an uninhabited island. He predicted that the babies would grow up speaking the so-called natural language; his bet was that it would be Hebrew. Apparently, his research idea didn't attract much attention. He never did conduct the study.

In addition to his belief that there was a natural language, King James obviously believed that language *ability* is innate. This is not the position of the theorists who stress the importance of biological forces in language development. The notion of innate *capabilities* does not imply that all human beings will develop a behavior regardless of the circumstances. But given the appropriate circumstances, what is natural for us to acquire—in this case, language—will naturally emerge. Thus, any discussion of interpersonal forces must involve *appropriate circumstances:*

1. Children must have *communication models* that they can observe.
2. Children must have *opportunities to interact* with these models..

This chapter includes a discussion of interpersonal forces in terms of these appropriate circumstances.

The essential ingredient in normal development of communication in children is exposure, from birth, to communication models. Obviously, before children can learn grammatical rules they must be exposed to the adult speech that follows the rules of their grammar. Before children can learn to emphasize the importance of their requests with gestures and body motions they must be exposed to adult communication that follows patterns of body movement. Family and friends are communication models from which children's communication is patterned. Even though children have innate capabilities of using language, they must still be exposed to language in order to discover its rules. Verbal and nonverbal communication patterns employed by communication *models* act as input into the child's communication system. During the child's important years in an elementary school, the teacher becomes another important model for the child's development of communication.

If conditions are just right, children grow up in an environment rich with communication. Conversations surround them. With the help of family members, friends, and teachers, children engage in conversations quite regularly. They have plenty of opportunities to interact with the important communication models in their environment. Though their contribution to the conversation may be a string of babbled sounds accompanied by a big smile, or a simple greeting, "Hi Dad," coupled with a little wave, their excitement at being included is obvious. The opportunities to communicate with others, to be included in conversations, describe the appropriate circumstance of *interaction*.

On the basis of the intrapersonal forces we discussed in Chapter 2—biological maturation and self-initiated practice and discovery—children are equipped to learn the language appropriate to their environment. Children's "equipment" must be triggered, however, by the communication input they receive from communication models and through interaction with these models. Figure 3.1 outlines the relationship of intrapersonal and interpersonal forces affecting children's communication development. Let's consider the model before discussing interpersonal forces further.

At the top of the model is the *input*, which contains "communication data": the verbal and nonverbal communication patterns of models, as well as children's interaction with these models. The input portion contains the interpersonal forces affecting

Communication data: (1) *communication models* provide the child with verbal and nonverbal language patterns "to be discovered"; (2) the child's *interaction* with communication models directs the development of communication.

(INTERPERSONAL FORCES)

Communication equipment: (1) the *biological* forces, including maturation of the brain, vocal apparatus, and body; (2) the child's self-initiated *discovery and practice* of language schemes (that is, the child's creativity with language).

(INTRAPERSONAL FORCES)

The child's communication: verbal and nonverbal language patterns characteristic of the child's stage of development and dependent on factors in the child's communication environment.

(COMMUNICATION DEVELOPMENT)

Figure 3.1. *The components of communication learning.*

communication development. Next in the model is *children's equipment*: (1) maturation of the child's brain, vocal mechanism, and body; and (2) the child's self-initiated discovery and practice of verbal and nonverbal language patterns. This equipment constitutes the intrapersonal forces affecting communication development. The *output* is represented by children's communication in its full form. The nature of children's communication, as found in the output, is certainly characteristic of their stage of development (based on maturation) and is dependent on factors in their communication environment.

Communication data, the child's equipment, and the emerging communication patterns of the child are the three components in our model of communication learning. The model draws together the intrapersonal and interpersonal forces affecting the development of communication in children. Our concern in the remainder of this chapter is to examine more closely the input portion of the model, which contains the communication data.

COMMUNICATION MODELS

Studies of child language development conducted in the United States have assumed that the mother is the major source of input (that is, the primary model) for the child's acquisition of his native tongue, English. For many American middle-class households, this assumption is probably valid. Cross-cultural studies that have tested the generality of the mother-as-primary-model assumption contain evidence that this assumption might not be true in certain countries, cultures, and social groups. Many studies have simply assumed that the mother was the primary model even though in many of the cases studied this was not true. In some instances the mother appeared to be most important, but in other cases the mother was rarely with the child and could not have been the primary model. In a ghetto community in California, for example, a child's siblings are key models for the child's development of language. In certain Chinese cultures, the grandmother may be the key figure in caring for the child and in the child's language development.

Whether the source of input is the mother, the sister, or another family member, the role of the communication model is about the same. The important factor is that children are exposed to "live" communication, which they can analyze and reproduce in some way. When children copy examples provided by adults or other children, we say they are imitating. Imitation may involve copying single words or phrases; for example, a two-year-old may copy (complete with intonation and bodily movements) adult swearing and cussing expressions—"Oh nuts" and worse. One of my boys has often imitated my body movements in communication; for example, at eighteen months Jeffrey was employing the pointing gesture for emphasis when he wished to communicate "no" to me. Viewing his communication is like viewing my own, and it can be a wonderful, although sometimes terrifying, experience.

Scientists who study imitation of models as a factor in children's development of communication do not agree about the exact role of the imitation process. It is not unusual to observe children's patterns and expressions that are carbon copies of those employed by adults; however, many of their attempts at imitation fail. Let's examine children's imitation of communication models from three perspectives: (1) the nature of imitation; (2) the role of practice and new language forms; and (3) the role of practice and solidification of old language forms.

the nature of imitations

Sometimes children's attempts to imitate result in a lengthy exchange that appears to lead them nowhere. Consider the following dialogue between a mother and her child.[1]

---

[1] David McNeill, "Developmental Psycholinguistics," in *The Genesis of Language*, eds. Frank Smith and George Miller (Cambridge, Mass.: The M. I. T. Press, 1966), p. 69.

Child: Nobody don't like me.

Mother: No, say, "Nobody likes me."

Child: Nobody don't like me. (eight repetitions of this dialogue)

Mother: No, now listen carefully; say, "nobody likes me."

Child: Oh! Nobody don't likes me.

As a tool for language instruction, imitation hasn't worked well in this case. Adults often admit that attempts to prompt imitations from children end in failure. Although copying seems to be a favorite game with children, their imitations often miss the mark. Why does this happen? It makes sense to suggest this: Although the child's imitation may not be an exact copy of what the adult says or does, it may approximate *what the child sees and hears.* One linguist concerned with grammar suggests that the child's failure to copy new grammatical forms in adult speech is based on the "relative impenetrability" of the child's grammar to adult models, even under the instruction (given by the mother's "no") to change.[2]

In other words, young children at any given stage of grammatical development think in terms of their own grammar and cannot do differently until their grammar changes. Although studies agree that it is important for children to hear grammatical speech, the role of imitation in children's development of grammar is not clear. It is quite possible that from the perspective of children's minds, communication models *change* as children develop. That is, as children develop verbal and nonverbal language, the input from models assumes a different form to their eyes and ears.

The same phenomenon that we just observed in children's verbal communication can be observed in their nonverbal communication. Young children often fail to employ the rules of communication distance (called proxemic rules) and space important in adult communication interactions. Young children seem to follow different rules for communicating "in space." For example, an adult usually conducts a social conversation at a distance of about four feet from another person. A young girl attempting to conduct social conversations like Mommy does may stand inches from you if you happen to be her lucky listener. Her attempts to copy the communication patterns of adults may fall short of doing exactly that. It is important to consider, however, that young children follow their own proxemic rules in communication. As they become incorporated more and more into the adult system, their patterns and rules approximate more closely those followed by adults in their family, community, and culture.

[2] Ibid.

It is important to note that children's imitations are very much affected by their perceptions of the communication patterns to be imitated. In other words, children's imitations are a product of their particular stages of development in verbal and nonverbal language. It makes little sense to view the imitating child from an adult's eyes and ears; instead, we have to "get inside" the child's eyes and ears to see and hear as he does.

With this perspective on imitation, let's examine two approaches to the role of imitation in children's development of language. One view suggests that practice in imitation leads to the *incorporation of new forms* (advanced verbal and nonverbal patterns); the second approach suggests that the key advantage of practice rests with the *solidification of old forms* (previously acquired verbal and nonverbal patterns). The evidence in both approaches is drawn primarily from the grammatical level of language. Evidence in nonverbal channels—such as communication space, intonation, and body motion—must be gathered in the future if a conclusive statement on the role of imitation in communication development is to be made.

practice and new forms

When children are imitating the speech of others, what forms are they practicing? Are these forms novel, or are they forms already learned? To be novel forms (for instance, new words or new grammatical structures), the forms must be absent from the child's "free" speech—that is, speech that does not appear to be a direct imitation of the speech of others. If imitation is a necessary condition for grammatical development, then children's speech with imitations should be grammatically more progressive or advanced than their free speech. Studies have demonstrated, however, that imitated speech and free speech are almost identical, in terms of complexity, for most children.[3] If children are not producing the progressive inflection, "he is running," in their free speech, chances are they will not imitate it. However, by exploring situations not explored by previous studies, future studies may provide evidence that challenges the nonprogressive nature of imitations in children's speech.

A young child's grammar seems to be impervious to change. The imitation-dialogue ("Nobody don't like me.") between a mother and her child demonstrates the failure of a child to employ a novel form.

---

[3] Susan Ervin, "Imitation and Structural Change in Children's Language," in *New Directions in the Study of Language,* ed. Eric Lenneberg (Cambridge, Mass.: The M. I. T. Press, 1965), pp. 163-89.

The only safe conclusion that can be drawn is that imitation in practice does not appear to contribute directly to the incorporation of novel (and thus more advanced) forms into children's language. On the other hand, novel forms *do appear* in children's speech. Their language does change, eventually. Children do profit from adult models, but how they profit is not clear.

Probably the most important aspect of imitation in regard to new forms is what psycholinguists have called *expansion* of the child's speech.[4] When adults imitate the child's speech but *expand* it, we have a kind of imitation in reverse. Quite often, adults repeat the speech of a young child; in doing so, they change or alter the child's utterance into a well-formed adult equivalent. Consider the following example of the expansion process:

Child: Daddy outside.
Adult: Yes, Daddy is working outside.

In this case, the adult filled out the sentence with the appropriate verb. Expansions typically include the prepositions, verbs, articles, and auxiliaries that young children may "omit." On the surface, these expansions seem to constitute a prime explanation of how a child develops a more complex grammar. After all, the expansions direct attention to the missing components of the child's sentence. There is one basic problem with this approach: many adults do not expand their child's speech, per se; instead, they may simply comment on the truth value of the child's sentence. In the latter instances adults may respond to the child's sentence only in terms of its truth or falsity and rarely in terms of its grammaticality, in an adult sense. Consider the following dialogue:

Child: Daddy play ball Markie?
Mother: No, he's busy!

In this case, the mother's response to the child's sentence was based solely on its probability of occurrence. Relating this finding to a theory of grammatical development, we would have to predict that the child who is subjected to truth-value (or probability) responses to his speech (rather than grammatical expansions) would develop language more slowly or would develop an inadequate grammar. Since this does not seem to be the case, we must be cautious in using expansion to explain grammatical development. About the only

[4]Roger Brown and Ursula Bellugi, "Three Processes in the Child's Acquisition of Syntax," *Harvard Educational Review*, XXXIV (1964), 131-51.

conclusion that we can draw from the study of adult expansion of children's speech is this:

> *Although many parents are motivated to expand the speech of their child for instructional purposes, it seems likely that the primary reason that adults expand a child's speech is to "check" their interpretation of the child's meaning. The expanded sentences are offered by the adult. The child can either accept or deny the adult interpretations.*

Taking the expansion process one step further—to the point where the child attempts to imitate the adult expansion—may prove to be an important criterion for the rapid development of a rich language in children. Dan Slobin examined children's imitations of adult expansions and found that about half of the imitations he studied were grammatically progressive.[5] Although children's imitations of adult speech do not typically contain new forms, their imitations of adult-expanded versions are more progressive. Slobin's studies focused on the speech of middle-class children, so generalizations beyond this population are impossible.

practice and solidification

Let's examine a second approach to the role of imitation. This view suggests that imitations constitute practice for already acquired forms of language. Once acquired, perhaps through the expansion process, new forms entering the child's language system must be practiced in order to become solidified in the system. The issue is whether or not forms receiving more practice become more stable than forms receiving less practice. Susan Ervin attempted to answer this question by examining the speech of children for the emergence of past-tense inflections.[6]

Initially, the child utters verbs with no tense markings for past or future action—for instance, a child saying "Daddy go" may intend a past, future, or present action. The first verbs to be inflected by children (to have tense markings added) are the "strong" verbs—that is, verbs such as "sit," "come," "go," and "run." The inflection of strong verbs necessitates total word changes (for instance, "go"/ "went" or "sit"/"sat"), not merely the addition of markings per se. "Weak" verbs, such as "look," "walk," and "laugh," are inflected in

[5] Dan Slobin, "Imitation and Grammatical Development in Children," in *Contemporary Issues in Developmental Psychology*, eds. N. S. Endler, L. R. Boulter and H. Osser (New York: Holt, Rinehart and Winston, 1967), pp. 437-43.

[6] Ervin, "Imitation and Structural Change," pp. 177-79.

the regular way. Studies reveal that weak verbs follow the strong verbs in the child's development of language.

Children usually say "He comed" or "I sitted" at the same stage in which they say "Daddy walked" or "I jumped." Utterances such as "Teddy goed to bed" do not simply drop out of the child's speech in a matter of weeks—or months, for that matter. Many such forms persist in the child's speech even into grade school. Children's earliest utterances involving the strong verbs tend to be consistent with adult inflections. Children say "He went," "I ran," or "Man came." The "regularizations"—such as "He comed" or "I sitted"—appear later in children's speech. In short, past tense appears *first* in correctly inflected strong (but irregular) verbs. At first glance, this finding may seem surprising. How can a child begin to acquire the more difficult strong verbs before he masters the regular weak verbs? The finding is not that surprising if we take into account the high frequency with which strong verbs occur in adult speech. Once a child begins to use verbs such as "came," "went," and "sat," he finds many opportunities to employ these verbs. The opportunities for the use of past-tense strong verbs are greater than the opportunities for their weak-verb counterparts. Consequently, the child receives much practice with strong verbs in the past tense. According to a solidification view of practice in child language development, these strong verbs should remain stable in the child's repertoire. Contrary to expectation, however, the correctly inflected strong verbs are soon replaced by the incorrectly (but regularly) inflected strong verbs. The strong verbs become very unstable, despite the great amount of practice they receive. The use of regular inflections for strong verbs (such as "He comed") has been called *overgeneralization:* that is, the child inappropriately extends regular endings to irregular verbs, thereby creating a kind of generalization beyond the rules.

Perhaps overgeneralization of strong verbs should be emphasized as a positive shift from strictly imitative behaviors in children to the more productive discovery behaviors that lead to the formation of *rules.* The discovery of language rules, an important aspect of the child's equipment (see Chapter 2), becomes a dominant strategy for learning the structure of a language. Further, it also makes sense to suggest that although weak verbs are individually less frequent in parental speech, surely the consistency of the past-tense marking on the many different weak verbs must impress the child greatly.

Whatever our explanation for the role of imitation in children's development of language, we know that children imitate the communication patterns of others constantly. Communication models, such as parents, siblings, friends, and teachers, are extremely important in children's development of communication. Only indirectly (through *expansion*) may imitations account for the appearance of new forms in the child's communication. Imitations do not appear to help in the solidification of such forms. But we know that imitation plays some role in the child's development of communication. It may be a crucial learning strategy in the child's acquisition of sounds and words. It may also be valuable in the child's acquisition of nonverbal communication. For example, the body motions accompanying adult speech are often attempted by young children. The results can often be amusing, particularly if the movement or gesture is a prominent one. To understand fully the role of imitation in communication development, we must conduct in-depth studies on children's development of nonverbal as well as verbal language.

In conclusion, communication models play an important role in providing *communication data*, which is analyzed by children's *communication equipment*. Although direct imitation of the model's language by children does not seem to account for children's language development, adult expansions of children's imitations, may in some way promote this development. The communication models—parents, siblings, friends, and teachers—are full-fledged users of the language to be acquired by children. The importance of children's interaction with such models is discussed next.

INTERACTION AND DEVELOPMENT

A second interpersonal force affecting children's development of communication is the interaction of children with their communication models. *Interaction* in this sense involves the flow of conversation between a child learning to communicate and others, and it plays an important role in the process of learning to communicate. The interaction process can be examined in terms of the language assistance provided by communication models:

1. Children are given information regarding the *content* of their language (the extension process).
2. Children are given information regarding the *structure* of their language.

the extension of children's speech: content

Our experience in talking with children reminds us how important it is to comment on what they say. We can help children understand how to use language if we respond to their utterances with comments, new ideas, questions, and evaluations. Courtney Cazden studied this technique of adult interaction with children, in the belief that such responses positively affect children's development of their language. She found this to be true.

Initially, Cazden called the technique "modeling." She reasoned that adults provide a type of full-fledged language in response to the child's more immature form of language. Later, she renamed the technique "extension." The extension of children's speech provides children with semantic information that "extends the meaning" of their utterances.[7] The parent, friend, or teacher who is extending the speech of children is doing something like this:

Child: Doggie bark. (when a dog is barking)
Other: Yes, but he probably won't bite. (or)
Maybe he is mad at the kitty. (or)
Barking is his way of saying how he feels.

Comments and ideas expressed in the adult's extension give children semantic information that is important to them in their development of language.

In her studies of the effectiveness of extension, Cazden reasoned that children who received daily extensions of their speech should progress more, grammatically, than children whose speech was simply expanded (expansion was discussed on pp. 46-47). Remember that expansion simply involves a grammatical filling out of the child's utterance, as in this example:

Child: Doggie bark.
Adult: Yes, the dog is barking.

The thought behind the Cazden study discussed above was that the value of extension information in child-adult interactions is far greater than that of expansion information. The results of Cazden's study indicate that *extension is an effective treatment in assisting young children (twenty-eight to thirty-eight months) in their development of grammar*. The expansion process, on the other hand, did not seem to produce grammatical progressions—that is, sentences that were more complex grammatically than those the child may have used before the treatment.

Even though Cazden's extension study involved only a small sample of children her results illustrate the Importance of adult-child interaction in the child's language development. The key point to be emphasized is that the nature of adult-child interaction may have a

[7] Courtney Cazden, *Child Language and Education* (New York: Holt, Rinehart and Winston, Inc., 1972), pp. 124-27.

strong bearing on development. The interaction should emphasize meaning—that is, semantic considerations of what the child is talking about. Many parents expand and extend their children's speech, but the important factor affecting the speed and ease with which children learn their language may rest in the richness of the extensions provided by parents and others. In other words, the more that adults truly interact with children, the more quickly and efficiently children may learn to use more complex forms of language. Adults must realize that children believe they have something important to say and that they seek reactions to their speech from adults.

mother-child interaction: structure

A second type of interaction assistance that children receive is found in the form of adult language, as opposed to its content. In recent years, several studies have investigated mother-child interaction in order to examine the mother's speech in terms of its structural assistance to her child. A study by Patricia Broen, which serves as the focus of the present discussion, closely evaluated the speech of mothers to their children. Broen predicted that a mother's language was somehow geared to the age of the child.[8] Thus, the language the mother used with her young child should have been far simpler than the language she used with an older child. The study assumed, and probably rightly so, that the mothers examined *did* play a major role in their children's acquisition of language. The families were of middle-class backgrounds and the parents had professional occupations.

Rarely have studies examined directly the nature of the language parents direct to children. We have assumed, because of the obvious omission of the subject from most discussions, that parental speech directed to children remains relatively constant over the years. The language of the mother has been assumed to be a rather stable factor; the unstable and changing factor is supposed to be the child's language. Broen's study revealed that the language a mother uses to her child may change almost as drastically as the child's language changes, in the course of mother-child interactions over time. Broen found that the language style of mothers with their younger children (eighteen to twenty-five months) was quite different from their style of language with their older children

[8] Patricia Broen, *The Verbal Environment of the Language-Learning Child*, American Speech and Hearing Assn. monograph no. 17 (Washington, D.C.: American Speech and Hearing Association, 1972).

(forty-five to ninety-four months), indicating that a mother adapts her language to her perception of what her child's should be sounding like. (Actually, a comparison was made of mothers' speech in three conditions: younger children, older children, and adults. Using three conditions resulted in more information about mothers' speech to children of both ages.)

Broen found the following generalizations to be true, regardless of the children's age:

1. Mothers talk more slowly to their children than they do to adults.
2. Pauses in mothers' speech to children are usually located at the ends of sentences, whereas pauses in their speech to adults are located almost anywhere within sentences, as well as at the ends of sentences.
3. The mother's vocabulary is geared to the child's vocabulary, but with adults her vocabulary size is far greater.
4. The sentence structures mothers use with children are of two basic types; sentence structure in mother-adult interactions is more varied.

Mothers, acting as communication models, adapt their language to children. This finding should not startle us: in observing adult-child interactions it is quite apparent that they differ in many respects from adult-adult interactions.

The most interesting comparison is between mother-younger child interaction and mother-older child interaction. With younger children (about two years of age) mothers tend to talk in brief sentences:

Child: See?
Mother: That's my purse.
Child: Mommy purse.
Mother: Put it here.

Dialogues of this nature are abundant in mothers' speech to their younger children. Rarely do mothers speak in complex sentence forms. Their sentences represent two basic patterns:

1. Imperative sentence (a command or request).
2. "Be" sentence, with "this," "that," "it," "there," or "here" as a major constituent.

In the dialogue immediately above, the mother used an imperative sentence, "Put it here," and a "be" sentence, "That's my purse." Imperative sentences to children usually start with the verbs, "look," "put," and "see." The "be" sentences (questions and statements) to young children look like this:

"What's in there?"
"It's a nice dolly."
"There is the box." '

When talking to their older children (four to eight years of age), mothers usually employ the same kinds of sentence structures—that is, imperative sentences and "be" sentences—but their sentences are more complex. The difference is in the extent of modification in the noun phrases. Consider the following sentences, which are typical of mothers' speech to older children:

Imperatives:

"Please put the purse on the big table."
"See the pretty little dolly."

"Be" sentences:

"What's in that big box over there?"
"That table is really big, isn't it?"
"There is a special treat in my purse."

Mothers adopt common sentence patterns in talking with their children. They expand these patterns into bigger sentences with greater modification when they talk to their older children. Mothers' speech to adults is far more complex, structurally.

In summary, mothers, and possibly all models, tend to provide a simple form of language for their children. The language used by mothers with their children reveals a process of development similar to that of children's language, although the speech of mothers is "slightly" more advanced. This adapted form of parental speech may or may not assist the child in acquiring language structures. The simpler forms of adult language may help the child in defining major linguistic units, such as the sentence, where pauses are always used to define the end of a sentence. Simpler sentences are undoubtedly easier for children to understand. Since the vocabulary of mothers is geared to their children's understanding, misunderstandings based on word meaning are not likely to occur.

Sentence structure can thus be the focus for interaction assistance. On the other side of the coin, however, the simpler forms of language may only slow children in their grammatical progression. If parents used more adultlike language with their children, would their children progress faster or better than children whose parents used the simpler forms of speech? Further research must be conducted to answer this question.

Interaction opportunities are important in children's develop-ment of language. Evidence suggests that the structure of models' language to children is geared to the structure of children's language. Those who talk with children often show in their language a kind of sensitivity to children's language. The child's progress in acquiring language is affected by the content and structure of the model's speech. When others extend the meaning of children's utterances, children seem to progress more rapidly in developing language structure. The structure of the model's speech in the interaction process may or may not play the key role in grammatical progression. A tempting conclusion about the role of interaction in children's development of language is this:

> *The semantic richness of a communication model's language (in inter-action with children) helps to advance children's language and its structure; syntactic richness may or may not help to advance language, but models usually gear their language structure to that employed by children.*

"DIFFERENT" COMMUNICATION ENVIRONMENTS

Thus far, in discussing various studies we have sometimes qualified our remarks according to the background of the children studied. Most of the studies were of children from white, middle-class socioeconomic backgrounds. A primary consideration of parents and teachers of children is the effect of different communication environments on children's development of language. Is children's communication a function of the type of communication environ-ment and its interpersonal forces?

Many child development experts claim that the quantity and quality of communication data in certain conditions of environ-mental deprivation (such as low socioeconomic background, large families, children in orphanages, and children from congenitally deaf parents) are so low and poor that they negatively affect the child's acquisition of communication. Many textbooks state that the environment drastically affects the nature of language development. Although it may seem tempting to accept this conclusion, we have to look at some evidence first. If children reared in conditions such as those just mentioned develop language quite regularly, then the supposedly poor environments do not really cripple the child's progress. A review of the studies considering the effects of "poor" environments on children's development of language leads us to a few basic conclusions.[9]

1. *Socioeconomic background:* Studies that compare the language of lower- and upper-class children fail to account for the influence of malnutrition and disease, which may delay the child's development. Those who conclude that there are language deficiencies (for instance, in vocabulary and sentence structure) in groups of lower social class are not necessarily correct from a developmental standpoint. Probably the only acceptable conclusion is that children from different social classes may acquire languages that are slightly *different,* but they still acquire such languages according to regular developmental schedules.

2. *Large families:* Studies indicate that the emergence of single-word utterances, phrases, and intelligible speech is no different for the first child than for subsequent children.

3. *Orphans:* Children reared in orphanages are frequently below average in speech and coordination when tested at age three; but when retested at six or seven years of age, these children have caught up with control populations, in terms of language.

4. *Congenitally deaf parents:* The language onset for children of congenitally deaf parents is not delayed, although the quality of vocalization of the preschool child from this dramatically abnormal environment tends to be different. If such children are exposed to communication models elsewhere, their development can be normal.

Communication environments can differ in rather important ways: for instance, socioeconomic class, language of parents, presence versus absence of parents, and size of family. Evidence indicates, however, that children from most kinds of environments will develop language normally, in the same stage-by-stage fashion. Although children sometimes progress more slowly in certain environments, they usually catch up at some point. Different communication environments do not affect development differently, per se; but different environments shape the form communication takes in the family, and, consequently, children's language is affected.

styles of family communication

According to Basil Bernstein, a productive approach to viewing communication differences as a product of the environment lies in the analysis of family communication styles: the particular language code that children acquire depends on the basic structure of the family.[10] Social roles within the family can take two basic forms:

[9] Eric Lenneberg, *Biological Foundations of Language* (New York: John Wiley and Sons, 1969), pp. 135-39.

[10] Basil Bernstein, "A Sociolinguistic Approach to Socialization: With Some Reference to Educability," in *Directions in Sociolinguistics*, ed. J. Gumperz and D. Hymes (New York: Holt, Rinehart and Winston, 1972), pp. 465-97.

1. *Person-oriented families:* The family has an *open* role system, such that each member of the family has discretion in the performance of his or her role. The more decisions allowed each member of the family (children included), the more chance each person will have to communicate personal choices. Communication in the open role system includes judgments (and reasons) as the basic content of talk. A child's personal qualities are often considered of great value. In an open-family style of communication, children socialize and learn to cope with abstraction, ambiguity, and ambivalence.

2. *Position-oriented families:* The family has a *prescribed* role system, and each member of the family has little choice in his or her role. Family roles are assigned rather than achieved, and are often prescribed by parents according to the age and sex of the child. Communication is less open because of the boundaries (an abundance of status-related rules) defined by the parents. A person's position in the family, according to age and status, often dictates his patterns of acting and communicating, and thus his social role, in the family. Because family roles are prescribed from a positional standpoint, communication cannot be open. For example, children do not have the right to ask questions about their place in the order of persons in their families. Disputes regarding roles and rules are often the focus of communication. Children do not learn to cope effectively with abstraction, ambiguity, and ambivalence, and their communication reflects this.

These two family styles of communication are very different from each other. In the person-oriented family, Bernstein discovered that language patterns are more elaborated in terms of meaning and structure. In position-oriented families, there is greater likelihood that children will develop a restricted language code. Since judgments and their bases are the basic content of the open family's talk, the child is in an excellent position to acquire an elaborated form of communication to accommodate this type of content. The child in a closed family is not required (or allowed) to question his or her social position; his experience in using elaborated forms of language is minimal. The restricted code is characterized by syntactically simple sentences and rather concrete meanings.

What this approach tells us as teachers and parents is that an understanding of children's communication is not possible without an understanding of the social system characterizing their family environment. The often-cited language "deficiencies" in children from certain environments are not so much deficiencies as differences in family structures and styles of communication. Bernstein also states that families with a person-oriented communication system are not constrained to use only an elaborated language. Restricted forms of language are also a part of their communication. But in families bound by position-oriented roles the elaborated code receives little or no practice. Children growing up in a closed family are less able to acquire the elaborated code as they grow up, unless they can do so in school. Thus, the school experience for children from position-oriented families is of supreme importance; the school is the only environment that will give this child practice in acquiring an elaborated form of language. In this sense, *teachers are extremely important communication models for children from position-oriented families.*

What can the elementary school program provide for children in order to help them acquire skill in both person-oriented and position-oriented styles of communication? The goal of communication instruction should be to give children the opportunity to communicate in various types of communication situations. Before instruction can be designed for children, however, the teacher must understand the nature of children's communication in both verbal and nonverbal channels. Parts II and III of this text present a comprehensive discussion of children's development of verbal and nonverbal communication.

SUMMARY

Interpersonal forces affecting children's development of communication are the communication models (such as parents, siblings, friends, and teachers) to which the child is exposed, and the type of communication interaction between the child and the model. To better understand the contribution of interpersonal forces to the total learning process, consider these three components of a model for communication learning:

1. *Input (interpersonal forces):* Children receive communication data; communication *models* provide children with verbal and nonverbal language patterns that they can discover, and their *interaction* with these models offers opportunities for their further development.
2. *Children's Equipment (intrapersonal forces):* Biological forces, including the maturation of the child's brain, vocal apparatus, and body, direct the course of development; further, children's self-initiated *discovery and practice* in language assist them in development.
3. *Output:* Children's communication is characteristic of their stage of development (maturation) and their communication environment.

The major interpersonal forces affecting children's development of communication are their communication models and their interaction with these models. First, communication models play an important role in providing communication data—that is, verbal and nonverbal language patterns characteristic of the full-fledged language system. Direct imitation of the model's language by children does not seem to account for their progress in communication development, but adult expansions of children's utterances ("filling out the grammar") may assist in the learning process.

Probably more important in children's language development is the nature of communication exchanges (interaction) with models. When others comment on children's utterances—suggesting ideas, asking questions, and making suggestions—they are extending the meaning of children's language. This technique is called extension and has been found effective in helping children acquire more complex grammatical structures. The language that mothers direct to their children appears to be structured like the child's language; studies have supported this tendency of mothers (and perhaps other models, as well). Consequently, the key interpersonal forces assisting development may rest more in the *content* of interaction than in the *structure* of interaction.

Different communication environments affect children's communication in important ways. However, environments thought to be detrimental—for instance, poor families, large families, and orphanages—do not appear to harm the general course of development. The important factors are clearly the presence of "live" communication models, ready to interact. But communication environments can differ in another way, which *has* been found to make a difference. The style of communication in a family depends on whether the members of that family have open or closed roles. In an open family structure, communication reflects concern for person-oriented roles. Members of the family (including children) are encouraged to talk openly and freely, asking questions and commenting on judgments and their bases. The result is a form of communication that includes elaborated language structures. In closed family systems, the position-oriented roles prescribed by parents present boundaries for behaving and talking. A member accepts his or her role and is not encouraged to challenge that role. Consequently, each person knows where he or she stands, based on sex and age. A more restricted form of language characterizes communication in this family. Because of the strong effect of the family style of communication on children, the most important model and environment for the child from the closed family system is the teacher in the school setting.

SUGGESTED READINGS

DEESE, JAMES, *Psycholinguistics*, Chap. 5. Boston: Allyn and Bacon, Inc., 1970.
SLOBIN, DAN, *Psycholinguistics*, Chap. 5. Glenview, Ill.: Scott, Foresman and Co., 1971.

II

THE CHILD'S COMMUNICATION SYSTEM: VERBAL DEVELOPMENT

Children acquire a communication system that allows them to function effectively in many important situations. A preschooler can convince his mother to invite his friends to their house for the day. A six-year-old can explain how a butterfly grows, using very precise language. A ten-year-old is able to quiet her whining three-year-old brother with a host of reasons why his whining is in vain. Children's ability to communicate effectively is based, to a great extent, on their mastery of verbal language skills.

Communication can be defined as the sharing of meanings. When we talk with someone, we share descriptions of people, events, ideas, and feelings that we have encountered. We share opinions, arguments, and pleas. The communication of meaning can be traced to the four basic levels of verbal language: sounds (phonology), words (morphology), structure (syntax), and semantics.

In Part II each level of verbal language is outlined in two ways: a definition of the level and a stage-by-stage account of how children learn that level. Children's verbal language development is viewed as a process that can best be explained in terms of the development of meaning, whether through phonemes, morphemes, syntax, or semantics. The best view of children's development of meaning is given through a stage-by-stage analysis, where each stage offers an explanation of children's meanings. Some of the stages of development that we cite are based on a multitude of studies; others are cited with the qualification that further confirmatory studies are necessary. Our purpose in each chapter is to present *what we know* about how children acquire a particular level of language. Studies conducted in the past decade or two have revolutionized our understanding of children's acquisition of language. The new information should be invaluable in helping parents and teachers understand their children.

Chapter 4 is an introduction to the four chapters that follow it. It argues that a competence-performance approach to the study of verbal language development is most productive. Children's development of language entails the acquisition of linguistic intuitions about how the language should sound. Five methods of study typically employed in research with children are explained with the help of examples.

Chapters 5-8 deal with the four basic verbal levels. Each chapter outlines one of these levels according to the typical stages of its development. The following sections stress the importance of each of these levels in the communication of meaning.

SOUNDS AND SENSE

The sounds we use in communicating are described by our language's phonological system. Chapter 5 adopts a modern view of phonology to explain children's mastery of speech sounds. That view is called the *distinctive-features* approach to language sounds. According to this approach, phonemes are defined according to "sound bundles" or distinctive features. We have tentatively advanced what we believe to be the stages of development in the children's mastery of these features.

The distinctive-features approach to children's mastery of English sounds is based on the premise that sounds can be considered learned once they appear in words that assist in the distinction of meaning. In essence, studies in the area of phonological development start with the emergence of meaningful communication. It is important to determine when those "first words" emerge so that we can begin our examination of phonemic mastery.

WORDS AND MEANINGS

When we think of meanings, we often think of the words available to communicate those meanings. Our vocabulary is usually considered our source of power for the communication of meaning. To a certain extent, this is true. Linguists suggest, however, that the basic unit of meaning is the *morpheme*, and that the study of children's development of meaning must focus on this unit. Basically, the morpheme is a minimal meaning unit, the smallest unit we can derive from a word that "says something," from the standpoint of meaning. Consequently, we have free morphemes, such as "cat," "word," and "enjoy," that can stand alone and convey meaning; but we also have bound morphemes, such as "-ed" and "pre-," that do not stand alone but still convey meanings. The study of morphological development focuses on children's acquisition of the meanings related to various bound and free morphemes.

Children's performance in school settings, as well as their behavior in social groups, is based on their ability to communicate meanings to others. Morphemes can be used to make fine distinctions among objects, events, feelings, and actions. Thus, children who are able to use morphemes to express fine distinctions in meaning will more successfully communicate their ideas, feelings, and attitudes to others. Vocabulary instruction has long been an important component of language arts instruction in elementary school years. It should continue, but in a more meaningful way that is in accord with developmental principles. In Chapter 6 the discussion of how children acquire meanings is from a morphological viewpoint. By analyzing the stages of morphological development in children, we can create more effective programs to build children's vocabularies (actually, their knowledge of meanings).

STRUCTURE AND MEANING

As children acquire complex sentence structures, they acquire a potential for communicating specific and subtle meanings. A sentence containing a high degree of modification and subordination of ideas is quite effective in communicating an idea vividly and accurately. Chapter 7 emphasizes the fact that children learn the syntax of their language in a stage-by-stage fashion. With little help from those around him, a child will eventually utter sentences that reflect the syntax of adult sentences. The most important assistance an adult can give young children acquiring syntactic rules is to employ language that uses these rules. Research has indicated that although it might help toddlers to use a form of "baby language" that is easier for them to copy, the use of any form of baby language for language-learning children may only hinder their development.

Chapter 7 is organized according to six stages in children's development of language structure. We based our selection of these six stages on information gathered from a host of studies on the emergence of structure in children's speech. Since the communication of meaning is accomplished by the use of various syntactic structures, teachers must be given a comprehensive view of syntactic development that covers all the language-learning years. Chapter 7 presents syntactic development in a comprehensive manner, beginning with early forms of toddler language and extending to the complex structures acquired in later elementary-school years.

SEMANTICS AND MEANING

Probably the most pressing problem in our everyday communication is that of sentence meanings. "What do you mean?" is a question asked again and again in our encounters with our family, friends, and strangers. Children acquire the semantic rules of their language in a slow but steady fashion. It takes children far longer to learn sentence meanings, for example, than to learn the sounds and structure of their language. Children have difficulty in saying what they mean primarily because their "dictionary of meanings" is not complete until they reach adolescence.

The dictionary of meanings for a young child is based solely on tangible, concrete properties. Consequently, a young child's messages involve meanings that are related to tangible and concrete properties as opposed to the more abstract and conceptual properties. For example, a child's meaning for "mother" may relate primarily to the more visible, concrete attributes of age, size, and the clothes she wears than to the more conceptual properties of child rearing, providing security and loving. A clear understanding of how children develop meanings as they progress cognitively is critical in our attempt to understand children's development of language. Chapter 8 examines children's cognitive development and explores the changes that take place in children's "meaning dictionaries."

4

children's language:
methods of discovery

"That not ice cream. Where my ice cream goed?"

Children's sentences such as these have traditionally been explained as including "mistakes." Current theories of child language development, however, regard the child as a capable speaker of his own rather "curious" language rather than a poor speaker of adult language. They argue that children actually *follow their own rules* in forming negative constructions, asking questions, producing past tenses of verbs, and so forth. These rules are not deviations or distortions of adult language rules; they simply differ from the rules adults follow. As the child progresses through his elementary school years his language gradually approaches that of an adult. Modern theorists explain language development in children in terms of the child's stage-by-stage and rule-by-rule acquisition of adult linguistic competence.

This new approach to studying child language is based on a distinction between *linguistic competence* and *linguistic performance*. The implications of this technical distinction for communication instruction in the classroom are very important. In fact, many authorities view children's reading, listening, speaking, and writing skills according to the competence-performance approach.

This chapter explores the distinction between linguistic competence and linguistic performance as applied to children's development of language. Our purpose in studying children's language is always to uncover an explanation for why children use particular forms of language, forms that are characteristically child-like. It is not enough that we understand what are in the forms of language that children employ; we must understand the nature of the language rules which prompt children to use their language as they do. Consequently, the competence model suggests that we must search for children's rules of a language, knowledge that we speak of in terms of linguistic intuitions. This chapter discusses five methods of uncovering children's linguistic intuitions that allow us to view their linguistic competence:

1. Check for regularities in usage.
2. Test for the extension of regularities to new instances.
3. Look for the child's self-corrections.
4. Ask indirect questions.
5. Ask direct questions.[1]

Before examining the discovery methods, let's outline the competence-performance distinction.

OUR INTUITIONS ABOUT LANGUAGE: OUR COMPETENCE

Every adult, native speaker of a language, whether that language is English, Russian, or Samoan, has certain linguistic "intuitions" about how his language should sound. These judgments represent our underlying knowledge of the *rules of language* and constitute what linguists have labeled *competence*. If we were asked to state our linguistic intuitions—for instance, why a sentence sounds right or wrong to us—we probably could not. But all of us speak as if we know what these rules are.

All of us have a fair understanding of intuition. We know that it refers to our capacity for guessing accurately, possibly without the ability to present solid reasons for what we believe to be true. We also know that sharp insight into a matter can be called intuition.

---

[1] These five methods are based on ideas provided in Dan Slobin, *Psycholinguistics* (Glenview, Ill.: Scott, Foresman and Co., 1971), p. 7.

Incidentally, it has been said that females possess an uncanny ability to perceive a situation and then predict what might happen. This sharp insight cannot always be explained—it's simply a "woman's intuition," right? And it's often correct. "Good guesses," "sharp insights"—these phrases capture the spirit of a linguistic intuition, as well.

When we hear ungrammatical sentences, such as those spoken by the child in the introduction to this chapter,

"That not ice cream. Where my ice cream goed?"

we notice that the utterances do not conform to adult rules. If pressed to explain why we can make this judgment, we might not be able to present a list of grammatical rules that have been broken, from an adult standpoint. Our sharp insight regarding the structure of English tells us, "Something is wrong!" We might fumble a bit in supporting our insight with reasons. Nevertheless, our judgment represents our intuition about how language should sound in order to mesh with the language patterns spoken in the community.

Our linguistic intuitions are guesses, but they are guesses based on top-notch, native experience with the rules of English. After all, we have spent many years of our lives learning language rules, so saying that linguistic intuitions are simply guesses does not reflect the rich experience we have had in acquiring them. Instead, we might say our intuitions represent solid judgments about what sounds right and what something means, based on our experience in the "business" of language learning.

intuition 1: "It's grammatical!"

Because you are a native speaker of English, you can distinguish well-formed sentences from ungrammatical strings of words. Consider the following:

1.   Rubber the active duckie threw the boy.
2.   The rubber boy threw the active duckie.
3.   The active boy threw the rubber duckie.

As an adult speaker of English, you had no trouble distinguishing which one was merely an unstructured string of words (sentence 1), which one followed grammatical word ordering but made little sense (sentence 2), and which one was a well-formed and meaningful sentence (sentence 3). (By the way, children attach great significance to little rubber duckies. Ernie, who lives on "Sesame Street," is never without his rubber duckie. It means a lot to him.)

In addition, you know when certain word sequences are not acceptable sentences. For example:

4. The boy who was active and that I knew threw the rubber duckie.

Something is wrong there, and you know it!

Your sense of grammaticality also includes some knowledge of what linguists call "degree of deviation" of sentences from English. For example, most of us would agree that the following sentences are scaled from top to bottom in terms of increasing deviation from English.[2]

5. The dog looks terrifying.
6. The dog looks barking.
7. The dog looks lamb.

A speaker's ability to make such distinctions is based on his grammatical intuition.

intuition 2:
"There's a difference in underlying meaning."

Adult speakers can also distinguish between sentences that look alike on the surface but differ in their underlying meaning:

8. The doll is easy to see.
9. The doll is eager to see.

The difference between sentences 8 and 9 becomes apparent if we analyze the relations between the words within each sentence. The doll is the subject of sentence 9—it is seeing "eagerly." In sentence 8, however, someone else is the actor—the doll is what can be seen. Our ability to assess relationships between nouns and verbs, to determine which noun is subject and which is object, and to identify which words modify other words enables us to distinguish differences in the underlying meaning of sentences.

Incidentally, five-year-olds will have trouble understanding the difference in meaning between sentences 8 and 9, whereas nine-year-olds will have no difficulty at all. A young child, when asked if a

---

[2] R. B. Lees, "Review of Syntactic Structures," Language, *XXXIII* (1957), 375-408.

blindfolded doll is "easy to see," will say "No" because "the blindfold is in the way." Obviously, the child has missed the point of the question and the meaning of the sentence: the child has assumed that the doll is "seeing," when in reality, the question asked whether the child was able to see easily. Children of elementary-school age are in the process of acquiring complex grammatical rules related to underlying sentence meaning. The development of these rules (stage 6 of the child's acquisition of syntax) is explored in Chapter 7.

intuition 3: "They're saying the same thing."

   Adult speakers can also distinguish between sentences that look different on the surface but are alike in underlying meaning:

   10. The elephant carried the man.
   11. The man was carried by the elephant.

There is no question in your mind that the elephant is the subject of both sentences—the man never "does the work." Experience with language tells us that these sentences are saying the same thing, even

Figure 4.1. *Passive sentence understanding: monster and boy.*

though the form is different. The difference in form is something we might be able to pinpoint if we recall our high school grammar. Sentence 10 is presented in an active form, whereas sentence 11 is written in a passive form.

Our intuition about the semantic relationship between active and passive sentence forms is based on learning and becomes a part of our linguistic competence. The linguistic competence of a four-year-old child may not include the ability to make such a judgment, however. As we will see in Chapter 8, preschoolers have trouble understanding the "meaning" of certain passive sentences. If young children are shown a picture of a monster chasing a little boy (see Figure 4.1) and are asked, "Does this sentence match the picture?"

12. The monster is being chased by the little boy.

the children might reply, "Yes, they match OK." Intuitions regarding semantic rules of a language take time to develop.

intuition 4: "It's ambiguous."

Adult speakers can judge whether or not a sentence is ambiguous. Some sentences have more than one interpretation:

13. Walking toddlers can be a pleasure.

This sentence could mean "Toddlers who walk can be a pleasure," or it could mean "It can be a pleasure to walk toddlers." The ambiguous verb in this sentence could be rewritten in two different ways:

14. Walking toddlers are a pleasure. (*They* look so cute, that is, until they get away from us.)

15. Walking toddlers is a pleasure. (The *activity* can be enjoyable, unless the wee ones have "ideas.")

Sentence 13 can be "read" two different ways by using stress and pause to illustrate differences in meaning. The words in both readings are the same, but the underlying meanings of the readings, as expressed in sentences 14 and 15 are different.

The study of linguistic competence attempts to account for all such linguistic intuitions that relate to grammaticality and meaning. Competence theorists do not try to explain how and why we use language in everyday situations. Instead, they attempt to explain what knowledge—that is, what linguistic intuitions—people must possess in order to make judgments about language. In this sense, competence is an abstraction—a model on which we base our language performance.

THE "REALITIES" OF LANGUAGE: OUR PERFORMANCE

Psycholinguist David McNeill once remarked, "Performance operates under constraints of memory, which is finite, and time, which must be kept up with."[3] Unlike its performance counterpart, competence is not at all concerned with time and memory, for competence is based on a computerlike memory with all the time in the world. The competence computer can generate any number of sentences but all that it guarantees is that these sentences follow the rules of grammar by which it was programmed. Consequently, a grammatical sentence generated by a competence model might be an endless "linguistic onion," fifty words long or longer, including complex constructions that could entail hours of decoding by a human being. The human speaker, unlike our competence "computer," has a limited memory capacity that does not allow for the production of long, extremely complex sentences. Furthermore, human speakers do not have hours in which to decode—they must understand and produce sentences "on the spot." A competence theory pays no attention to the complexity or length of a sentence it generates. (Remember that computers have huge memories.)

Such a theory does not account for what we actually say or why we say it as we do. We need a performance theory to do this job. Performance studies have indicated, for example, that it is easy enough to produce or understand a sentence with one other sentence embedded in it. Here is a case in point.

The rubber duckie that the boy threw squeeks.

"The boy threw (the rubber duckie)" is embedded in "The rubber duckie squeeks." Even two embeddings are not particularly difficult if you concentrate, but three or more embeddings become nearly impossible for most speakers. Try this one.

The rubber duckie that the boy that his dog who was frisky fetched threw squeeks.

It's one of those linguistic onions (a weird one, too) that our

---

[3] David McNeill, "Developmental Psycholinguistics," in *The Genesis of Language*, ed. Frank Smith and George Miller (Cambridge, Mass.: The M. I. T. Press, 1966), p. 17.

competence computer might produce. This sentence is simply too taxing on our memory to produce or understand "correctly." We would probably express our observations of the boy, his rubber duckie, and his frisky dog by means of other, more "acceptable" sentences.

Because our practical concern is with oral language performance, we must "live with" human limits on performance. The competence model has no limits whatsoever; people, however, "make human-like errors under less-than-ideal conditions in their language performance."[4] Defining memory boundaries is crucial in any theory of performance. Further, "factors [such as] fatigue, switching of attention, distractibility, emotional excitement, drugs, and so on, affect linguistic performance in many ways not envisaged by the model of competence."[5]

Our starting point in studying children's language is not at the level of performance factors such as memory and attention. Instead, we first have to uncover the child's linguistic competence—the network of rules that govern the utterances he can produce and understand. Once we have a pretty good idea about the structure and form of children's sentences, we can propose performance explanations that might account for these structures. Consider, for example, these three-word sentences produced by a typical two-and a-half-year-old child:

"Mommy go bye-bye."
"Bobbie fall down."

These sentences must first be explained in terms of the syntactic rules the child seems to follow in putting words together in this way.

First question: What is the nature of the competence model governing children's sentences at this stage of development?

We can then propose relevant performance factors, such as the child's short-term memory capacity, that might account for the apparent three-word "limit" that is so typical of young children's sentences.

Second question: What psychological factors explain the form and content of the child's linguistic competence at this stage of language development?

Performance studies are difficult to design. Psychological techniques that "probe" the human mind are complex and require

[4] Slobin, *Psycholinguistics,* p. 7.
[5] Ibid.

the full cooperation of the person being tested. It can be extremely difficult to get a child to cooperate in a testing situation of this nature. More important, psychological tests that rely on human performance for information yield only *guesses* about how our mind is working when we produce or understand a sentence. Neurological equipment that could directly examine the human mind, electronically and chemically, would result in less guesswork. Some day soon, we will probably be able to "watch" the child's brain in action as it works to produce that three-word sentence.

Our most logical starting point in the study of children's language is linguistic competence: What are the methods of tapping children's linguistic intuitions? The following methods help us discover a child's linguistic competence at any particular stage of development.

TAPPING CHILDREN'S LINGUISTIC INTUITIONS: FIVE METHODS

A grammarian is concerned with studying linguistic competence, as exhibited by adult speakers. The method relies on the tapping of adults' linguistic intuitions. A grammarian studying children's language competence is confronted with a very difficult task. Consider the following attempt to tap a linguistic intuition (of grammaticality), an attempt that two linguists, Roger Brown and Ursula Bellugi, thought relevant to Adam's competence.

Interviewer: Now Adam, listen to what I say. Tell me which is
    better . . . some water or a water.
Adam (two-year-old):   Pop go weasel.[6]

Two-year-olds do not make very good native informants for providing intuitions. Slobin has suggested that there are several methods for discovering the linguistic intuitions of children (or adults, for that matter), in addition to the *direct-question* method used with Adam.

check for regularities in usage

The first method for tapping children's intuitions about language involves analyzing their speech regularities. The regularities

---

[6]Roger Brown and Ursula Bellugi, "Three Processes in the Child's Acquisition of Syntax," *Harvard Educational Review*, XXXIV (1964), 133-51.

or patterns are noted, recorded, and explained in terms of rules. Consider the following sentences typically produced by children.

1. "Allgone shoe"
2. "Allgone Mommy."
3. "Allgone hot."

In these three sentences, the message or sentence was composed of "allgone" plus the object word. On a regular basis, children select the descriptive word "allgone" to modify "shoe," "Mommy," and "hot." Children could not have been "reducing," or simplifying adult sentences in these instances; adults would not produce complete sentences with these words, in an order resembling the children's order. Rather, children follow their own rules of sentence production. By observing regularities in children's speech, then, such rules can be uncovered.

test for the extension of regularities to new instances

A more stringent method of demonstrating the existence of a rule is to search for the extension of regularities to new instances. A good example of this method is that employed by Berko in her landmark study of child language, which we discussed briefly in Chapter 2. Persuaded by the regularity of childlike utterances such as "he goed" and "two mouses," Berko created a nonsense language of words such as *wug* and *bing*. Cartooned pictures of a fat little bird (a wug) and a man standing on the ceiling (binging) were used to elicit responses in this way.

> This is a wug. (picture of one wug)
> Now there is another one. (picture of two wugs)
> There are two of them. They are two_____.
>
> This is a man who knows how to bing. (picture of man standing on ceiling)
> He is binging. He did the same thing yesterday. What did he do yesterday?
> Yesterday he_____.[7]

Children followed their own rules in forming plurals ("wugs") and past tenses of verbs ("binged"). Since the children had never heard these words before, Berko and other theorists concluded that children are able to produce new forms in a regular fashion, based on a knowledge of grammatical rules.

------

[7] Jean Berko, "The Child's Learning of English Morphology," *Word*, XIV (1958), 150-77.

look for self-corrections

A third method of uncovering linguistic intuitions requires evidence that a child has a "normative sense of rules." In some situations, it is apparent that a child can judge whether or not an utterance is correct according to some linguistic standard. A child's sense of grammaticality can be observed in this three-year-old-girl's "self-corrections."

"She had a bad headache like me had . . . like I . . . like I did."

This child was monitoring her speech in accordance with rules she simply "knew." In this case the standards were adult rules. In other examples the same girl may adjust her speech to follow her own rules rather then adult rules.

"Why . . . Why . . . Why people have not . . . Why people have no tails?"

After realizing that her attempt to follow adult rules was not working out so well, she changed her utterance to conform with her own rules for negative questions.

ask indirect questions

A series of studies by Carol Chomsky illustrates the fourth method of tapping children's linguistic intuitions. Her ingenious approach concerned the understanding of *grammatical relations* by children from five to ten years of age.[8] The interviewer presented children with a blindfolded doll and asked this question (recall sentence 8 on p. 66):

"Is this doll easy to see or hard to see?"

Most five-year-olds insisted that the doll was "hard to see." The interviewer then asked the children:

"Would you make her easy to see?"

The children simply removed the doll's blindfold. When asked, "Why is she easy to see now when she wasn't before?" the children usually pointed to the blindfold and said, "Cuz it's off now." The point here is that these children did not understand the grammatical relations between the words of this sentence. Only the nine-year-olds in her study understood that the blindfold had nothing to do with the

---

[8] Reprinted from *The Acquisition of Syntax in Children from 5 to 10* by Carol Chomsky by permission of The M. I. T. Press, Cambridge, Massachusetts. © 1969 by The M. I. T. Press.

correct answer to the question. As a whole, children between five and eight years of age gave mixed responses: some children understood the construction but others did not. The children that did not respond "correctly" were probably following another rule (or set of rules) in understanding this sentence. The object of child language study, then, is to detect the rules that children *do* follow in producing and understanding sentences.

ask a direct question

The most stringent method for tapping children's linguistic intuitions, other than asking them to state the intuitions explicitly, is to ask them direct questions. Linguists depend heavily on this method in formulating a theory of adult competence, but as we saw from Adam's "pop go weasel" response, this method may not be very productive with young children. According to Slobin, "the ability to make such overt grammatical judgments is late to develop in childhood."[9]

Armed with these five methods of determining the rules children follow in using language, developmental psycholinguists have begun to characterize the stages of language development in children. Though not specifically defined in terms of children's chronological ages, these stages represent periods of development in the child's pursuit of adult linguistic competence. By tapping the linguistic intuitions of children, scientists can postulate constructs of children's language competence at successive stages of development. Generally, all children pass through such stages, regardless of their income level, home environment, or cultural background; and they all do so at about the same time in their life.

Most of the information presented in Chapters 5-8 is based on one or more of these five methods. These methods have allowed theorists to account for the development of verbal language in children, thus paving the way for psychologists and neurologists to explain *why* children's language develops as it does.

SUMMARY

The study of children's verbal language is based on the competence-performance distinction. Linguistic competence refers to our underlying knowledge of the rules of a language, knowledge that we speak of in terms of linguistic intuitions—how a sentence sounds and what it means to us. Our judgments about grammaticality, sentence meaning, and sentence ambiguity constitute our linguistic intuitions:

[9] Slobin, *Psycholinguistics*, p. 54.

1. "It's grammatical."
2. "There's a difference in underlying meaning."
3. "They're saying the same thing."
4. "It's ambiguous."

Linguistic performance concerns the study of human factors that explain why we use language the way we do. The limitations of our memory in producing and understanding sentences constitute one performance factor. Others include shifts of attention, distractions, and the like. Once we have characterized the structure and form of children's utterances, we can begin to explain why the child speaks as he does—we can study his linguistic performance.

The starting point in child language research has been the examination of children's linguistic competence at successive stages in their language development. We explored five methods of tapping children's linguistic intuitions:

1. Check for regularities in usage.
2. Test for the extension of regularities to new instances.
3. Look for the child's self-corrections.
4. Ask indirect questions.
5. Ask direct questions.

These five methods are employed by researchers who study the sounds, words, syntax, and semantic development in children's language.

SUGGESTED READINGS

SLOBIN, DAN, *Psycholinguistics*, Chap. 1. Glenview, Ill.: Scott, Foresman and Co., 1971.

WOOD, BARBARA, "Competence and Performance in Language Development," *Today's Speech*, XXI, No. 1 (1973), 23-30.

CHAPTER

5

the sounds
in children's communication

Young children are capable of making hundreds of different sounds. In addition to those they use in their speech, children can make the sounds of animals, horns, racing car engines, and police sirens. Parents are familiar with that steady stream of noise and sound that flows from their children's mouths all day long. Even infants are versatile in their production of sound: they produce many of the sounds that will appear some time later in their speech, but they also produce some exotic sounds resembling German gutterals, French "r" sounds, and African clicking sounds. The more exotic sounds soon disappear, probably because they are not reinforced by parents.

From a vast repertoire of *possible sounds*, children learn to communicate with a *basic set of sounds* appropriate to their language. The sounds of speech, called phonemes, are the basic building blocks of a language. Sounds are combined to form words, and words are combined to form sentences. So the heart and the start of the language learning process must be an understanding of how children acquire that basic set of sounds that are appropriate to their language community. Although it might be said that specific sounds do not express our ideas in communication ("It's really words

76

and sentences!"), a detailed discussion of speech sounds must be considered for two important reasons:

1. Phonemes constitute the core of any language used for communication, and we must therefore know what they are and how children learn them.
2. Phonemes are often the focus of attention in understanding a child's speech because (a) the child's speech sounds are often different from adults', and we may not know what the child is saying; (b) the child's speech may involve phoneme errors, and we must understand the nature of these errors; and (c) the child may speak a dialect of English, which involves the use of phonemes that are different from standard English phonemes, and we should be aware of these differences.

A solid understanding of phonological development is crucial to our understanding of children's language development. The following discussion of children's acquisition of sounds may become a technical one for those without a background in the study of phonetics. Still, to understand how children learn to speak, we must be aware of the step-by-step process by which they acquire speech sounds; this entails a discussion of the specification of speech sounds.

The sound system of any language includes a core of building blocks—phonemes—for the communication of ideas. In order to understand how children learn the phonemes of their language, we must understand how speech sounds are *specified*—that is, how they are defined and explained by linguists. All of the symbols for the sounds of English are not found in our alphabet. Fortunately, we can turn to the linguist, who defines and describes all speech sounds according to their distinctive features.

Children acquire speech sounds in a surprisingly short period of time: the majority of sounds children will use in their communication are acquired in their first few years of life. After the fourth birthday, children struggle with the more "difficult" sounds but encounter very few communication problems in the struggle. They can get along without total mastery of all the sounds of their language.

Recent studies have shown that the more difficult-to-learn sounds for children, regardless of their native language, are the sounds that are more complex from a linguistic viewpoint. The sounds that children learn last are are also the sounds that linguists consider *rare*, in terms of their occurrence throughout the world. Children's utterances such as these:

"Yook at the wabbit chasing the turtle!"
"Pease, may I have mow candy?"

reflect difficulty with the /l/ and /r/ sounds of English. According to linguists, these two English sounds are not found in all languages of the world. Furthermore, in order to describe the linguistic characteristics of these two sounds, as compared to other sounds that appear in all languages, linguists need to employ a greater number of features in their descriptions. In the more technical sense, the /l/ and /r/ sounds are "marked" for a significant number of features. The sounds which are common to all languages of the world (for example, /p t k s n/) are marked for just one feature, by contrast. In the language learning process, whether the language is Russian, English, or German, children first acquire a basic set of sounds common to all languages and then learn the sounds that are more characteristic of their native language. Young children (for instance, at the early elementary level) who are struggling to acquire the more complex sounds have learned a sufficient number of sounds to communicate effectively with their parents, their friends, and others.

It is important for parents and teachers to be aware of *how* the children learn the sounds of their language. A strong awareness of the learning process will aid teachers or parents in both understanding children's speech and assessing their progress. Before exploring how children acquire speech sounds, we must understand two important subjects: (1) the physiological processes necessary for making speech sounds; and (2) the basic characteristics of the sounds children must learn.

PROCESSES NECESSARY FOR SPEECH

Four processes are necessary for the production of speech sounds: respiration, phonation, resonation, and articulation. When we speak, we usually don't think about these processes; we take them for granted. Instead, we probably focus our attention on what we are saying or how we are saying it. We can perhaps best appreciate the importance of these processes by considering the unusual situation of a speaker who, for some reason or other, has lost one of the four processes, either temporarily or permanently. To clarify these four processes, let's consider Figure 5.1, a diagram of the speech production mechanism.

respiration

Obviously, respiration (breathing) is essential for life, but it also acts as the energy source for human speech sounds. The lungs (see Figure 5.1) send air through the trachea to the oral and nasal cavities, which modify the air for speech purposes. To better realize the

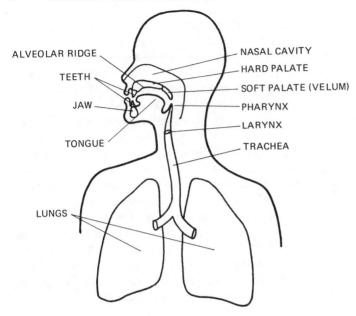

ALVEOLAR RIDGE
TEETH
JAW
TONGUE
LUNGS

NASAL CAVITY
HARD PALATE
SOFT PALATE (VELUM)
PHARYNX
LARYNX
TRACHEA

Figure 5.1. *The speech production system. Adapted from Frederick Williams,* Language and Speech: Introductory Perspectives *(Englewood Cliffs, N.J.: Prentice-Hall, Inc., 1972), pp. 31-32.*

function of respiration in speech, try to visualize the difficulties you encountered if you have had the wind knocked out of you. When this happens, it becomes nearly impossible to produce any kind of speech sound. Your energy source is momentarily cut off, and you are incapable of sustaining the stream of air necessary for speech.

phonation

Phonation is the process of giving a "voice" to the stream of air. The phonation process makes the stream of air audible so that others can hear what you are saying. Contrast the audible nature of speech with the inaudible quality of whispering, which involves no phonation. The voicing for speech results from vocal-fold vibration at the larynx, where the stream of moving air is changed into acoustic energy.

The process of phonation is easily illustrated by a simple contrast. When we tell someone to be quiet without saying precisely that, we can say "shhhh." After we open our mouth so that a doctor can examine our throat, we follow the physician's command by saying "ahhhhh." Both the "shhhhh" and the "ahhhhh" sounds are related to primary speech sounds, although we don't employ such prolonged versions of the sounds in our speech. There is a certain quietness to the "shhhhh" sound—that is, it is not "voiced." On the other hand, the "ahhhhh" sound does not have this quietness; it is a voiced sound primarily because phonation is occurring. We can feel where phonation takes place by putting a hand on our neck near the vocal folds, commonly referred to as the Adam's apple. In the case of the "shhhhh" sound, there is no vibration. But with the "ahhhhh" sound, we feel the movement— the vibration—connected with phonation. Now consider a situation where a person is temporarily unable to speak because of a phonation problem. The best example of this is what is commonly called laryngitis. This malady can happen for any of several reasons, but the outcome is usually the same: a general loss of the phonation process due to injury or stress of the vocal folds. The speech of a person with laryngitis is whispered and sometimes difficult to understand. This is because many of our speech sounds require phonation: all of the English vowels are voiced, as are many of the consonants.

resonation

The third process necessary for producing speech sounds is resonation. Our ability to make different speech sounds is limited without this process. We need a speech process that allows flexibility in the kind of continuous sound we can produce. Resonation is the modification of the voiced stream of air. We accomplish resonation by varying the shape of the oral cavity: we can do so by moving the jaw and the tongue, for example.

To understand better the process of resonation, try this. Produce the "ah" sound and then vigorously move your jaw up and down and from side to side. Notice what happens to the "ah" sound. It changes with each movement, and you produce other sounds, such as "aw" or "uh." Now do the same thing but move your tongue as well. You will notice that other voiced sounds emerge—for instance, "ee" or "ehh." The process of resonation allows you to produce different continuous speech sounds.

To understand the importance of resonation, visualize (or recall, if you were a "victim") what it would be like to have a full set of braces in your mouth. What would be your initial reaction? You may be afraid to move your mouth very much—the braces might "pull" in just the wrong places. Consequently, you become cautious in moving the jaw from one position to another—movements necessary for producing various resonation qualities in speech sounds. The sounds that are affected the most noticeably are the vowels. Instead of producing a full range of vowels, which requires varying degrees of mouth opening, you produce a limited range of vowel sounds. This limited set of vowel sounds will not contain the vast differences in resonation characteristics that choir directors always insist upon.

articulation

The fourth process necessary for producing speech sounds is articulation. Contact between *mobile articulators* (for instance, tongue tip, tongue, and lips) and *fixed articulators* (for instance, alveolar ridge—the gum ridge behind upper teeth—soft palate, and hard palate) accounts for our consonant sounds (see Figure 5.1). Contact is made, for example, between the tongue tip (mobile articulator) and the alveolar ridge (fixed articulator) for the /t/ sound. Normally, we are not conscious of touching the tongue tip to the alveolar ridge; the movement is a natural, unconscious one. If we pay close attention to the movement, however, we can feel the contact. Tactile feedback assures us that we have made the movements necessary for the production of /t/.

To illustrate what happens when you lose your ability to receive tactile feedback—and, in turn, how that affects your articulation—recall the last time you had a cavity filled by a dentist. If novocaine was administered, you may have lost all feeling in your mouth. Tongue twisters became impossible; in fact, all articulation seemed sloppy. Your speech seemed "lazy" because the movements were slow. You may have thought your entire tongue had become swollen. Maybe it was too "heavy" and cumbersome for speech. The problem was not one of swelling, however. The drug simply deprived you, temporarily, of the feedback from the nerve pathways near the surface of the articulators. You couldn't feel the contact between articulators; this lack of feedback affected your speech, or more specifically, your articulation.

Given these four basic processes in the production of speech sounds, we are ready to explore the characteristics of speech sounds from the distinctive-features viewpoint.

CHARACTERISTICS OF SPEECH SOUNDS

Before we describe the sound acquisition process, we must understand the nature of the sound system children must learn. Recent advances in phonological theory have led to the description of speech sounds according to *distinctive features*.[1] This method is based on

[1] Noam Chomsky and Morris Halle, *The Sound Pattern of English* (New York: Harper & Row, 1968), pp. 163-235.

the articulatory contrasts inherent in the production of speech sounds. According to the distinctive-feature approach, there is a set of features (characteristics of sounds) that we can hear if we are trained to listen for them. A feature, such as voicing, is either present (+) or absent (−) in a particular sound being described. As you can see, the system is binary: essentially, a sound either *does* or *does not* have the feature being considered.

This binary system analyzes all the sounds in all the languages of the world. Some of the proposed features distinguish each sound from all other sounds—across languages. Theorists have discovered that all languages possess a common set of features and that differences among languages can be seen in terms of a smaller set of "unshared" features. Distinctive-feature theory suggests that English, for example, can be described according to nine features appropriate mainly to consonants and five features geared to the discrimination of vowels. This set of fourteen features classifies all the sounds in English, so that the feature-description of any one English sound is different in some way from the feature-description of any other English sound.

When children learn their native language, they master the features, not the specific sounds per se. Phonological theorists argue that children's acquisition of a language can best be described in a feature-by-feature mode. Thus, you can see why it's essential that students of children's communication first master the distinctive features of English. It's simply the logical starting point.

feature 1: consonantal

This is the basic feature, and it describes the consonantal nature of a sound. If there is a constriction or obstruction inside the oral cavity during the production of a sound, then the sound is consonantal. The constriction can occur at a number of places:

A. *Lips:* /m/ as in "mat"
             /p/ as in "pot"
             /b/ as in "bat"

B. *Tongue to upper teeth:*   /θ/ as in "teeth"
                               /ð/ as in "bother"

C. *Lower lip to upper teeth:*   /f/ as in "fine"
                                  /v/ as in "vine"

D. *Tongue to alveolar ridge:*   /t/ as in "tin"
                                  /d/ as in "dim"
                                  /s/ as in "sip"

/z/ as in "zip"
/n/ as in "nip"
/l/ as in "lip"

E. *Tongue to hard palate:*   /š/ as in "ship"
/ž/ as in "measure"
/č/ as in "chip"
/ǰ/ as in "judge"
/r/ as in "rage"

F. *Tongue (back) to velum:*   /g/ as in "goat"
/k/ as in "coat"
/ŋ/ as in "ring"

The sounds in categories A through F (actually, the majority of English consonants) are described as "+consonantal." All other sounds in English (that is, the nonconsonantal sounds) are designated "−consonantal." The nonconsonantal sounds are all vowels, such as /u/ ("push") and /ū/ ("pool"), and the glides (for instance, /y/ as in "yet").

feature 2: vocalic

The majority of consonant sounds in English, which are examples of feature 1, involve a constriction in the oral cavity. Vocalic sounds do not involve such constriction. The vowels of English are defined by the vocalic feature, that is, sounds involving spontaneous voicing from the vocal folds. A few of the consonant sounds are classified as vocalic as well as consonantal, primarily because they involve a smooth flow of air coupled with a slight constriction. The /l/ and /r/ sounds, just classified as consonantal because of the obstruction, are also classified as vocalic because of spontaneous voicing. How can sounds be described by features 1 *and* 2? You might say that the /l/ and /r/ sounds, called "liquids," have the *qualities* of both features and are thus defined by both.

Another group of sounds, called "glides," is a curious one.

/h/ as in "house"
/y/ as in "yet"
/w/ as in "will"

Since there is no major constriction in any of these sounds, we must classify them as nonconsonantal (feature 1). In addition, there is no spontaneous voicing associated with these sounds, the criterion of the vocalic feature. Thus, the glides do not exhibit the qualities of either the consonantal or the vocalic features, and we designate them

−consonantal and −vocalic. With our first two features, we can classify sounds into four different categories, using the "+" and "−" markings of distinctive-feature analysis to differentiate these sound groups.

		features	
sound category	*examples*	*consonantal*	*vocalic*
consonants	/b/, /d/	+	−
vowels	/u/, /ū/	−	+
liquids	/l/, /r/	+	+
glides	/h/, /y/	−	−

Now we are ready to introduce several other distinctive features.

feature 3: nasal

When the velum, or soft palate, is lowered to the back of the tongue, a passageway to and through the nasal cavity is opened. Sounds produced by the opening of the nasal cavity are described by the feature of nasality. Three English consonants are described by the nasal feature:

/m/ as in "meat"
/n/ as in "neat"
/ŋ/ as in "ring"

Consequently, the nasals are classified as +consonantal, −vocalic, and +nasal.

feature 4: coronal

The corona, the front part of the tongue, is crucial in the articulation of some consonants. A speech sound that depends for its articulation on the movement or positioning of the corona is described by the coronal feature. Recall that three categories of sounds in feature 1 involved tongue (coronal) constriction.

Category B. Tongue to upper teeth: /θ/, /ð/.
Category D. Tongue to alveolar ridge: /t/, /d/, /s/, /z/, /n/, /l/.
Category E. Tongue to hard palate: /š/, /ž/, /č/, /ǰ/, /r/.

In the production of these sounds, the corona participates actively in the constriction of the stream of air through the oral cavity.

feature 5: continuant

The +consonantal distinction, you will remember, refers to the constriction of the air flow in some way. But some consonantal constrictions are more obvious than others: for instance, there is greater constriction or blockage in the /t/ sound than in the /f/ or /z/ sounds. Sounds involving a maximum constriction in the oral cavity are noncontinuants (−continuant), and sounds produced with a minimum constriction are described as +continuant. Consequently, the /t/ would be classified as −continuant, whereas the /f/ and /z/ would be +continuant. Sound groups that are typically described as continuant are:

1. The fricative sounds (sounds that are characterized by frictionlike energy or hissing): /f/, /v/, /θ/, /ð/, /s/, /z/, /š/, and /ž/.
2. The liquids: /l/ and /r/.

Noncontinuants include three consonant groups:

1. The nasals: /m/, /n/, and /ŋ/. (air flow through mouth is blocked although nasal flow is "continuous.")
2. The stop sounds (sounds that involve an abrupt stop of air): /p/, /b/, /t/, /d/, /k/, and /g/.
3. The affricates (sounds that have qualities of the fricative and the stop; linguists agree, however, that the stop portion of an affricate "overpowers" the fricative (continuant) portion, so the affricates are noncontinuants): /č/ and /ǰ/.

feature 6: voicing

Whenever the process of phonation occurs in the production of speech sounds, the feature of voicing is present. All vowels are marked by +voicing, as are consonant sounds that involve vocal-fold vibration. Liquids, glides, and nasals are all characterized by +voicing. Some of the stops, fricatives, and affricates are +voicing, but others are −voicing. In fact, the voiced and nonvoiced pairs can be listed as follows:

sound category	examples	voicing
stops	/b/, /d/, /g/	+
	/p/, /t/, /k/	−
fricatives	/v/, /ð/, /z/, /ž/	+
	/f/, /θ/, /s/, /š/	−
affricates	/ǰ/	+
	/č/	−

feature 7: anterior

Sounds produced in the front of the oral cavity are called anterior; sounds produced in the back of the mouth are called nonanterior. The dividing line is at the alveolar ridge, just behind the upper teeth (see Figure 5.1). Sounds articulated at the alveolar ridge (or forward of it) are +anterior: for example, /t/, /f/, and /s/. Sounds articulated behind the alveolar ridge are −anterior: for instance, /g/, /š/, and /č/.

feature 8: strident

Whenever the following two conditions exist, the sound is classified as strident.

1. The constriction in the oral cavity produces a long hissing sound due to the forcing of air through a long, narrow passageway shaped by the tongue.
2. The hissing air then hits another constriction point (usually the upper teeth or upper lip) to produce a second noise source (a secondary hissing).

For example, when you produce a /v/ sound, the teeth-to-lip constriction produces a hissing sound. The air coming through this constricted passageway is forced into the upper lip, producing a second source of hissing. Two hissing sounds are present in strident sounds.

All fricatives and affricates are +strident except for the two "th" sounds, /θ/ and /ð/. These sounds involve a corona-upper teeth constriction, which produces the primary hissing. But a constriction point for the secondary noise source is simply not there.

Now let's take a final look at the fricative sounds and distinguish among them, feature by feature.

fricative sounds	*voicing*	*coronal*	*strident*	*anterior*
/f/	−	−	+	+
/v/	+	−	+	+
/θ/	−	−	−	+
/ð/	+	−	−	+
/s/	−	+	+	+
/z/	+	+	+	+
/š/	−	+	+	−
/ž/	+	+	+	−

feature 9: lateral

When the corona contacts the palate (the roof of the mouth) during articulation, and the sides of the tongue are lowered at the same time, the resulting sound is a lateral. The /l/ liquid is described as +lateral, and its fellow liquid, /r/, is −lateral.

With these nine features all of the consonant sounds of English can be differentiated from one another. Table 5.1 does just this. As we indicated earlier, several other features can be used to describe sounds in other languages or more detailed versions of the sounds we introduced. But our present list of nine is sufficient to discriminate among all English consonant sounds, so we will stop here. Features 10-14 differentiate among the vowel sounds of English.

Table 5.1. *Distinctive features of English consonants.*

FEATURES	z	s	ð	θ	d	t	v	f	b	p	š	ǰ	č	g	k	w	h	y	l	r	m	n	ŋ
Consonantal	+	+	+	+	+	+	+	+	+	+	+	+	+	+	+	−	−	−	+	+	+	+	+
Vocalic	−	−	−	−	−	−	−	−	−	−	−	−	−	−	−	−	−	−	+	+	−	−	−
Nasal	−	−	−	−	−	−	−	−	−	−	−	−	−	−	−	−	−	−	−	−	+	+	+
Coronal	+	+	+	+	+	+	−	−	−	−	+	+	+	−	−	−	−	−	+	+	−	+	−
Continuant	+	+	+	+	−	−	+	+	−	−	+	−	−	−	−	+	+	+	+	+	−	−	−
Voiced	+	−	+	−	+	−	+	−	+	−	−	+	−	+	−	+	−	+	+	+	+	+	+
Anterior	+	+	+	+	+	+	+	+	+	+	−	−	−	−	−	+	−	−	+	−	+	+	−
Strident	+	+	−	−	−	−	+	+	−	−	+	+	+	−	−	−	−	−	−	−	−	−	−
Lateral	−	−	−	−	−	−	−	−	−	−	−	−	−	−	−	−	−	−	+	−	−	−	−

feature 10: high

Figure 5.2 is a chart of the major English vowels. Note that the vowels with the highest tongue position are at the top of the chart. These vowels have the narrowest passageway through which air can

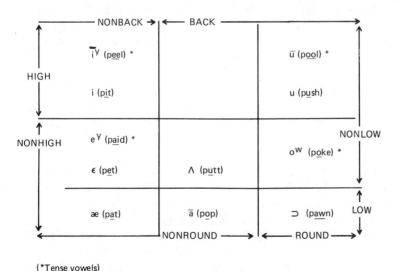

(*Tense vowels)

Figure 5.2. *English vowels and their features.*

resonate and escape during vowel production. Only four vowels, /īy/, /i/, /ū/, and /u/, are described as +high; the rest are −high.

feature 11: low

The vowels involving the widest passageway for air to escape during vowel production are called the low vowels: /æ/, /ā/, and /ɔ/. They are described as +low, and all other vowels are −low. Consequently the vowels which are not classified as +high and +low are called nonhigh and nonlow (−high and −low), respectively.

feature 12: back

The vowels produced mainly in the back of the oral cavity are called back vowels (see Figure 5.2) and are designated +back. The /ū/, /u/, /oʷ/, /ɔ/, /ʌ/, and /ā/ sounds are +back; the rest of the vowels are nonback (−back).

feature 13: round

Vowels that require the lips to be rounded during production are labeled +round. The back vowels, with the exception of /ā/, are +round. The /ā/ vowel is nonround (−round).

feature 14: tense

If the production of a vowel involves muscular tension, particularly in the tongue, the vowel is described as +tense. The muscular tension is usually coupled with a longer time spent in production. Compare, for example, the longer duration of /īy/ in "peel" (+tense) with the /i/ in "pit" (−tense). In Figure 5.2, tense vowels are marked by an asterisk (*).

Let's analyze the English vowels according to distinctive features, as we did the English consonants. Table 5.2 summarizes such an analysis.

We have just examined fourteen distinctive features that characterize a total of thirty-three English sounds. Let's examine one of these sounds, the /t/ sound, more closely. This consonant occurs, for instance, in "tip," "still," and "mat." The /t/ sound varies, however, in each of these words. If you hold your hand in front of your mouth while producing these three words, you will feel a puff of air in "tap," a weaker puff of air in "still," and practically no puff of air in "mat." The key point of similarity among these three sounds is this: there are no pairs of words in English that have

Table 5.2. *The distinctive features of English vowels.*

		FEATURES				
vowel	sample word	high	low	back	round	tense
/iʸ/	m<u>ea</u>t	+	–	–	–	+
/ĭ/	m<u>i</u>tten	+	–	–	–	–
/eʸ/	m<u>a</u>te	–	–	–	–	+
/ɛ/	m<u>e</u>t	–	–	–	–	–
/æ/	m<u>a</u>t	–	+	–	–	–
/ʌ/	m<u>u</u>tt	–	–	+	–	–
/ā/	b<u>o</u>ttom	–	+	+	–	–
/ū/	b<u>oo</u>t	+	–	+	+	+
/u/	b<u>oo</u>k	+	–	+	+	–
/oʷ/	b<u>oa</u>t	–	–	+	+	+
/ɔ/	b<u>ou</u>ght	–	+	+	+	–

All vowels are defined as −consonantal and +vocalic.

different meanings but differ only in the type of /t/ sound produced. When words that differ according to only one sound result in different meanings, as in "t̲ap" and "c̲ap," then we have different *phonemes.* A class of sounds considered equivalent by a language is called a phoneme. The three /t/ sounds are instances of the phoneme /t/ but are different *allophones* of /t/. Our discussion of children's acquisition of sounds focuses primarily on phonemes, not allophones.

Children acquire speech sounds according to the phonemic contrasts (features) in English. The acquisition process occurs according to a feature-by-feature schedule, not a phoneme-by-phoneme schedule. The reasons for using the feature-by-feature approach are these:

1. Children learn phonemes in "packages" that bear a striking resemblance to distinctive features.
2. The acquisition process for children speaking all languages follows this feature-by-feature schedule, in which common features are mastered first, cross-culturally.
3. Children with speech problems, which are typically called articulation problems, have trouble with features, not with specific phonemes per se.

Thus, the relevant method of analysis must be in terms of features.

THE BEGINNING OF SOUND ACQUISITION

Infants produce speech sounds in their first year of life, particularly in the *babbling* phase. Sometime after their first birthday, infants begin to produce *meaningful speech* which is typically launched by their "first words." Let's examine these two periods—babbling and meaningful speech—to see when and how the acquisition process is launched. We will discover that the acquisition process does not begin in the babbling period, a belief quite common in more traditional theories of speech development. Instead, the learning of phonemes (really, distinctive features) does not begin until the meaningful speech period. Let's see why this is the case.

the relation of babbling to speech

During the second half of their first year of life, infants produce a wide variety of speechlike sounds. This stage of development is called babbling. Among these babbled sounds are many not found in the native language the children will acquire. As we discussed earlier, it is not uncommon to hear infants of English-speaking parents use German gutteral sounds, French "r" sounds, and "click" sounds characteristic of African languages. When children master their native language, these sounds disappear, probably because they are not used by people around them. Those sounds "reinforced" by the speech of others become a part of the language system that the child will soon use.

The traditional studies of sound development in children presented a misleading picture of development. They focused on the first year of life and made these conclusions:

1. Consonants develop from the back of the mouth to the front of the mouth. For instance, younger infants vocalize sounds such as the /k/ in "key" before they vocalize the /t/ in "tea."

2. Vowels develop from the front of the mouth to the back of the mouth. For example, younger infants vocalize the /i ^{y}/ vowel before the /ā/ vowel.

The problem arises when we examine the course of development in the child's second year of life. The direction of development is exactly the opposite: the first-appearing consonants are those formed in the front of the mouth, and the first-appearing vowels are those formed in the back of the mouth.

The back consonants and the front vowels, the first ones to be babbled, are the last to be incorporated into the child's meaningful speech. Opposite trends in development during the babbling period and the meaningful-speech period suggest the lack of a relationship between babbling and phonemic development. The traditional studies presented teachers and parents with a misleading picture of the child's development. That is, traditional charts of sound development from three to twelve months were useless in predicting the incorporation of a sound into the child's linguistic system. In fact, the charts told a story that was almost opposite the true course of development.

The lack of importance of babbling in speech development has been argued from several standpoints:

1. *Since the order of appearance of sounds in a child's babbling does not match the order of appearance of sounds in meaningful speech, what relevance does babbling have to speech development?*

2. *Sounds with which the child may have serious difficulty later in the second year of development may have been babbled frequently in the first year. Thus, the babbling period tells us little about development.*

3. *There appears to be a discontinuity in development during the transition from babbling to meaningful speech. In fact, there may be a period of "silence" when the child passes from one stage to the other—a rather curious happening.*

4. *In medical case studies of children who hadn't "said a word" until they were eight years old, the children often did not begin with babbling; they simply began with meaningful speech.*[2]

The babbling period, previously regarded as the child's practice period for learning sounds, appears to have little importance in the acquisition of phonemes. However, recent studies on the prosodic features of language have hinted that the babbling period may be extremely important in children's mastery of the intonation and stress of spoken language. Chapter 10 explores this idea in detail.

In short, the babbling period appears to have little bearing on the child's development of the sound system of his language. The meaningful-speech period, which occurs sometime after the first birthday, launches the acquisition of phonemes.

meaningful speech: first words

The child's first "words," no matter which language the child speaks, are often "mama" and "papa" (or "dada"). Roman Jakobson discussed this phenomenon in an article entitled "Why 'Mama' and 'Papa'?"[3] Jakobson examined the "nursery forms" of young children across the world. In particular, he studied those "first

[2] Eric Lenneberg, "Understanding Language Without the Ability to Speak," *Journal of Abnormal and Social Psychology*, LXV (1962), 419-25.

[3] Contained in *Child Language: A Book of Readings*, ed. Aaron Bar-Adon and Werner F. Leopold (Englewood Cliffs, N.J.: Prentice-Hall, Inc., 1971), pp. 212-17.

words" referring to the mother and father. Interestingly, he found that the words in baby talk for the mother and father are close, phonemically, to mama and papa *in all languages.* In the minds of all parents, the obvious reason for the appearance of "mama" and "papa" in their little girl's early speech sounds something like this:

> *We are the most important people in the child's life, and we use these words constantly with our child—naturally, she is going to "recognize" us first when she starts to talk.*

In fact, parents are quite upset when "mama" and "dada" are not the first words of their child: "Something must be wrong; maybe I'm doing something I shouldn't—she doesn't even say my name."

The conclusion of Jakobson's article was that the early appearance of mama-papa words in infants' speech can probably be explained by either of these possibilities: (1) all languages have created baby-talk terms composed of sound combinations (that stand for mother and father) that "fit" the child's first "meaningless" sounds; or (2) the child's utterance of either sound combination may reflect his first bit of phonemic knowledge, but it is not necessarily related to the recognition of Mom and Dad. It's probably fortunate that most mothers and fathers haven't read the Jakobson article; otherwise, they might find their child's early and brilliant speech efforts more difficult to get excited about.

meaningful speech: first phonemes

Studies conducted in recent years have focused on children's acquisition of the *phonemic system* of their language. Sometime after the emergence of "first words," children regularly put sounds together in communication. The specific order of appearance of these sounds is important to note, but reasons for this order of appearance are of greater value to theorists. An explicit theory of phonemic development has existed for over thirty years, as outlined by Roman Jakobson. Jakobson's writings were not translated into English for some twenty-five years, however. It's unfortunate that we haven't had the advantage of his thinking to direct us toward more meaningful studies of children's speech.

Until Jakobson's writings were translated, investigators had typically observed children's production of sounds, counted them, and noted how old the children were when they produced the sounds. Consequently, we were given charts of development that claimed ten-month-old infants had mastered ten phonemes of English. Such claims are incorrect, however, based on Jakobson's conclusion that phoneme acquisition cannot begin before the meaningful-speech period. Mastery of phonemes before age one, then, is nearly impossible.

To characterize the child's acquisition and development of the phonemes of a language, we must employ a method based on the appearance of meaningful speech. Such a system is part of Jakobson's distinctive-feature approach to phoneme acquisition. This approach is based on the idea that children master the phonemes of any language by learning certain characteristics or "distinctive features" of the sounds, such as vocalic, voicing, and strident. The next section outlines the child's acquisition of the distinctive features of English phonemes.

The basic methodology in the study of phoneme acquisition is the observation of regularities in the child's utterances. (You may recall from Chapter 4 that this is one of five methods employed to study children's competence in language.) The method is accompanied by very powerful criteria for inclusion in the phonemic system, however. In Jakobson's system, for example, a phoneme is not "counted" unless it appears quite regularly in the child's speech *and* appears in a combination of phonemes that conveys a consistent meaning to others. In most cases meaningful speech begins in the child's second year. This method will become clearer as you read the examples below.

The distinctive-features approach defines all phonemes in terms of their features. Some features are reasoned to be more complex than others, so that the phonemes they define are also more complex. Because the features are ordered in complexity, so are phonemes. The greater the complexity, the more difficult the phoneme is to acquire. Consequently, the distinctive-features approach is extremely helpful in accounting for how (and in what order) children acquire the phonemes of their language. In the initial stage of phoneme development, the approach is concerned with "filling the gap" between two extreme sounds, "ah" and "p." Why these two sounds? Why do we call them "extreme"? The "ah" ($/\bar{a}/$) vowel is a sound that is formed in the back of the mouth, involves the complete opening of the vocal tract, and has a maximum amount of acoustic energy. The $/p/$ consonant sound is almost the opposite of $/\bar{a}/$: it is formed in the front of the mouth, involves the closing of the vocal tract (at the lips), and has virtually no acoustic energy (that is, it is nonvoiced). In a sense, then, the $/\bar{a}/$ is an optimal vowel and the $/p/$ is an optimal consonant. Each is an extreme example of its type, and the contrast between them is as great as one could imagine.

We can't be misled by a young child's mere *production* of these sounds, however. We must carefully observe the context of their utterance. Does the child say "papa" for his father, a toy, *and* his milk? If so, these sounds (/p/ and /ā/ do not distinguish meaningful messages—a necessity for phoneme "status." Before we can say that phonemes are acquired, "differentiation" is necessary. The space between /p/ and /ā/ must be filled with another contrast. Jakobson's studies revealed that the contrast that launches phonemic development in most children involves the /p/ and the /m/ sounds.

The oral-nasal distinction between /p/ and /m/, both of which are produced with the lips, allows the production of a phoneme-contrast necessary for the distinction of meaning. By duplicating the sound combinations (oral + /ā/) and (nasal + /ā/) we obtain "papa" and "mama." Now we have two possible words, and it seems reasonable to assume that for the child these words convey meaning distinctions. When an adult or parent hears a young child say them, and if they are uttered in the appropriate contexts ("papa" for father, "mama" for mother, and neither for toys or milk), then we can be pretty certain the phonemic system is beginning to develop. Yet notice the cautious language in the last two sentences: "possible words" and "we can be pretty sure." According to Jakobson's article, "Why 'Mama' and 'Papa'?" these sound combinations might not reflect the child's ability to make a meaningful distinction between mother and father. It might simply be that for some physiological reason the child finds these sound combinations easiest to produce. This is why it is crucial to examine the contexts in which the sounds are produced.

The /ā/ vowel in "mama" and "papa" has not yet achieved the status of a phoneme; it merely supports the two consonants, /m/ and /p/. The /ā/ vowel serves another function in the child's acquisition of the phonemic system: it establishes a syllable in speech. Rhythm in speech can be observed as the child says "mama" or "papa." The /ā/ provides the longer speech sound—a vowel—that allows rhythmic duplication of sound combinations. In fact, most of the child's first words are duplications of a consonant and vowel combination—for instance, /māmā/, /dædæ/, /bīy̆bīy̆/ (baby), and /wɔwɔ/ (water).

meaningful speech:
mastery of distinctive features

Recent studies of phoneme mastery have taken the approach of analyzing children's speech for these two regularities:

1. The phoneme must be correctly produced by the child, in terms of articulatory movements and acoustic characteristics (that is, its "sound").
2. The phoneme must be produced correctly in initial, medial, and final word positions. (For example, the /p/ must be produced correctly in "pat," "apple," and "tip".)

Because the phoneme must be produced correctly in all word positions (that is, all allophones must be "mastered"), recent charts of phonological development portray the child acquiring sounds at what appears to be a slower rate than that portrayed in earlier charts of phoneme development. Table 5.3 lists the sequence of mastery of the consonant phonemes in English.[4] By understanding this chart, you will find it easier to grasp the feature-by-feature approach to the acquisition of speech sounds.

Table 5.3. *Children's mastery of phonemes, according to age.*

AGE OF MASTERY	PHONEMES
3 years	/b/, /m/, /n/, /f/, /w/, /h/
4 years	/p/, /d/, /g/, /k/, /y/, /l/, /t/
5 years	/v/, /s/, /z/, /š/, /ž/
$5\frac{1}{2}$ years	/č/, /r/
6 years	/j/
6+ years	/θ/, /ð/, /ŋ/

Adapted from Paula Menyuk, *The Acquisition and Development of Language* (Englewood Cliffs, N.J.: Prentice-Hall, Inc., © 1971), pp. 78-79.

Phoneme mastery: consonants. Our knowledge of children's mastery of phonemes is based mainly on information gathered in production studies, that is, studies in which children's utterances are analyzed for phoneme output. Studies based on phoneme perception (that is, children's ability to differentiate among phonemes) have recently been launched, but there are too few such studies upon which we can base conclusions. Eventually, the total picture of phonological development will necessarily include both production and perception information.

Table 5.3 illustrates the general trend in children's production mastery of phonemes in all word positions. The chart shows that certain sound types are acquired earlier than others. For example, phonemes mastered *by four years of age* are typically these:

1. Voiced and voiceless stops: /b/, /p/, /d/, /t/, /g/, and /k/.
2. Nasals: /m/ and /n/ (/ŋ/ is mastered only in initial and medial word positions.
3. Glides: /w/, /h/, and /y/.

Only one fricative (/f/) and one liquid (/l/) have emerged by the age of four. Phonemes mastered *after the fourth birthday* include these sound types:

[4] My discussion of phoneme mastery, including Table 5.3, is based on Paula Menyuk, *The Acquisition and Development of Language* (Englewood Cliffs, N.J.: Prentice-Hall, Inc., 1971), pp. 78-79.

1. Fricatives: /s/, /z/, /ʃ/, /ž/, /v/, /θ/, and /ð/.
2. Affricates: /č/ and /ǰ/.

The liquid /r/ is mastered at the age of five-and-a-half, and the late-to-appear nasal /ŋ/ is mastered in the final position after the age of six.

   To explain further this sequence of mastery, theorists have had to "look inside" the sound types mastered at each age level to see what features have emerged.

Feature mastery: consonants. To obtain a better understanding of feature mastery, let's look inside the sound types that are mastered early. For example, the stop sounds that are mastered first demonstrate the emergence of the *voicing* feature. The voiced and nonvoiced pairs of stops are acquired in a package, although the voiced stops (/b/, /d/, and /g/) tend to appear before their voiceless counterparts (/p/, /t/, and /k/). Paula Menyuk has examined typical sound substitutions appearing in the speech of normal children without speech problems. Her studies suggest that the voicing feature appears to be the one least likely to account for substitution errors in children's speech.

   In fact, a comparison between substitution errors and data on the order of acquisition suggests a feature-acquisition chart similar to Figure 5.3. Support for the feature-by-feature acquisition scheme can be seen in the two-way analysis of the substitution data and the order

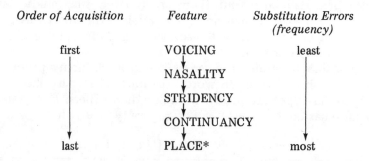

*Although we have not considered the place feature in our discussion, we have considered features related to the place of articulation (for instance, anterior, coronal, lateral). The usual substitution error related to place is simply the production of a phoneme in the wrong place in the mouth—for example, production of /g/ in "go" with the tongue on the alveolar ridge, resulting in "doe," instead of production of the /g/ sound with the tongue (back) touching the velum.

Figure 5.3. *The emergence of consonant features. Adapted from Paula Menyuk,* The Acquisition and Development of Language, *(Englewood Cliffs, N.J.: Prentice-Hall, Inc., © 1971), pp. 77-79.*

of acquisition data: the early-to-appear features are those which involve fewer phoneme substitutions while the later-to-appear features involve the greater number of phonemic substitutions. The striking negative relationship between acquisition and substitution errors provides evidence in support of the distinctive features system, itself. Although few studies propose a complete developmental chart for all the consonantal features outlined earlier in this chapter, we can examine a basic set of features that have been analyzed from two perspectives.

The features children acquire in their first five years can be contrasted in one important way: absolute versus relative. Certain features have the quality of a "this or that" distinction—a dichotomy; let's call them *absolute*. Other features have the quality of "varying degrees of this or that"—a more complex scale of values; let's call them *relative*. Consider the following features: (1) voicing, (2) nasality, and (3) continuancy. A phoneme is either voiced or nonvoiced, a clear dichotomy. Nasality works in about the same way: a sound *is* or *is not* nasal. Both voicing and nasality are absolute features and are acquired early by the child. The best example of a relative feature is continuancy: the *degree* of constriction of the air flow determines whether a sound is or is not a continuant. Continuants are acquired later. In short, theorists have suggested that the absolute-versus-relative quality of a feature may have some bearing on the order of feature acquisition.

Another possible explanation for the order in which features are acquired in children's development of speech is based on an ease-of-articulation model. The movements necessary for nasality and voicing, for example, may be easier to accomplish than the more complicated movements necessary for strident and continuant sounds. Studies have even compared the number of articulatory muscles involved in the production of various phonemes, suggesting that muscular involvement may explain the order of mastery.

The foregoing section on feature mastery is brief and somewhat tentative, primarily because theorists are just beginning to tackle the subject. Nevertheless, this discussion should give you a glimpse of a new approach being explored vigorously by phonologists interested in basing their theories on developmental data from children. Next, let's discuss the emergence of vowel phonemes and features, a far more tentative subject.

Feature mastery: vowels. Vowel mastery is slightly different from consonant mastery in the sense that once the child is able to produce a few consonant phonemes, the vowels begin to emerge at once and feature differentiation occurs rather quickly. Figure 5.4 illustrates the acquisition pattern of four of the five vowel features.

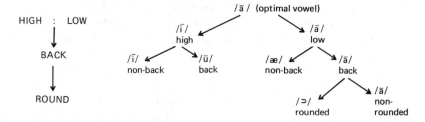

Figure 5.4. *Mastery of vowel phonemes and features.*

Following the appearance of the first "optimal" vowel, /ā/, the high-low distinction appears with /ī/ and /ā/. Then, the high vowel "splits" into the nonback /ī/ and the back /ū/, and the low vowel splits into the nonback /æ/ and back /ā/. Sometime later, the round /ɔ/ appears in contrast with the nonrounded /ā/, mastered earlier. An examination of the chart suggests that the order of appearance for vowel features is something like this: first, high and low; next, back, and, finally, round (and probably tense). Few theorists attempt to explain the order of mastery of vowel features, except to say that the features of position (high, low, back) may appear before the features related to musculature (round, tense).

SPOTTING PHONOLOGICAL PROBLEMS IN CHILDREN'S SPEECH

In 1971 The American Speech and Hearing Association published a survey indicating that the most prevalent language deviancy among school-age children is *articulation problems*. Such problems involve phonological production that is inconsistent with normal developmental patterns. Table 5.3, which outlines phoneme mastery, demonstrates that a seven-year-old child is probably capable of producing all the English phonemes correctly. If a child speaks with phonemic substitutions—for instance; if she says "wabbit" for "rabbit"—she *may* or *may not* have a phonological problem, as the label, "problem," depends on the child's developmental schedule and her age.

A child who is acquiring language normally makes substitutions for the late-to-appear distinctive features. A four-year-old child who says "wabbit" for "rabbit" is making a rather predictable substitution of /w/ for /r/ and probably does not have an articulation problem. The continuant /r/, which is +coronal and +anterior, is late to appear and is not fully mastered until the age of about five-and-a-half. Remember also that the continuants are generally mastered after four years, except for the glides—/w/, /h/, and /y/. In the above instance, the child has substituted the glide /w/, an early-to-appear phoneme, for the more "difficult" /r/ phoneme. The /w/ is not differentiated by the place markings of +coronal and +anterior, as is the /r/. If a seven-year-old always substitutes /w/ for the /r/ in "rabbit," then we might ask whether or not the child has an articulation problem.

Young children do not randomly substitute one phoneme for another when they produce sound substitutions. Instead they substitute an already learned feature for one not yet acquired. Usually, the phoneme that has been substituted has a feature in common with the *target phoneme* (the phoneme predicted by adult usage). For example, children may substitute the early-to-appear continuant /w/ for the later-to-appear /l/—as in "yewwow" for "yellow." In this case both phonemes are continuants, but the /w/ and the /l/ differ in "place": the /l/ is +coronal, +lateral, and +anterior, whereas the /w/ has no such markings.

Common articulation errors may involve phoneme substitution. For example, the /l/ and /r/ sounds are often replaced with /w/-like sounds, and the /s/ and /ŝ/ phonemes are frequently replaced by /θ/-like sounds. Examples of these substitutions are:

/w/ for /l/: "yewwow" for "yellow"
/w/ for /r/: "wunning" for "running"
/θ/ for /s/: "thilly" for "silly"
/θ/ for /s/: "thur" for "sure"

Children diagnosed as having an articulation problem typically make such substitutions, but if they are asked to differentiate between the sets of phonemes, they can often do so correctly. Consequently, many children with articulation problems have deficiencies in *output* (speech) but not *input* (hearing or perceiving differences). Some children have input problems as well as production (output) problems. If children cannot "hear" a difference between /w/ and /l/, for example, they require more extensive language therapy than children who can make such discriminations.

An effective way to analyze potential articulation problems in school-age children is to follow these steps:

1. Listen carefully to samples of the child's speech and record in writing the words that are misarticulated. Record the phonemes you hear (the incorrect phonemes). In another column, record the target phonemes (the correct phonemes).

2. Find the target phonemes in other word positions in the child's speech, and again record the sounds you hear. Does the child make errors in the other

word positions? In the case of the child who substitutes /w/ for /r/ in "rabbit," does this child produce the following words without errors: "hairy" (medial position) and "core" (final position)?

Words	Phoneme Employed	Target Phoneme
wabbit/rabbit weady/ready	/w/	/r/
thaw/saw thing/sing	/θ/	/s/

3. Consult Table 5.3 to see how "different" the child is with respect to the age of mastery, remembering that this chart contains the average ages for mastering phonemes in all word positions. Only if the child varies from the chart *significantly*—that is, by more than one year—ask for assistance from a speech clinician. Remember that the chart represents norms, and children can be developing their phonemic system more slowly than the norms but still be progressing normally. For example, Table 5.3 suggests that /r/ is usually mastered by the age of five-and-a-half, but some children develop /r/ nicely at the age of seven.

PHONOLOGICAL DIFFERENCES
RELATED TO DIALECTS

Puerto Rican and black children were, until a few years ago, frequently diagnosed as having articulation problems. Even today, some teachers and therapists perform articulation therapy with children who speak black English or Spanish English. Although children of these ethnic backgrounds do speak a phonological version of English that is *different* from standard English, it is incorrect to say they have "articulation problems." Although a black child may say, "Come wif me" (substituting the /f/ phoneme for the /θ/ phoneme), so may the adult "standard speakers" in his speech community. The substitution does not relate to an underlying articulation problem; rather, it represents a dialect difference.

From the viewpoint of standard English, children who speak black English or Spanish English use substitute phonemes for standard phonemes. These phonological differences have no relation to articulation problems because the children's target phonemes are drawn from their native language and are often different from English phonemes. For example, the phonological structure of Spanish does not make extensive use of consonant clusters occurring in the final position of a word; for example, the final /k/ and /s/ in "tracks" are merged in /træs/. This difference does not result from an articulation error of omission; rather, it is a basic dialect difference. In black dialect the vowels /i/ and /ɛ/ may not be differentiated before a final nasal sound; for instance, phonemic differences between "pin" and "pen" do not appear (both are /pin/). Black English, as well as Spanish, makes little use of final consonant clusters; such clusters are often reduced (for example, "bold" becomes "bole"). Asking a black or Spanish-speaking child to discriminate or produce phonemes not representative of the phonology of his target language is an issue very different from asking English-speaking children to change English phonemes that are misarticulated. Many current educational philosophies argue against such demands.

An important point to remember about the dialects some children employ is that the phonology, morphology, and syntax of the dialects are based on their target languages. In the case of a Spanish dialect spoken by Puerto Rican children, the target language is Spanish. An investigation of the features (sounds and syntactic structures) of Spanish predicts many of the dialect features. Differences are explained by the target language. If standard English is the target language for judging Spanish and black speech, then the dialects appear deficient. But when the phonological features of Spanish and black languages are used as criteria, Spanish and black children are on the mark, with no articulation errors or language deficiencies.

The elementary school teacher must know about the linguistic differences in the speech of minority-group children. Articulation therapy is not an appropriate solution for dialect differences. One would expect a percentage of black and Spanish children to demonstrate articulation errors above and beyond dialect differences. The teacher must work with the therapist to distinguish differences from deviances. If the school employs a bidialectal form of language instruction, dialect differences will be the focus of instruction.

SUMMARY

Phonemes are the sounds of speech, the basic building blocks of a language. Children's phonemic systems are virtually complete by the time they enter the first grade. Prior to that time, children communicate effectively with progressive versions of the adult phonemic system. Even three-year-olds communicate effectively with their incomplete set of sounds. Young preschoolers learn their phonemic system in an orderly fashion, feature by feature.

After a basic discussion of the four processes necessary for the production of speech sounds—respiration, phonation, resonation, and articulation—we outlined the distinctive features of English. We examined the nine consonantal features—consonantal, vocalic, nasal, coronal, continuant, voicing, anterior, strident, and lateral—and then the five vowel features—high, low, back, round, and tense.

Phonological acquisition begins in the meaningful-speech (or "first-words") period, which occurs sometime after the child's first birthday. The babbling stage that precedes this period seems unimportant in the learning of phonemes. Although it is most reasonable to chart the development of phonemes according to age levels, theorists suggest that the child actually learns distinctive features, or associated phoneme bundles. Children appear to master features in an order that ranges from absolute to relative features: voicing, nasality, and stridency (all absolute), and then continuancy and place (relative).

Children with articulation problems often substitute one phoneme for another, omit a phoneme in a word, or distort a phoneme in some way. Although many speech-sound substitutions (such as /w/ for /r/) are normal for preschool, kindergarten, and first-grade children, such substitutions are not normal for older children. With the younger children there is really no articulation problem, but with the older ones there may be. One way to spot potential articulation problems is to follow these three steps in analyzing the child's speech:

1. Record the incorrect sounds in the words that are misarticulated.
2. Keying on the target phoneme, record the phonemes the child produces for the target phoneme in other word positions.
3. Compare the child's phonological performance with a chart showing normal development in the mastery of phonemes. If there is a *significant* difference, consult a speech clinician.

A far more pressing problem, because it has received inadequate attention over the years, relates to children speaking different dialects of English. Black and Puerto Rican children speak a form of English in which phonemes often differ from those in standard English. However, dialect differences should not be equated with articulation errors. Research and common sense indicate that the speech of minority-group children reflects "standard" phonological features of their "standard" native language.

SUGGESTED READINGS

McNEILL, DAVID, *The Acquisition of Language: The Study of Developmental Psycholinguistics*, Chap. 9. New York: Harper & Row, 1970.

MENYUK, PAULA, *The Development of Speech*, pp. 3-44. New York: Bobbs-Merrill, 1972.

CHAPTER

6

words in children's communication

Children ask for the names of everything, figuring that if they know the name or the words they will better understand a spoke on a bicycle wheel or a shadow that follows them. To explain something to children, we give them the words that allow them to talk about the thing or idea. From our experiences in communication we know that words are strongly tied to the meanings we wish to convey. Children learning to communicate ask their parents, friends, and teachers to help them understand words and their meanings.

An eighteen-month-old child communicates with as many as fifty different words. A four-year-old, on the other hand, may produce well over 2,000 different words and probably understands many more. Because of children's increased exposure to words from a very early age, which is perhaps due to their exposure to television and other social situations, the number and diversity of words in a preschooler's vocabulary is often so great as to be astonishing.

The current approach to children's acquisition of words is different from that of earlier years. Instead of counting the *words* in a child's vocabulary to obtain an estimate of the potential meanings at the child's command, researchers are taking a more penetrating look at *meanings* children ascribe to the words they use. You might think that these two approaches are similar: studying words is the same as studying meanings, right? But that's not the case: children may have a particular word in their vocabulary from age two through age twelve, but what they mean when they use that word may change drastically over that ten-year period. Today, theorists account for children's acquisition of meanings at successive stages of development.

Our meanings for words relate to things, actions, feelings, concepts, and relationships that are around us. Words can be used to signify that "monster," the action of "hurrying," the feeling of being "all alone," the concept of "sharing," and the relationship of "under." Most of us assume that when children use a word they know our meaning(s) for that word. But research has found this assumption to be false. Children's word meanings change as they age: their early meanings are often very unlike adult meanings.[1] A young girl who is told to "share," for example, believes that sharing means giving a toy away. She doesn't like to give it away so she doesn't wish to share. In a sense, the child is right in ascribing the action of giving to sharing because there is "give and take" in our adult meaning of "to share." But the child sees only the giving and decides that it's not for her.

Children also use words in a very general way rather than in a highly differentiated manner. A child using the word "water" may assign a very general meaning (or set of attributes) to water. The child's behavior is often the best indicator of what these attributes are. If all forms and states of water are treated in the same manner, we have evidence that the child's meaning of "water" is only a general one. For example, water to an eighteen-month-old boy simply means something to drink. He has no fine distinctions among types and functions of water, so he tries to drink everything that looks like water: hot water, dirty lake water, and even toilet water. An adequate account of the child's vocabulary at any stage of development, then, should include a description of the meaning(s) assigned to the word "water" and not simply the word itself.

Before exploring children's acquisition of word meanings, we must understand the words linguists use to talk about words. Linguists rarely say they are investigating words in language; instead, they analyze *morphemes*. The morpheme is the smallest unit of meaning in language, and the study of morphemes is called *morphology*.

---

[1] We discussed an important example of this phenomenon in Chapter 1 when we considered children's developing morality. Remember that we stressed the differences between children's and adults' meaning of the word "good": children think of this word in terms of *duty*, whereas adults consider it to mean *goodness*. As children develop, their meaning approaches the adult meaning.

WHAT IS A MORPHEME?

A morpheme is a basic unit of meaning composed of one or more phonemes. Many words in our language are single morphemes, but others are composed of two or more morphemes. In fact, some of the words we use every day—common words—contain multiple morphemes (for example, "newspaper" and "going"). Basically, there are two types of morphemes:

1. *Free morpheme:* a meaning unit that can stand alone to convey meaning ("kitty," "doggie," "car-car").
2. *Bound morpheme:* a meaning unit that must be attached to a free morpheme to "make sense"; examples of bound morphemes are prefixes, infixes, and suffixes (for instance, "pre-," "-ed," "pro-," "-ing").

Free morphemes are meaning units that cannot be subdivided into more basic meaning units. They are often considered base-words in our vocabulary. Examples are "monster," "hurry," "alone," "share" and "under."

We can combine free morphemes to produce compound words. Compound words such as "airplane," "blackboard" and "motorcycle" contain two free morphemes. In each instance, two minimal meaning units are joined together to form the compound word: "air" + "plane"; "black" + "board"; and "motor" + "cycle." When children first use compound words, they do not know that they are combining two minimal meaning units, as such. A study of compounding (to be discussed later in this chapter) shows that preschoolers have very general meanings for compound words. Their early meanings do not reflect an understanding of both free morphemes. When asked why a blackboard is called a "blackboard," a four-year-old child may simply way, "Because," reflecting little understanding of the meanings. A five-year-old boy may answer, "Because we write on it," basing his understanding of the compound word's meaning on the meaning of one of the free morphemes. A six-year-old child might have the insight to respond, "Because it's a black thing we write on." The older child has assigned a meaning to each of the free morphemes in explaining the compound word. Although it is not accurate to say that the meaning of a compound word (or any multiple-morpheme word, for that matter) equals the sum of its parts, in general the meaning of multiple-morpheme words is derived from its components.

The *bound morpheme*, unlike the free morpheme, cannot stand alone to convey meaning. Its meaning—remember, it *is* a minimal meaning unit—is derived from its attachment to a free morpheme. Many words we use have bound morphemes attached to free morphemes—for instance, "walk*ed*," "*pre*view," "cat*s*," "Jane*'s*," "work*er*,"and "nice*ly.*" What are the meanings of such bound morphemes? Let's take a look!

1. "Walk*ed*": "-ed" means that the action took place in the past—it happened before I am saying the word.
2. "Cats": "-s" means more than one, or plural, in terms of quantity.
3. "Jane*'s*": "'s" means possession—that this person owns something or has something.
4. "Work*er*": "-er" is the agentive form, meaning "one who does something" in this case, one who works.
5. "Nice*ly*": "-ly" atrributes the quality of the free morpheme ("nice") to a person's action, as in "works nicely."

Bound morphemes that are frequently studied in children's communication are tense endings, plural endings, agentives, and possessive endings. Studies of children's language reveal that there are certain stages of development in acquiring both free and bound morphemes.

To test your understanding of morphemes, figure out how many morphemes are in each of the following words, and determine whether each morpheme is free or bound.

1. viewfinder
2. going
3. properties
4. indirect
5. interest

Word 1 is composed of two free morphemes, "view" and "find," and one bound morpheme, "-er." The "-er" ending is the agentive form. In word 2 we have one free morpheme, "go," and one bound morpheme, "-ing." The "-ing" verb inflection indicates the present progressive form of the verb—that is, the action is taking place right now. The plural bound morpheme, "-ies," is added to the free morpheme, "property," to form word 3. Word 4 has the prefix, "in-," attached to the free morpheme, "direct." The "in-" prefix, in this case, has a negative meaning. Word 5 might have fooled you: the "in" beginning might have led you to propose that the word contains a bound and a free morpheme. This is not the case, however, because the "in" does not have a meaning function in the word "interest." We cannot break down this word into smaller meaning units and still preserve the meaning of the word itself. "Interest" contains one free morpheme and cannot be further divided without "fracturing" the original meaning of the word.

In studying children's language, the importance of the distinction between bound and free morphemes is this: if meaning is the focus of analysis in typical frequency counts of a child's vocabulary, then both bound and free morphemes must be taken into account. Children who have a vocabulary of 600 different words might have a morpheme count of over 600 because of the multiple-morpheme constructions in their vocabulary. The study of meanings must focus on the +600 morphemes and not on the 600 words, per se. Of even greater importance is that we view these morphemes in terms of children's meanings rather than adult meanings.

One of the most effective approaches in the study of morphological acquisition in children has been the use of nonsense words to test children's development of bound and free morphemes. A child is shown a picture of a funny little animal called a "wug" and then shown a picture of two "wugs" (recall the Berko method, discussed on p. 72.) Of course, the appropriate response is that there are "two wugs," the plural ending /z/ being added appropriately. Children have a meaning for this plural morpheme because they can apply the bound form to this new instance in a nonsense language. Analyzing common words that children say every day may not reveal their understanding of bound morphemes; instead, it may reveal that they are good at copying plural forms. The kind of approach just described, involving the use of a nonsense language, fits the discovery method described in Chapter 4.

Our discussion of the child's acquisition of morphology will first concern the acquisition of meanings for free morphemes. Why do children learn meanings in a particular order and fashion? What are the stages of development that explain the growth of the number of free morphemes in a child's vocabulary? Answering these questions will be our concern in the first part of this chapter. Then, we will consider the child's development of bound morphemes. How do children learn the appropriate inflections for plurals, verb tenses, possessives, and derived forms? Just as there are stages in children's development of free morphemes, so there are stages in their acquisition of the bound morphemes.

LEARNING WORDS:
FREE MORPHEMES

Most parents are curious about what their child's first words will be. Will it be "mommy" or "daddy," or will it be something else— perhaps "doggie," "car," or "light"? In the back of their minds they hope their child's first words will refer to them, and according to our discussion in Chapter 5, the chances of this happening are great. Children's first phoneme combinations exhibit certain regularities, one of which is the pairing of a closed consonant with an open vowel. Consequently, sound combinations such as "papa," "dada," and "mama" are likely to appear as first words. Roman Jakobson has warned us that such sound combinations might not be the child's first meaning units, however. Rather, these sounds may at first exist without meaning, which explains why many infants call their father, a chair, and food by the same name—"dada."

the first word

At what age do children utter their first meaningful word? In a landmark review of twenty-six studies of the first words of children, Darley and Winitz concluded that on the average, children say their first word at about one year of age.[2] If children don't say their first word by eighteen months of age, they might have some type of physical, mental, or hearing impairment.

All investigations of first words must contend with difficulties. The problems in defining and in reporting the age of the first word are many. It might seem to be an easy procedure—just ask the mother what her child's first word was and when it happened. Often, however, parents so eagerly anticipate their child's first word that they report early babblings as words when the child has no meanings for these babblings. That these babblings happen to coincide with objects, persons or events is enough evidence for the parent to conclude that the first word has appeared. The problem is that this so-called word may stand for many things. The only way a researcher can test this is to study children over a long period of time to see if they use words only in highly specific situations. This observational approach requires the recording of all sound combinations so that the appearance of the first word (after constant testing to see that the word is used appropriately) is associated with a particular age.

Some observers define the child's first word as the first spontaneous utterance that has meaning. But how do we know whether or not the child has given meaning to the word? Often, the word's meaning is inferred by adults in the absence of supporting evidence. The criteria for evidence in first-word studies are as varied as the studies themselves. Some studies use mothers' reports, others use only words uttered for the tester, and a few have no real criteria at all. Consequently, the age at which the first word appears, considering the twenty-six studies cited by Darley and Winitz, ranges from about nine to sixteen months for normal children—that is, children without physical defects, behavior problems, or deviant IQs. The range is so great probably because of the different meaning

[2] Frederick Darley and Harris Winitz, "Age of First Word: Review of Research," *Journal of Speech and Hearing Disorders*, XXVI (1961), 272-90.

criteria employed, as well as differences among the samples of children studied (differences in social class, parental background, sex, and so forth). Darley and Winitz have captured beautifully the problems in first-word research:

> In summary, it would seem that the use of operational definitions of the first word have been so consistently different from investigator to investigator as to be an important source of error in reported age of appearance of the first word. Coupled with it are other sources of error: the inadequacy of parental records; the fallibility of parents' memory; parents' "wishful hearing," "optimism," and "pride"; and the infrequency and meagerness of sampling of infants' vocalizations by observers rather than parents.[3]

Generalizations about the appearance of first words are difficult to make if one considers such serious shortcomings. Darley and Winitz referred only to the better-controlled studies of the past in concluding that boys and girls begin to talk at about the same time, as measured by the age of appearance of the first word. Further, children with physical, mental, and behavioral problems say their first word significantly later than "normal" children.

The first words of infants have several important characteristics, which M. M. Lewis attributes to a universal "baby language."[4] These characteristics extend to children of all countries speaking all languages. Lewis discovered six fundamental sound combinations, or "words," that characterized his "international language of babies": "mama," "nana," "papa," "baba," "tata," and "dada." These "words" are simple sound combinations consisting of duplicated consonant phonemes with the open vowel, "ah." That these sounds appear among "international" first words is not surprising when we consider Jakobson's explanation for the emergence of phonemes in the child's language (discussed in Chapter 5). Recall that the voicing and nasality features emerge first. Baby-language words contain evidence of the emergence of these features.

Lewis probably carried his explanations for these first words too far when he advanced his notion of "phoneme meaning." For example, Lewis suggested that nasal sounds mean a sense of urgency related to need satisfaction. Consequently, the /m/ and /n/ phonemes in "mama" and "nana" (a term for a nurse or grandmother-caretaker) are supposed to mean urgency. The labial and alveolar stop phonemes (/p/, /b/, /t/, and /d/) are supposed to mean contentment, and are reserved for events (for instance, "tata," which

[3] Ibid., p. 283.

[4] M. M. Lewis, *Language, Thought and Personality* (New York: Basic Books, Inc., 1963), pp. 13-19, 33-35.

connotes a waving game) and persons ("dada," meaning play with daddy). The velar stop consonants /g/ and /k/ are supposedly associated with comfort or excitement (for example, "gaga" signals comfort and "goggie" for "doggie" means excitement). It is difficult to accept the idea that phonemes mean feelings and activities, but Lewis found the idea a plausible and exciting one. There is no evidence to support the phoneme-meaning idea; it's a tenuous one, to be sure.

Because the first words of most children are related to their mother or father, Lewis conducted a study of infants' use and understanding of the word "mama" over a period of several months.[5] The records of infants' conversations with parents revealed that a clear identification of *word with person* takes much longer than one might think. For example, a twelve-month-old boy gave a piece of crust to his mother when she said, "Give mummy crust." One month later gnawing on a crust the same child, in the presence of both parents, was first told "Give daddy crustie." The child offered it to his mother. Then, when told, "Give mummy crustie," he turned around and gave it to his father. There was not a stable association between the word "mummy" and his mother.

Two principles help explain the development of first words related to mother and father:

1. *Children's first words have both cognitive and affective components: "mummy" can be both a person and someone with a very positive (or negative) emotional value.*

2. *Children's first words are usually situational rather than symbolic: at first, a word does not stand for* something; *instead, it relates to a general set of* circumstances.

Accordingly, Lewis was convinced that a child does not acquire a symbolic and cognitive meaning of "mummy" until about eighteen months, even though they seem to understand the word much earlier.

Approval words. A better approach to the study of early words is to study words in an important developmental context. Lewis's study of early words and ethical development is very revealing in its focus on "yes" and "no" as approval-disapproval words.[6]

At first, the nonverbal cues related to "No" and "Yes" are sufficient to affect a child's behavior. A smile may keep a young girl going and a frown may stop her quickly. When language emerges, a

[5] Ibid., pp. 37-38.
[6] Ibid., pp. 42-46.

child behaving in an acceptable way still needs no more than a smile or a nod. But a child behaving unacceptably may need more than a frown. The only thing that may work—a most powerful instrument of behavior change—is the parent's admonitory "No!" directed to the child in a loud, abrupt voice with a falling pitch.

"No!" enters the child's linguistic experience earlier than "Yes!" One child responded to "No!" at nine months and used it at nineteen months, but responded to and used "Yes!" as late as twenty-one months. At first, children's understanding of both "Yes!" and "No!" appears to be situation-bound. Either of these words may elicit an appropriate response almost automatically. Consider this behavior of Gregory (our youngest son) at about one year of age:

> Gregory began to reach for an ashtray filled with cigarette butts. As he reached, I said "No!" Immediately, he pulled his hand back and looked at me. Again he tried to reach for the ashtray, and again I said, "No, it's hot." He pulled his hand back and looked at me a bit longer this time. I looked back at him and he began to whimper.

That Gregory always stopped his movements after I said "No!" showed that he had a basic understanding of "No!" as "Stop that!" His whimpering indicated that the situation was unpleasant for him; quite possibly, he wanted to explore the objects even if they were hot. Some months later, we noticed that he attempted to touch the ashtray again. This time, as he began to reach for the ashtray this sequence of events occurred:

> Gregory reached for the ashtray, and almost out of habit I said "No!" Gregory pulled his hand away and said "Ha" ($/h/ + /\bar{a}/$), possibly the word "hot." I nodded my head in agreement and praised him for his perceptive remark. Rather than stopping with that, he again reached for the ashtray. This time I simply showed my reaction in my face (with wide-open eyes and rounded mouth). Again he said "Ha."

This example of Gregory's understanding of "No!" shows a far greater grasp of its meaning. Recently, we witnessed the final step:

> Gregory pointed to the ashtray, and without reaching for its contents he said "Ha." I agreed with him, saying "Yes it's hot." Then, as if he had just figured it out, he said "No no!"

Gregory had acquired a meaning for "No!" that reflected thinking rather than an automatic response to the word, per se.

The same pattern of development occurs for "Yes"; as we mentioned earlier, although "Yes" takes longer to emerge. At first, the "Yes" response of parents may be best considered as part of the greater context containing "no" responses. Children acquiring a meaning for "Yes" may do so in playing with objects, waiting for either a "yes" or "no" answer for each of their actions. Later, they may verbally anticipate what their parents will do and act in accordance with the reply. The following is typical of young children in search of a meaning for "Yes":

> A child is playing with objects on a table. She is allowed to play with the coaster, the magazine, and the book but not the glass vase. She points to the vase and with a rising intonation says, "OK?" When her mother replies "No!" she points to the permitted book and her mother says "Yes!" Then she receives "Yes!" responses to the magazine and coasters. She repeats her requests several times for each object.

She now has acquired a way of communicating that involves seeking permission instead of simply going ahead with an action and awaiting approval or disapproval.

Consequently, the meanings of "No!" and "Yes!" have taken rather drastic changes over the child's early months. "No!" is one of the child's first words to undergo such drastic changes in meaning. The changes are in the child's behavior in relation to the word and the situation and in the presence (versus absence) of future planning in the child's behavior.

Functions of first words. In addition to words for mother/father and yes/no, children's first words relate to any number of objects, persons, actions, or events. We can begin by listing them according to an adult word-class scheme:

Nouns		*Verbs*	*Adjectives*	*Prepositions*
(objects)	(persons)	go	pretty	up
		look	good	down
car	Mommy	sit	nice	on
dog	Daddy	run	bad	off
light	baby			
bottle	Grandma			

This type of classification falls short of saying something meaningful about the child's communication, however. Instead, it seems realistic to say that first words *perform many different functions,* depending on the communication context—the events surrounding the word. In fact, differences in the meanings of first words are best understood in terms of *functions* and not word classes, according to Paula Menyuk.[7]

[7]Paula Menyuk, *Sentences Children Use* (Cambridge, Mass.: M.I.T. Press, 1969), pp. 25-29.

The following are typical functions of children's first words:

1. *Declarative:*   a. "(Look at the) car."
                        b. "(I'm being) bad."
2. *Imperative:*   a. "(Look at the) light!"
                        b. "(You be) nice (to me)!"
                        c. "(Pick me) up!"
3. *Interrogative:* a. "(Is that a) light?"
                        b. "(Will Daddy) go?"
                        c. "(Is the light) on?"

Notice that a particular word class, such as noun or preposition, can appear in more than one function category. To consider first words according to their grammatical form class is insufficient in terms of understanding children's *intentions.* The major functions of children's first words are to declare, to exclaim, and to question. Words from any adult form class (adjectives, nouns) can be employed in each functional context. Clues for determining the function of a child's word are found in the prosodic features of his voice (pitch changes, emphasis, and loudness) and in his bodily movement.

The content of first words, irrespective of their function, is usually things, persons, actions, and events closely related to the child's immediate life. For instance, if families expose a young child to animals, chances are many of her first words will be names of animals. Furthermore, if moving things fascinate the child, as they do most children, you can be sure that words for moving objects—for example, "airplane," "car," "truck," "taxi," "bus"—will constitute a large portion of the child's early vocabulary. That even babies are fascinated with lights seems to explain why "light," "off," and "on" appear in the early vocabularies of most children.

In summary, first words serve three major functions: *declaring* the presence of some thing or event, *exclaiming* about that thing or event, and *asking* for it. Now, our most important concern is the child's development of meanings associated with words that serve such functions.

changes in meaning: expansion and contraction

Children do not simply acquire meanings in a word-by-word fashion. Instead, a child may learn one meaning of a word, then another meaning for the same word, and then even another. The process of meaning development involves what Lewis calls "progressive adaptation," in which word meanings *expand* and *contract* under the influence of a child's interaction with other persons.[8] The key to

[8] Lewis, pp. 47-57.

understanding the child's acquisition of words, then, is to understand the expansion and contraction processes in meaning development.

Expansions of meaning are among the most characteristic features of children's speech. Lewis discusses some rather clever, and often bizarre, examples of expansion. One boy (just beginning to talk) called a duck, "quack." Then the boy applied "quack" to water, probably because ducks and water "went together." Next, he used "quack" to refer to birds and insects on the one hand and to liquids on the other hand. Some time later, having seen an eagle on a French coin, he named other coins "quacks." In another example, a little girl was told that the full moon she saw through her window was a "moon." That evening, she called a round biscuit she was eating, "moon." Thereafter, she applied the word to cakes; round marks on paper, in books, and on walls; the letter "O"; and other round drawings.

These examples illustrate the initial process of expansion in the child's acquisition of words. After learning a word the child applies the word to other things and events that seem to be similar or related to that word. This extension of a word to new contexts is often amusing to adults: the extension may make some degree of sense, but the relationship is often quite remote.

Another example cited by Lewis illustrates the child's progression to the second stage of meaning development—the *contraction* of meaning. A little boy who was given the name of an airplane and subsequently called one a "pay pay." Several days later he saw a kite and called it a "pay pay," probably expanding the meaning of airplane ("pay pay") to "flying things." Once he learned that a kite was called a "kite" and not a "pay pay," his word for airplane was then restricted to airplanes. After the expansion of meaning to new objects and events, the process of meaning contraction begins; eventually, the word-referent relationship is almost one-to-one. Figure 6.1 illustrates expansion and contraction in Timmy's acquisition of animal words, as outlined by Lewis.[9] The words in quotation marks represent those Timmy used at each stage of development. Notice that "tee" first stands for three different animals (a cat, a small dog, and a cow), based on expansion. Later, contraction prompts different animal names: "pushie," "goggie,"and "moo-ka."

The foregoing discussion has focused primarily on one-word (free-morpheme) utterances. Our next topics are the child's understanding of compound words, which theoretically contain two free morphemes, and bound morphemes; examples are drawn from Berko's landmark study.[10]

[9] Ibid., p. 51.
[10] Jean Berko, "The Child's Learning of English Morphology," *Word*, XIV (1958), 150-77. Reprinted by permission of the author and publisher.

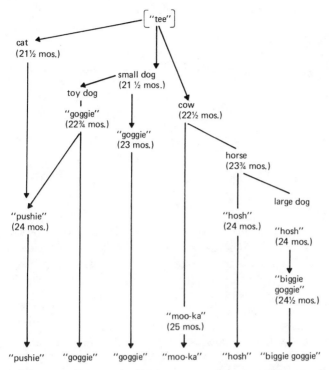

Figure 6.1. *The expansion and contraction of meanings for animal words. Table II from Chapter 3 of Language, Thought, and Personality by M. M. Lewis © 1963 by M. M. Lewis, Basic Books, Inc., Publishers, New York.*

compound words

A brief look at compound words and what children think about them will give us further insight into the child's mind, from the standpoint of morphology. Although the subject of compounding represents only a small portion of the total picture of meaning, we include it here primarily because it gives us a glimpse into the child's mind that we, as adults, often miss. Furthermore, the results are often humorous.

In her landmark study of "wugs" (inflectional endings), which we discussed in Chapter 4, Berko included a modest study of children's understanding of compound words. The children were preschoolers through first graders. They were asked why they thought a compound word was so named. The compound words studied were these:

1. afternoon
2. airplane
3. birthday

4. breakfast
5. blackboard
6. fireplace
7. football
8. handkerchief
9. holiday
10. merry-go-round
11. newspaper
12. sunshine
13. Thanksgiving
14. Friday

Some of these compound words appear more difficult to analyze than others; in fact, some of them seem slightly unfair. Berko used a control group of adult subjects in her analysis of children's responses.

Berko proposed four stages in the child's acquisition of meaning(s) for compound words:

1. *Identity:* a statement of the form, "an x is called an x because it's an x."
2. *Salient feature or function:* a statement that accounts for a feature or function of the compound word but is not related to either morpheme.
3. *Word-related salient feature (function):* a statement that accounts for a salient feature (function) and is related to one of the two morphemes in the compound word.
4. *Etymological:* an account of both morphemes and their meanings. Each stage of development is discussed and illustrated by examples.

Identity: stage 1.   The preschoolers provided very few responses, but when they did identity responses were the most common. When asked, "Why is a fireplace called a 'fireplace'?" the preschoolers typically answered, "Because" or "Because it's a fireplace." Identity responses do not demonstrate an understanding of the components of a compound word. Instead, they seem to reflect a young child's feeling that *words* are related to *things* "because that's just the way it is." The older children gave very few identity responses. Apparently, this type of response is restricted to preschoolers.

Salient feature or function: stage 2.   "A blackboard is a blackboard because you write on it." This response takes into account a function of the compound word, but the child does not relate that function to either morpheme, "black" or "board." A salient feature response to "Why is sunshine called 'sunshine'?" might be this: "Because it's very bright." Both of these responses indicate a child's basic understanding of word meaning but relate to the totality of the compound word, not to one of the two morphemes contained in the word. The children are attempting to provide some kind of reason in naming, even though their stage 2 responses represent rather weak reasons for calling something by a certain name. A few of the preschoolers were able to provide salient feature (function) responses. The older children provided many more.

Word-related salient feature (function): stage 3. As in stage 2, the third stage of development involves the child being able to state a salient feature or function of the compound word. The difference is that the feature or function corresponds with one morpheme in the multiple-morpheme construction. For example, most of the children giving an answer for "fireplace" said it is called that because "you put fire in it." In this case, the salient function in the child's response matches the first morpheme in the compound word. A child's ability to answer in this fashion might be explained in part by the nature of the compound word. The word "fireplace" may be far easier to analyze in a word-related way than, let's say, the word "birthday." That "birthday" is tied both to one's *birth* and to a *day* might not be important to the child. What *is* important to the child on a birthday is the "you get presents and cake"—a stage 2 response. Only the older children (the first graders) were able to understand compound words according to a word-related salient feature or function.

Etymological: stage 4. A small percentage of the children's responses and most of the adults' responses were etymological, taking into account both morphemes and their meanings. The number of etymological responses was greatest for "Thanksgiving," probably because teachers talk with children about its word-related meaning. About one fourth of all etymological responses were for this word. Berko noted that despite instruction, however, 67 percent of the children answering this item said it was called Thanksgiving "because you eat lots of turkey," a stage 2 response. The etymological responses offered by the older children were filled with their "private" meanings for the compound words. These explanations were unrelated to the word's history or to conventional usage, but represented marvelous attempts by the child to explain the linguistic puzzles. Examples make the point clear:

> "An airplane is called an 'airplane' because it's a plain thing that goes in the air."
> "Breakfast is called 'breakfast' because you have to eat it fast when you rush to school."
> "Friday is a day when you have fried fish."
> "A handkerchief is a thing you hold in your hand and you go 'kerchoo.' "

Eventually, children learn to understand the meaning of compound words from an etymological viewpoint, but in the process they often assign personal meanings in their explanations. Instruction in the classroom often focuses on ascertaining the meanings of compound words by analyzing the meanings of the morphemes contained in them.

LEARNING WORDS: BOUND MORPHEMES

In the same study, Berko employed a nonsense language in examining children's acquisition of various bound morphemes. Inflections such as plural endings, possessives, past tense, and present progressive were to be attached by the child to nonsense words, as in these examples:

> A man who stands on the ceiling knows how to "bing"; if he did the same thing yesterday, then yesterday he————(past tense).

> One funny-looking bird is called a "gutch," and two of the same are called————(plural).

Cartooned drawings of the actions or things were used in conjunction with the lead-sentences and questions. Figure 6.2 shows Berko's prompt cues for the plural of "wug."[11]

THIS IS A WUG.

NOW THERE IS ANOTHER ONE. THERE ARE TWO OF THEM.
THERE ARE TWO____.

Figure 6.2. *Berko method for the plural morpheme– allomorph /-z/. Reprinted by permission of the author and publisher from* Word, *Vol. 14, 1958, p. 154.*

Because the children were able to add inflectional endings to nonsense words, Berko concluded that children learn to master morphological rules of bound morphemes. Older children had apparently internalized the bound-morpheme rules and could apply them to new instances of a "language." Recent studies have supported this major finding.

The children knew just what was being asked of them. When they were given a picture of a man "spewing" (an odd picture of a man with a steaming pitcher on his head) and told, "He did the same thing yesterday—yesterday he _____ ," many responded, "spewed." Often, the children pronounced their inflectional ending with great care so that the examiner would not miss it. At times, the children said, "That's a tough one" and pondered before answering. The children seemed to understand and enjoy the linguistic task.

Berko's major findings were these (1) boys and girls did equally well on the test; and (2) for many of the morphemes examined there was significant difference in performance when comparing the younger and older children. By age six or seven, the children appeared to have mastered most of the bound morphemes studied, except for the more difficult ones (such as comparative-superlative adjectives and diminutive forms).

Let's examine each of the bound morphemes that Berko analyzed. For comparative purposes, we'll give examples of nonsense words and "real" words included in the study. These were the bound morphemes examined:

1. plural
2. past tense
3. present progressive verb
4. possessive (singular and plural)
5. derived adjective
6. comparative and superlative adjective
7. diminutive
8. progressive and derived agentive

plurals

Most of us think that to pluralize we simply add "s." In reality, there are a number of ways to add a plural morpheme. The selection of the appropriate plural morpheme (that is, the appropriate allomorph) depends on the phonemic ending of the free morpheme and the type of free morpheme being pluralized. *Allomorphs* are equivalent forms of a single morpheme (for instance, the plural), just as allophones are equivalent forms of a phoneme. Consider the following examples of plural allomorphs:

1. dog + plural = dog + /z/
   boy + plural = boy + /z/
2. cat + plural = cat + /s/
   lip + plural = lip + /s/
3. face + plural = face + / ə z/
   dish + plural = dish + / əz/
4. wolf + plural = wol + v + /z/
   leaf + plural = lea + v + /z/
5. child + plural = children
   mouse + plural = mice

Berko's study was concerned primarily with testing children's understanding of the more regular plural morphemes (forms 1-3 in the above list). Children formed the plural of "heaf" by adding /s/, and their response was ruled correct. Most of the adults in Berko's study changed the final sound of "heaf" to /v/ and then added the /-z/ allomorph. This response was also considered correct. Both the children and the adults were following "reasonable rules" in pluralizing. The adults simply related "heaf" to words such as "leaf," applying form 4 instead of form 2.

The following generalizations characterize children's acquisition of the plural morpheme:

> *1. All of the children—even the four-year-olds—found the plural bound morpheme a rather easy one to work with. The /-s/ and / -z/ forms (forms 1 and 2 in the above list) were significantly easier for all of the children than the /- əz/ form. Children did better with "wug," "lun," and "heaf," adding /-z/, /-z/, and /-s/, than they did with "tass," "gutch," and "niz." For the latter three examples, the child would have had to add the /- əz/ bound morpheme, and apparently this was more difficult.*
>
> *2. The first graders did significantly better than the preschoolers on many examples of the plural morpheme. Berko concluded that children's ability to select the appropriate plural allomorph for a free morpheme probably improves with age.*

Berko considered the performance of the younger children surprisingly good; they were able to add the appropriate allomorph to the free morpheme in several instances. How could they do this? Berko advanced two explanations: (1) children learn morpho-phonemic rules early—for example, they know that words ending in a voiced phoneme are pluralized with a voiced plural allomorph; (2) because it is "easier" to combine phonemes that are "alike" (for instance, in terms of voicing), children followed this principle. Given either explanation, the children's excellent performance on the

Berko test prompted many theorists to reconsider their practice-based explanations of children's acquisition of words and inflections.

Paula Menyuk studied children's ability to add plural endings to the more difficult irregular words in English.[12] She discovered that children pluralize the irregular forms (forms 4 and 5 in the list above) the same way they do the regular ones (forms 1 and 3). For example, five-year-olds and six-year-olds often create the following plurals:

1. house + plural = house
2. people + plural = peopleses

Notice that the final phoneme in "house" is /s/, a plural sound. Why *add* an /-s/ allomorph when the word already ends in a plural sound? So the children added no ending. At other times, they were redundant in use of *plural markers*, Menyuk's way of referring to plural allomorphs. The attachment of only one plural allomorph to "people" might not be enough—so, why not add two to make sure?

Children acquire the plural allomorphs in the order listed above: first they acquire form 1, then form 2, and so forth. The period of acquisition is from about three years to seven years of age. After the child completes the second grade, his speech usually reflects appropriate use of plural endings in all word contexts. Studies with nonsense words have produced results similar to those using "real" words. The age levels for the studies with nonsense words have been slightly lower than those employing actual words, however.

verb tense

There are a number of ways to indicate verb tense. Studies have shown that children have differing degrees of difficulty with the following tense endings:

1. go + present participle = go + ing
2. walk + past = walk + /t/
   play + past = play + /d/
3. paint + past = paint + /əd/
4. play + present, third-person singular = play + /z/
   paint + present, third-person singular = paint + /s/
   dance + present, third-person singular = dance + / əz/
5. come + past = came
   go + past = went

Again, as with the plural allomorphs, the tense endings are generally acquired in the sequence listed—form 1 is acquired first and form 5

[12] Menyuk, pp. 58-64.

last—which corresponds to the order predicted by the increasing difficulty of the forms from a linguistic viewpoint.

The tense morpheme acquired the earliest is the present progressive form. A child who is shown a man who knows how to "zib" can say he is "zibbing" before he can indicate the past tense. After the present progressive form is mastered, the simpler /-t/ (for "rick") and /-d/ (for "spow") past-tense allomorphs (form 2) are learned. Later, the more difficult /- əd/ form (form 3) is attached to words such as "mot" and "bod."

The third-person singular forms (form 4) required for the present tense of "loodge" and "naz" were difficult for the children. Only half of them responded with appropriate bound morphemes. Improvement with age was minimal, so apparently this tense form is difficult for young children. The fifth type of tense marking was missed most often: none of the preschoolers knew the past-tense form of "ring," and only a few of the first-grade children knew it.

Apparently, children acquire the ability to add appropriate tense markers to verbs in a form-by-form fashion. The present progressive marker is the first to be added appropriately, even by preschoolers. Next, children can form the simpler past-tense endings. In the process of adding tense markers, however, children often add them redundantly, probably to insure that tense has been accounted for; for instance, the past tense of "push" is "pushted," and "wash" is "washted." The past tense forms for "came" and "go" are, of course, "camed" and "goed," according to young children. The *regular rule* applied in these examples is the /-d/ allomorph (form 2 in the above list of tense endings). By the end of second grade, children are able to apply the appropriate present progressive or past-tense markers to the verbs of their language.

Peter Herriot devised a comprehension task to test children's understanding of present, past, and future tense.[13] Children from ages three through six were shown two activities at a time. Each of the two activities showed Wally the Woodpecker (a bird attached to an aluminum pole by a spring mechanism) in one of three conditions:

1. perched at the top of the pole: future condition
2. tapping his way down the pole: present condition
3. resting at the bottom of the pole: past condition

Children were shown two of the three conditions and then asked to select which "Wally" fit the nonsense verb form given by the tester.

[13] Peter Herriot, "The Comprehension of Tense by Young Children," *Child Development*, XL (1969), 103-10.

In one trial, for example, one Wally was shown tapping his way down the pole; the other Wally was shown resting at the bottom of his pole. The children were asked, "Which one has glinged?" Of course, the Wally resting at the bottom of his pole "has glinged," not the Wally tapping his way down. Herriot found that children comprehended verb tense as early as three years, particularly the past and present verb forms. Three-year-olds understood the future tense only when it was paired with the past tense, however. The six-year-olds consistently understood the future tense when it was paired with either the past or present conditions. Herriot concluded that children understand verb-tense morphemes at a very early age but have some difficulty with the future tense, even at six years of age.

possessives

> This is the wug who owns a hat. Whose hat is it? It is the ＿＿ hat. Now there are two wugs. They both own hats. Whose hats are they? They are the ＿＿ hats.

In the first instance the child is asked to supply the singular possessive form of "wug." The /-z/ allomorph is appropriate. The plural possessive is a bit more difficult: the /-z/ allomorph already existed as the plural form, so the *zero allomorph* (no additional ending necessary) is appropriate. Surprisingly, many of the children responded appropriately. It was the adults in Berko's study who had fun with the plural possessive of this form. Many adults said the plural possessive of "wug" was "wugs's," probably applying the plural possessive distinction applied to proper names (as in "Lyons's" or "Woods's").

Plural and singular possessives are acquired at about the same time. Even preschoolers were fairly successful in forming both the singular and plural possessives of "wug" and "bik." The difficult possessive form was the /-əz/ attached to free morphemes ending in /s/ or /z/. For example, children had greater difficulty adding the possessive form to "niz" than they did to "wug" or "bik."

adjective forms

What would you say if you were shown a picture of a dog covered with green spots and told, "This is a dog with quirks on him. He is all covered with quirks. What kind of dog is he? He is a ＿＿ dog"? Of course, you would call him a "quirky dog," deriving an adjective from the noun, "quirk." Now, assume that you are shown three pictures—one dog has just a few quirks, one has a moderate number of quirks, and the third has many quirks—and are told, "This dog (first picture) is quirky. This dog (second picture) is _____ . And this dog (third picture) is the _____ ." You probably have no trouble supplying the comparative and superlative forms of the adjective: "quirkier" and "quirkiest."

Berko discovered that no statistical count was necessary to compare children's performance with the comparative and superlative forms: only one child in the entire study responded appropriately. The rest of the children didn't understand the question. When a child failed to give the first answer, the experimenter supplied it: "quirkier." The hope was that the superlative form would be easier to supply when the comparative form was given by the tester. Under these conditions some of the older children supplied the superlative form.

When asked to derive the adjective form, adults were unanimous in their response—"quirky dog." Most of the children formed the compound word, "quirk dog." None of the children added a bound form to the free morpheme, "quirk."

Young children are unable to produce derived adjective forms or comparative and superlative adjective forms. Although their speech may contain examples of such forms, the "rules" for deriving them are probably not learned until sometime after six years of age. Often, a language arts curriculum will offer instruction on adjective forms in the second or third grade with the hope of assisting the child in the acquisition process.

other word forms: diminutive and agentive

A man who "zibs" for a living is called, quite obviously, a "zibber." To form the agentive, all we do is add the /-er/ inflection to the verb. But what would you call a very tiny "wug"? How about a "wuglet"?

Adults unanimously said that a man who "zibs" is a "zibber," but only 11 percent of the children responded with this agentive form. Most of the children gave no answer at all; a few said he would be a "zibbingman" or "zibman," compound forms that the adults didn't employ.

For the diminutive of "wug," 50 percent of the adults said "wuglet." Others offered "wuggie," "wugette," and "wuggling." None of the children employed a diminutive bound morpheme; instead, they formed compound words such as "baby wug," "teeny wug," and "little wug." Two children were extremely creative: they said that the diminutive of "wug" was "wig"; in doing so they were possibly using sound symbolism to convey meaning (that is, the narrow vowel stands for the smaller animal).

Children, even preschoolers, are able to convey the meaning of the diminutive and agentive forms. Their responses are, however, composed of multiple free morphemes rather than a derived form (that is, a free morpheme plus a bound morpheme). In their elementary-school years children become more familiar with derived forms, particularly if instruction is offered.

SUMMARY

The primary focus of research on the child's acquisition of words is the acquisition of *meaning*. Children learn the meanings of *free morphemes*, typically understood as items in a vocabulary, and *bound morphemes*, which consist mainly of inflectional endings.

The child's "first word" is acquired sometime around twelve months and usually refers to his mother or father. First words usually involve duplication of a consonant-plus-vowel syllable, as in "mama," "dada," and "tata." Infants and young children have meanings for many words, such as "yes" and "no," but these meanings change as the child develops. His word meanings become less dependent on the situation at hand. He learns to use words to accomplish various functions: to declare, to question, and to exclaim.

Table 6.1. *Children's development of morphology.*

STAGE		STARTING AGE
1.	*First words:* for parents, objects, and so forth; they serve declarative, imperative, and interrogative functions	12-18 months
2.	*New words*: added through expansion and contraction (vocabulary building)	3+ years
3.	*Early bound morphemes* 1. plurals 2. possessives 3. verb tense: a. present progressive 　　　　　　 b. simple past 　　　　　　 c. third-person present 　　　　　　 d. irregular past 　　　　　　 e. future	5+ years
4.	*Compounding* 1. identity 2. salient feature 3. related feature 4. etymological	4-6+ years
5.	*Later bound morphemes* 1. adjective forms: a. comparative 　　　　　　　　　 b. superlative 2. deriving 3. diminutives 4. agentives	6+ years

Once children have acquired a few words in a vocabulary, they add new words according to two acquisition processes:

1. *Expansion:* Children apply a word they know to other objects or events similar to that word.
2. *Contraction:* Children decrease their use of one word for several objects or events in a concept class by giving new names to members of that class.

Later, children learn to understand compound words in a step-by-step fashion, beginning with an identity process and progressing to an etymological process.

Bound morphemes begin to emerge in preschool years. The plural and possessive allomorphs and the present progressive verb endings are mastered first. The more difficult tense endings, such as the irregular past and the future, take more time to develop. Adjective forms and other bound morphemes begin to emerge in the child's early elementary years. Table 6.1 is a stage-by-stage chart of morphological development in children.

SUGGESTED READINGS

LEWIS, M. M., *Language, Thought and Personality*, pp. 1-50. New York: Basic Books, 1963.

MENYUK, PAULA, *The Acquisition and Development of Language*, pp. 82-88. Englewood Cliffs, N.J.: Prentice-Hall, Inc., 1971.

——, *Sentences Children Use*, pp. 58-64. Cambridge, Mass.: M. I. T. Press, 1969.

CHAPTER

7

the syntax
of children's communication

Compare the imperative utterances of Gregory and Jeffrey:

Gregory (eighteen months): Cookie! (points to cookie jar)

Jeffrey (three years): Mommy, give me a chocolate chip cookie *now*, please!

Although both children have about the same chance of receiving the cookie, it is clear that the sentences they use in requesting it are drastically different. Gregory is communicating his interest in a sentence-like word coupled with a pointing gesture (to the cookie jar) and a demanding intonation pattern in his voice. Jeffrey's request also includes emphatic nonverbal cues (just look at his face), but his utterance reflects an ability to join words together to communicate his intention. Joining words to form sentences is based on knowledge of *syntax*, and Jeffrey has syntactic abilities that Gregory is just beginning to acquire.

A child learns the syntax of his language when he is able to (1) join words into sentences and (2) understand multiple-word sentences said by others. Consequently, syntactic ability relates to the production and comprehension of relationships expressed in sentences. With a handful of words and a few syntactic rules for combining those words, even two-year-olds can produce a host of different sentences. Furthermore, they can probably understand an endless number of sentences others produce because they are able to divide up their sentences into basic syntactic segments. Children's language begins to blossom when they acquire syntactic rules that allow them to understand and produce an infinite number of sentences related to almost any subject matter.

Syntax gives children two important powers of language:

1. *Productivity:* the ability to produce and understand an infinite number of utterances related to subjects of communication.
2. *Creativity:* the ability to create new utterances—that is, sentences the child has never heard before and is not copying.

Although many adults believe that a person's power in communication stems mainly from an extensive vocabulary, linguists argue that syntax surpasses morphology in enabling children and adults to be productive and creative in language use. The study of syntactic development in children is a crucial one because it gives us sharp insights into how children think and talk. Children begin to acquire the syntax of their language at about eighteen months of age, but the acquisition process extends through the elementary-school years. In their study of syntactic development linguists observe how language emerges from infancy, and this gives them a better understanding of how adults use language. Thus, developmental data from children help to shape linguistic theories in a very important way.

Children of elementary-school age have acquired most of the syntactic rules of their language. Their sentences are almost as complex as the ones adults use. During the elementary-school years children learn the more complex structures of language and the more complicated syntactic rules. They learn the syntax for their communication in a stage-by-stage fashion. Although most children pass through the various stages at about the same age, studies have indicated that a child's *developmental rate*—and not his age—is the most critical indicator of his progress in acquiring syntactic rules.

Few texts have characterized the stages of syntactic development in children from start to finish. In fact, the relevant literature focuses on one particular period of development or one syntactic structure. Our purpose is to explore all of the stages of syntactic development. Our information is based on scientific studies of children of all ages speaking different languages.

From the standpoint of production, there appear to be six major stages of development in children's acquisition of syntax:

Stage 1. *The sentencelike word:* children communicate relationships by using one word plus vocal and bodily cues. (twelve months to eighteen months or two years)

Stage 2. *Modification:* children communicate relationships by modifying a topic word with another word. (eighteen months to two years)

Stage 3. *Structure:* children employ complete subject-predicate structures to communicate relationships. (two years to three years)

Stage 4. *Operational changes:* children perform changes—for instance, in word order—on the basic sentence structure that enables them to communicate more complicated relationships. (two-and-a-half years to four years)

Stage 5. *Categorization:* children refine their sentences with a more particular choice of words, reflecting a complex system for categorizing word types. (three-and-a-half years to seven years)

Stage 6. *Complex structures:* children use the more difficult structures of a language—that is, the structures that involve complicated syntactic relationships. (five years to ten years)

Although these stages of development are usually defined by the ages indicated, these ages are merely typical of children's development. As we stated earlier, a child's rate of development plays a far more important role in explaining his progress than does his chronological age. There is an overlap in ages for the various stages of development. This simply means that children may be deeply involved with learning something in one stage while beginning to acquire rules in the next stage.

THE SENTENCELIKE WORD: STAGE 1

Although we typically think of syntax as the joining of words to form an utterance, some theorists believe that this definition disregards the first "bit" of syntactic knowledge acquired by children in the sentencelike-word stage. Most children go through this stage between their first and second birthdays. The peak time in the child's use of sentencelike words is usually around eighteen months of age. Let's begin with an illustration of this stage of development.

Imagine a seventeen-month-old girl looking into her toybox. Her mother, standing next to her, has suggested that she find something to play with.

Child (pointing to a teddy bear and turning her head toward her mother and smiling): Mommy?

The interrogative contour—the upward inflection in the child's voice at the end of the sentencelike word—does not signal a child confusing her teddy bear with her mother. The child is quite a bit smarter than that. She is probably asking her mother to give her the teddy bear because it's out of her reach; it's as if she were saying, "Mommy, can you get it for me?"

Children begin to communicate verbally by using the sentence-like word. If the context of the sentencelike word is not known by the listener, its meaning is ambiguous. Sentencelike words are one-word utterances used by children in a variety of situations to mean a number of different things. Usually, the meaning of the sentencelike word is clear to anyone present: it can be decoded with the aid of facial and vocal cues and knowledge of the communication situation.

The sentencelike word accomplishes three basic functions (briefly discussed on pp. 112-13), which are related to three sentence structures: (1) the emphatic or imperative statement; (2) the question; and (3) the declarative statement. Most people think that the child's first single words are labels of objects, persons, and actions. This is simply not true. The child is doing more than simply labeling aspects of his environment. Instead, his sentencelike word can serve a number of *assertive functions.* Here are some examples of these functions:

Sentencelike word	Utterance	Sample interpretation: assertive function
car (noun)	"Car!"	Child telling you to look at car.
	"Car?"	Child asking if that's a car.
	"Car."	Child saying it's a car and not something else.
sit (verb)	"Sit!"	Child telling someone to sit down.
	"Sit?"	Child asking permission to sit down.
	"Sit."	Child describing someone sitting.
nice (adjective)	"Nice!"	Child insisting that he's nice, not naughty.
	"Nice?"	Child asking if he is being nice.
	"Nice."	Child describing someone as nice.
on (preposition)	"On!"	Child telling you to turn on the light.
	"On?"	Child asking if the record player is on.
	"On."	Child asserting that the light is turned on, not off.

It is easy to understand why the young child has communicative power even though his ability to produce sentencelike words is modest. With four simple words he may be capable of communicating twelve sentence intentions.

We can increase the number of functions if we consider the fact that young children are also capable of communicating emotion in their sentencelike words. David McNeill claims that children are capable of communicating positive or negative emotion in a single word.[1] The emotion is conveyed through nonverbal cues. For instance, a loud voice can signal disapproval whereas a soft voice may indicate approval. "Mama" said with a soft voice has a quite different meaning from "mama" said with a loud voice. Consequently, our twelve functions can be expanded to account for the child's ability to communicate levels of emotional meaning.

Children may not articulate the sentencelike words according to adult standards (for example, a child may say "ight" for "light"), but their intonation contours closely resemble those an adult would use. The context of the sentencelike word may be babblings, and so the child's speech may sound like gibberish and appear meaningless. But the *prosody* (stress and intonation) and *body movement* (such as pointing and raised eyebrows) that accompany the word are definitely adultlike. Because it seems that elements are being combined to form the sentencelike word, we could describe this utterance according to an elementary syntactic rule:

sentence = word + prosodic element + body movement

In a sense children are *combining* structural elements in this stage, even though not all the elements are words, per se. The prosody and body movements can be called *markers* because they help interpret the meaning of the lexical item (the word).

The "word-plus-markers" rule characterizes the first stage of syntactic development. The young child may only have the capacity to store in her memory the properties of a single word, not a group of words. The other elements to be combined with the word could not require "memory space" to the extent that a word does. In fact, the more critical elements of the sentencelike word are the markers and not the word. In many instances, children can utter a nonsense word with the appropriate prosody and movement and thereby communicate meaning. It makes sense, then, to place heavy emphasis on prosodic and movement markers in this first syntactic rule.

Why do children use particular words for their "sentences" in this stage of development? Children may select key words from adult

[1] David McNeill, *The Acquisition of Language: The Study of Developmental Psycholinguistics* (New York: Harper & Row, 1970), p. 21.

sentences to use as their sentencelike words. These words are probably stressed by adults in one or more of the following says:

1. loudness
2. pitch difference
3. hesitations (duration cues)
4. movements (pointing, raising eyebrows, nodding head, opening eyes wider)

The emphasis can also be conveyed by demonstration. For example, a father may wish to explain to his son that the light can be either "off" or "on." The father's physical demonstration accompanying his explanation—turning the light switch from one position to the other—is a means of emphasizing "on" and "off." Thus, the adult uses the very markers (prosody and body movement) that his son will eventually use in his sentencelike words.

The most critical question for the linguist is whether or not the sentencelike word is really a sentence, grammatically speaking. An argument in favor of sentence "status" reads something like this:

1. Since most of the child's single-word utterances consist of nouns rather than members of other grammatical word classes; and

2. since all basic grammatical relations (in an adult grammar) contain nouns; and

3. because the nouns of the child's single-word utterances function in terms of these basic grammatical relations:

utterance	interpretation	grammatical relation
a. "door"	"Close the door."	object of verb
b. "eye"	"Water is in my eye."	object of preposition
c. "baby"	"The baby fell down."	subject of sentence

4. then it seems possible that the child has developed the concept of a set of grammatical relations in the single-word sentence.

Although experts do not agree about whether grammatical relations appear this early, we know that the child can express grammatical relations in multiple-word utterances in the next stage of syntactic development.

MODIFICATION: STAGE 2

When a child is able to combine words in the modification stage, he understands a basic set of grammatical relations. The development of multiple-word sentences, often called "patterned speech," does not reflect simply the acquisition of grammar; rather, it indicates the use of patterned speech to express grammar. This stage of development typically begins after eighteen months of age.

At sixteen months a boy may ask for more candy by saying "Candy!" At twenty months the same child is more explicit in his request: "Want more candy!" As the child ages the sentence expands, growing like a mushroom:

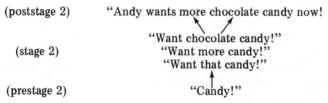

(poststage 2)   "Andy wants more chocolate candy now!

"Want chocolate candy!"
(stage 2)   "Want more candy!"
                         "Want that candy!"

(prestage 2)   "Candy!"

Obviously, the child's needs are expressed better by the expanded versions of the sentencelike word. Psychologists suggest that the short-term memory of two-year-old children is probably greater than that of sixteen-month-children. Thus, older children are able to store two or three words for their sentences, whereas sixteen-month-old children may be capable of storing only one word. Studies of children's short-term memory lead us to believe that it grows fast in preschool years. Because children can remember more and more words in a sequence, it follows that they can create longer and longer sentences. In other words, children's *productive span*—their ability to repeat items in series—is somewhat limited prior to the modification stage. It appears that an increase in children's productive span is associated with the onset of the modification stage.

The words composing the sentences of the modification stage tend to be the content words—the nouns, verbs, and adjectives—of adult sentences. As in the sentencelike-word stage, the words used by children in the modification stage are probably those stressed by adults in their sentences. The order of words in the multiple-word sentences of this stage usually matches the order in adult sentences. For example, the child's sentences,

"See shoe."
"That cookie."
"Want milk."

preserve the word order adults would use in expanded versions of these sentences. Sequences such as "Shoe see" or "Milk want" are usually not present in children's speech.

The sentences in the modification stage are usually two or three words long. Those who have studied the sentences produced by children in this stage have obtained amazingly similar sets of sentences from the children studied. The same words and sequences of two and three words are reported over and over again. Yet theorists do not agree in their explanations of why the child produces sentences as she does in this stage of development. Let's examine two explanations of the modification stage: the pivot-open approach of Martin Braine[2] and the modifier-topic approach of Jerome Gruber.[3]

the pivot-open approach

Braine's explanation of early sentences is based on the child's knowledge of two grammatical classes:

1. *The open class:* the largest group of words, which usually contains content words; a member of this word class can stand alone as a sentence; when a child learns a new word, it is first admitted to this class.
2. *The pivot class:* a smaller class of words, usually contains function words; a member of this word class cannot stand alone as a sentence; new members are slow to be accepted by this class.

Words typically belonging to these word classes are as follows:

pivot	*open*
see	shoe
that	milk
pretty	baby
allgone	doggie
nice	Mommy

To create sentences with members of the pivot and open word classes, the child has three options, which are related to three syntactic rules:

Option 1. sentence = open class word only
Option 2. sentence = pivot word + open word
Option 3. sentence = open word + open word

Let's take a look at examples of each possible word combination:

Option 1	*Option 2*	*Option 3*
1. "Doggie."	1. "See doggie."	1. "Mommy shoe."
2. "Shoe."	2. "Allgone doggie."	2. "Baby milk."
3. "Milk."	3. "Pretty Mommy."	

[2] Martin D. S. Braine, "The Ontogeny of English Phrase Structure: The First Phase," *Language*, XXXIX (1963), 1-13.

[3] Jerome Gruber, "Topicalization in Child Language," *Foundations of Language*, III (1967), 37-65.

The option 1 sentences are one-word sentences in which the word is selected from the list of open words. Options 2 and 3, then, describe the modification rules in stage 2 of children's syntactic development. The option 2 sentences involve the placement of a pivot word before an open word. This option seems to reflect children's ability to modify an open word with a pivot word. Option 3, on the other hand, seems to involve modification related to possession— "Mommy's shoe" or "baby's milk."

Braine's approach is based on the rather simple assumption that children are capable of classifying the words they learn into pivot and open classes. Criticism of the pivot-open approach focuses on this assumption. Critics argue that the classification scheme makes sense from an adult standpoint, but giving children credit for formulating such classes by themselves seems questionable. The word classes appear to be far too abstract for children to create. Some critics have suggested that the word classes need to be revised. Such revisions have focused on the pivot class.

Dan Slobin has suggested that the pivot class is far too vague and abstract to account for how children create sentences. According to his revision of the pivot class, *task words* can be coupled with the open word. There are five task words, and they accomplish a variety of intentions:

1. To modify: *pretty* Mommy; *my* book; *good* baby; *allgone* milk.
2. To locate or name: *there* Daddy; *see* kitty; *it* box; *that* car.
3. To describe an act: *away* horsie; *on* TV; *off* light.
4. To demand: *more* milk; *want* candy; *give* toy; *please* juice.
5. To negate: *no* water; *don't* help; *not* that.

Children understand the nature of the five tasks; they know they can use certain words to modify, describe, locate, demand, and negate, and they know which words accomplish these functions.[4] In essence, Slobin's approach is *functional* rather than purely grammatical, like Braine's. Because of its functional orientation, it seems to fit better with explanations of a child's capabilities at this stage of syntactic development.

the modifier-topic approach

In the sentencelike-word stage, the single word was described as having an assertive rather than a labeling function. The single word becomes the topic of the child's utterance. In the modification stage,

---

[4] Slobin's ideas (in press) are discussed in Paula Menyuk, *The Acquisition and Development of Language* (Englewood Cliffs, N. J.: Prentice-Hall, Inc., 1971), p. 101.

according to Gruber, sentences revolve around a topic word. The child's progress in the modification stage can be characterized as an advancement from the use of *performatives* to the use of *reportatives*. In other words, the progress is from demanding or indicating something about a topic to modifying that topic.

In the modification stage, the child first produces sentences that do not seem to attribute any characteristic to the topic of a sentence. Instead, these early sentences demand or indicate something about the topic of the sentence. Such sentences are called *performatives* and resemble predicate constructions in which the subject of the utterance is understood (omitted). Instead of saying "That's my doggie," the child says "My doggie." Rather than saying "I want candy," the child says "Want candy." In all cases, the child is demanding or indicating something about the topic word.

Performative sentences communicate the child's needs and interests in the here and now. Rarely does a performative relate to an event of the past or future. Performatives are of four major types; the first three are related to the basic grammatical relations discussed in stage 1, and the fourth type is a new function. Examples of each category of performative are as follows:

1. *Declarative:* big boat; pretty Mommy.
2. *Question:* want milk?; ride bike?
3. *Imperative:* give toy; more milk.
4. *Negative:* no truck; not allgone.

The performative sentence is followed by the child's production of the *reportative* sentence. This sentence involves the modification of a topic word, but in an adultlike construction that includes a subject and predicate:

> "Kathy going."
> "Jimmie fall down."
> "Mommy allgone."
> "Car back."

The topic (the subject of the sentence) is followed by a modifier, which is either part of a verb construction or acts like a predicate complement. Linking verbs—as in "Kathy *is* going"—are not included, and past-tense inflections are not employed—a child will say "Jimmie *fall* (past tense) down." Because reportatives are far more sophisticated sentences than performatives, they perhaps signal the child's transition into the next stage of syntactic development—structure. Children rarely use reportatives until they are experienced in the use of performative sentences.

In summary, children in the modification stage are able to join words together in four major types of sentences: declaratives, imperatives, questions, and negatives. Children join two or three words together for particular reasons, but the utterances seem incomplete. The third stage of development adds the element of "completeness" to the syntactic process: subject-predicate sentences are used consistently to reflect more complicated syntactic relationships.

STRUCTURE: STAGE 3

The multiple-word sentences of the structure stage are the child's first sentences that clearly follow the structural rules of a language. This stage begins between two and two-and-a-half years of age. Paula Menyuk describes the child's development from modification to structure as gradual; it often includes an intermediate stage in which the child struggles with structure.[5]

For example, consider the child's stage 2 sentence, "No play." This sentence simply strings two words together to show negation. The child's sentence in stage 3 might be this: "I won't play." This sentence has both a subject and a predicate and contains what linguists call structure. Stage 3 utterances typically include subjects and predicates, whereas Stage 2 utterances usually resemble predicate-only constructions.

In the structure stage the child's sentences include subjects and predicates. The child's progress is often like this:

stage 2	intermediate	stage 3
"Big boat."	"That big boat."	"That's a big boat."

Notice that the child's first attempts to incorporate structure do not include many of the grammatical features of a complete subject-predicate sentence—for instance, a linking verb. The following are examples of each sentence type; they show a child's progression into the structure stage:

sentence type	stage 2	intermediate	stage 3
declarative	"Big boat."	"That big boat."	"That's a big boat."
negative	"no play."	"I no play."	"I won't play."
question	"See toy?"	"Mommy see toy?"	"Do you see the toy?"
imperative	"No touch!"	"You no touch!"	"Don't touch it!"

Considering any one of the sentence types, the child's progression

---

[5] Menyuk, *The Acquisition and Development of Language*, pp. 103-9.

from stage 2 to stage 3 represents the incorporation of a complete subject-predicate relationship into the sentence.

In the process of incorporating structure, the child's sentences undergo drastic changes, which involve more than merely adding a subject. Verbs also change: phrases or predicate phrases now include auxiliary verbs, linking verbs, and modals ("can," "do," "will"):

"Daddy go." ⟶ "Daddy is going."
"No fall down." ⟶ "I'm not falling down."

They also include inflections such as the present participle, as in *"going."* Pronouns not previously used in questions ("See toy?") are now used: "Do you see the toy?" Pronouns previously used in imperatives ("You no touch!") are omitted: "Don't touch!"

In short, children begin to incorporate the structures of their language. They are able to replace noun phrases with pronouns and verbs with verb phrases. Their subject-predicate sentences begin to look like adult constructions. A number of differences between sentences in the intermediate stage and stage 3 indicate, however, that something else begins to happen. For example, the stage 2 sentence, "No play," changes in several ways to resemble an adultlike sentence:

"No play." ⟶ "I no play." ⟶ "I won't play."

In the first sentence, "No play," we see the negative element, "no," simply attached to the verb. After the subject of the sentence is added in the intermediate stage, the negative element is transformed (no→not) before it is incorporated into "I won't play." Many stage 3 sentences contain transformations called *operational changes*, which characterize the fourth stage of syntactic development. In this case the "no" is transformed into "not," and the modal ("will") is added appropriately.

OPERATIONAL CHANGES: STAGE 4

A rather complex stage in the development of syntax relates to a child's ability to perform operations on the basic structure of a sentence. These operations involve word-order changes, tense and modality changes, permutations, and inversions. The child's use of transformations starts sometime after the second birthday and continues through preschool years. Basic operational changes are learned by about three-and-a-half or four years of age. Three operational changes characterize this stage of development:

1. *The conjunction operation:* the joining of a modifier and topic to produce a sentence, or the conjunction of two sentences.
2. *The embedding operation:* placing elements within a subject-predicate structure.
3. *The permutation operation:* changing the order of elements within a subject-predicate structure.

conjunction

When the child conjoins elements to derive a sentence type, the child is making the operational change called *conjunction*. Consider the following examples of conjunction change; the child is adding an element to a basic sentence:

basic sentence	added element	sentence with conjunction
"Read it."	"my book"	"Read it, my book."
"Daddy go?"	"where"	"Where Daddy go?"
"Toys break."	"no"	"No toys break."

The conjunction transformation simply involves the addition of an element to the subject-predicate sentence. Notice that the word order of the basic sentence is not disturbed. In the second operational change, embedding, the child takes apart the basic sentence for further operational changes.

embedding

Embedding involves the placement of words within the basic sentence, which contains the subject-predicate relationship. Consequently, the three sentences just discussed might look something like this, before and after embedding:

before embedding	after embedding
"Read it, my book."	"Read my book."
"Where Daddy go?"	"Where Daddy did go?"
"No toys break."	"Toys did not break."

In this stage of development children are able to incorporate new elements, such as negatives, into the basic sentence.

permutation

When word order must be changed, as in converting a declarative sentence into a question, permutation must be employed. Consider this development of a question:

1. "Man here?" (The question mark is simply attached through intonation.)
2. "Man is here?" (A linking verb is embedded, but the question mark is still attached.)

3. "Is the man here?" (The permutation transformation is made.)

In questions 1 and 2, the rising inflection conveyed the question intent. With the inversion of the subject ("man") and the linking verb ("is"), after the embedding of "is" into "Man here?" the question is communicated in the order of the words as well as in the rising inflection. Here are two other examples of permutation with questions:

before permutation	after permutation
"I can go, too?"	"Can I go, too?"
"The milk is allgone?"	"Is the milk allgone?"

Permutation explains the child's ability to form negative sentences as well. Consider the following progression:

1. "No do it." (attachment of "no" element)
2. "I no do it." (structure + embedding)
3. "I no can do it." (further embedding—of modal, "can")
4. "I can't do it." (permutation)

Following the embedding of "no" and "can," the order of these two words is inverted to produce sentence 4.

Studies have characterized children's progression in the use of negatives and questions as a development from *attachment* to *structure* to *transformation*. This development can be pictured as follows:

attachment	structure	transformation
"No sit there."	"You no sit there."	"Don't you sit there."
"What this?"	"What this is?"	"What is this?"

By about four years of age children reflect in their sentences an ability to perform necessary operational changes, even though many of the sentences may still sound "wrong" (as in "Give me some piece of candy."). Stage 5, categorization, assists them in further development.

CATEGORIZATION: STAGE 5

A five-year-old child uses sentences that show an understanding of noun phrases, verb phrases, and complex adverbial clauses. The kindergarten child uses complete sentences that incorporate several adultlike word classes—for instance, nouns, pronouns, adverbs, and adjectives. As members of each word class multiply, however, the child begins to realize that members of a word class are not alike in all respects. Further *categorization* of the words within word classes is necessary.

The categorization stage begins in later preschool years and continues through the early elementary years. Word classes take on further subdivisions: for example, nouns become either singular ("child") or plural ("children"). Categorization of a word as singular or plural dictates the proper selection of a determiner and verb to use with the noun:

"That *child is* happy." (singular)

"Those *children* are happy."(plural)

Some nouns are mass nouns and others are count nouns, for instance, "milk" is a mass noun whereas "toy" is a count noun. Selection of the appropriate determiner depends on whether a word is categorized as a mass or a count noun:

"She has some *milk.*" (mass noun)

"She has some (many) *toys.*" (count noun)

Verbs are categorized as either transitive (taking a direct object) or intransitive; "make" is transitive and "go" is intransitive. Categorization of the verb helps determine whether or not an object is used and which modifiers are appropriate:

"Help me *make* it."   (transitive)

"I *am going* there."   (intransitive)

In addition, prepositions are categorized according to time and place so that appropriate use can be made of prepositional phrases:

"He slept *during* the game."   (time)

"He went *to* the game."   (place)

Children who have not mastered the rules of categorization produce sentences such as these:

1. "This things are heavy."
2. "Help me go the bicycle."
3. "Daddy took me at the circus."

In the first sentence, the child has inappropriately classified the subject noun as singular and selected the singular determiner for the sentence. Sentence 2 illustrates the selection of an intransitive verb ("go") instead of a transitive verb ("ride"). The third sentence shows the child using a preposition of time instead of a prepositional phrase of place.

In the child's struggle to master the rules of categorization, he goes through four periods of acquisition,[6] as listed below. Paula Menyuk's studies indicate that the process of acquisition is fairly consistent among children and that a striking correspondence exists between age and acquisition period.

Period 1. Nursery-school children frequently omit the word class or modifiers. (ages 3-4)

Period 2. Kindergarten children substitute an inappropriate word class. (age 5).

Period 3. First-grade children use the correct word or modifier redundantly to "insure appropriateness." (age 6)

Period 4. Second-grade children (and older children) use word classes correctly. (age 7+)

Table 7.1 portrays the periods of development within stage 5 for four word classes.

The examples listed in Table 7.1 demonstrate children's increased sensitivity to what linguists call the "context-sensitive" rules of a language. For example, the determiner to be joined to a noun or the preposition to be joined to a noun phrase must *agree* with the noun context. Consequently, prepositions must be sensitive to either time or place, just as determiners must be sensitive to mass or count nouns. The selection of words within a word class must be based on the linguistic context. Children learn the context-sensitive rules of categorization in their early school years.

COMPLEX STRUCTURES: STAGE 6

Many of the structures of our language are difficult and deserve careful attention when we use them. These complex structures are the focus of syntactic learning for children between five and ten years of age. When children begin to acquire the more complex structures of their language, the method of checking for regularities that is employed frequently in studying stages 1-5 does not bear fruit. To assess whether or not children understand the structural differences among the command, request, and promise verbs, more direct methods of research are necessary. Children may produce appropriate utterances for each verb, but they may produce a battery

[6] Paula Menyuk, *Sentences Children Use* (Cambridge, Mass.: M. I. T. Press, 1969), pp. 32-52.

Table 7.1. *The child's development of categorization.*

WORD CLASS	PERIOD 1: OMISSION	PERIOD 2: SUBSTITUTION	PERIOD 3: REDUNDANCY	PERIOD 4: MASTERY
plural noun	"Books heavy."	"This books are heavy."	"These books they're heavy."	"These books are heavy."
mass noun	"I want soap."	"I want many soaps."	"I want some lots of soap."	"I want some soap."
transitive verb	"Help me—the bicycle."	"Help me go the bicycle."	"Help me ride it, the bicycle."	"Help me ride the bicycle."
preposition of place	"Daddy took me circus."	"Daddy took me at the circus."	"Daddy took me there to the circus."	"Daddy took me to the circus."

of sentences that is inadequate if we are testing their full knowledge of these verbs. Consequently, stage 6 research employs the question technique.

To illustrate the problem, let's examine three verbs that take an object and a complement verb:

1. *Command:* "I told Bill to leave."
2. *Request:* "I asked Bill to leave."
   "I asked Bill (for permission) to leave."
3. *Promise:* "I promised Bill to leave."

When you use the command verb "told," the complement verb, "to leave," relates to Bill, not you. The request verb, "ask," relates to either you or Bill, depending on whether the verb, "ask," involves a request for permission. The English language has several *command* verbs (for instance, tell, order, force, compel, require) two *request* verbs (ask and beg), but only one *promise* verb. The promise verb is very different from the ask and tell verbs. A sentence with "promise" has a complement verb that relates to the subject of the sentence in the main clause—never to the object. You are the one who must "leave" if the promise is used—not Bill. Linguists call the promise verb an exceptional case in the English language.

Carol Chomsky conducted a series of research studies investigating the more complex structures of English, including the verb, "promise." She studied children from five to ten years of age and demonstrated that elementary-school-age children are still acquiring the more complex structures of their language. Let's examine three of the complex structures studied by Chomsky:

1. The doll is *easy to see.*
2. Donald *promises* Bozo to lie down.
3. Mickey Mouse *asks* Bozo to go first.

easy to see

Consider the following experimental situation. A child is given a doll that is wearing a blindfold. The experimenter begins to talk to the child.

Experimenter: Here's Chatty Cathy. Can you tell me whether she's easy to see or hard to see.

Child: Hard.

Experimenter: Could you make her easy to see?

Child: (removes blindfold)

Experimenter: Can you tell me why she was hard to see in the beginning?
Child: 'Cause she had this over her eyes.[7]

Obviously, the child related the action of "seeing" in the initial question to the doll, not to himself. Although the linguistic considerations that distinguish "easy to see" (from, say, "eager to see") are many, it seems clear that a five-year-old child is not able to determine the subject of the sentence or the subject of "see." There is a great deal of variability in *when* children acquire the complex rules necessary for interpreting the "easy-to-see" structure, but most children acquire this structure between five-and-a-half and nine year of age. Children nine years and older know this structure perfectly.

promise

We described the promise verb as a problematic one in our language. Its linguistic considerations include rules over and above those normally required for most verbs. Chomsky calls "promise" a *nonconforming verb.*
At first, the child knows what a promise is but understands the structure of promising in a very specific context only. Consider this interview with Kathy (five-and-a-half years old):[8]

Tester: What do you do when you promise somebody something?
Kathy: When you don't fool.
Tester: OK now, if you were going to promise your teacher that you will listen very carefully, what would you say to your teacher?
Kathy: I'd say, "I will." (adequate response)
Tester: Good. Now, if you were going to promise your friend to come over and play this afternoon, how would you say that? What would you say?
Kathy: I'd say, "Come over and play with me." (not an adequate response)

Children of five and six years of age, such as Kathy, know what a promise involves and have learned some of the syntactic structures related to promising. Nevertheless, they understand the promise verb only in a highly specific sentence. For example, the phrase, "that *you* will listen," is more specific than the phrase, "to come over," in indicating *who* will promise.
An older child understands the structures of promising better

[7] Reprinted from *The Acquisition of Syntax in Children from 5 to 10* by Carol Chomsky by permission of The M. I. T. Press, Cambridge, Massachusetts. © 1969 by the M. I. T. Press.
[8] Adapted from C. Chomsky's *The Acquisition of Syntax*, pp. 32-41.

but can occasionally be "tripped up" in performing correctly. Consider this interview with Peter (age eight): [9]

Tester: Can you tell me what you would say to your friend if you promise him to call him this afternoon?

Peter: I would say, "I'll call you up this afternoon."

Tester: OK, now. Here is Bozo and here's Donald Duck. (gives Peter the dolls) Donald tells Bozo to hop across the table. Make him do it.

Peter: "Bozo, hop across the table." (makes Bozo hop.)

Tester: Good. Now, Bozo promises Donald that he will do a somersault. Can you make him do it?

Peter: "I'll do a somersault, Donald." (makes Bozo do it)

Tester: Very good. Now Donald promises Bozo to hop up and down. Make him do it.

Peter: "I promised you you could do it." (making Bozo hop [wrong one!])

Tester: Would you do that again? Donald promises Bozo to hop up and down.

Peter: "I promise you you can do it." (again, making Bozo hop)

Peter did very well until the tester omitted all the syntactic cues from the fourth question. Then Peter made the wrong doll (Bozo) do the hopping. Peter is in one of the final stages of acquiring the "promise structure."

Similar to the "easy-to-see" structure, the promise structure is acquired slowly by some elementary-school children. Not until age nine do all children fully understand the "promise" verb, although some children do so as early as age seven.

ask

Chomsky employed three cases of "ask"-versus-"tell" verbs to test children's understanding of the more difficult "ask" verb. Whereas "tell" is acquired fairly early, "ask" causes a number of difficulties. Consider the three cases:

Case 1: Ask (tell) Bill what time it is?
Case 2: Ask (tell) Bill his (your) first name?
Case 3: Ask (tell) Bill what to feed the doll?

At first, children confuse the two verbs, interpreting both as "tell" verbs. Consider Eric (age six), who imposes a "tell" interpretation in all cases: [10]

[9] Ibid.
[10] Ibid., pp. 41-102.

Tester: Ask Bill what time it is.

Eric: It's two o'clock.

Tester: Tell Bill your first name.

Eric: Eric.

Tester: Ask Bill his last name.

Eric: Smith.

Tester: OK, now, ask Bill what to feed the doll.

Eric: Feed him cake!

Another child (age eight) understands "ask" for cases 1 and 2 but has trouble with the case 3 "ask":[11]

Tester: Ask Bill what time it is?

Jill: What time is it?

Tester: Good, now, ask him his last name.

Jill: What's your last name?

Tester: Fine. Now, tell Bill what to feed the doll.

Jill: Feed the doll liver.

Tester: OK, ask Bill what to feed the doll next.

Jill: Feed the doll ice cream.

Children acquire the "ask" verb in a stage-by-stage fashion, first learning case 1, then case 2, and finally case 3. Incidentally, some ten-year-olds have difficulty with the "ask" verb, showing that the acquisition of this verb is sometimes slow.

In order to summarize the child's development in stage 6, we have reviewed the stage-by-stage acquisition of complex structures. The "eager-to-see," "promise," and "ask" structures develop slowly. Stage 6 information is based mainly on the work of Carol Chomsky. In a similar study, Frank Kessel found that children acquire the "ask-tell" and "easy-to-see-eager-to-see" distinctions somewhat earlier than Chomsky has indicated.[12]

SUMMARY

An important aspect of children's communication is the syntax of their language—that is, the rules of word order and arrangement.

[11] Ibid.

[12] Frank Kessel, "The Role of Syntax in Children's Comprehension from Ages Six to Twelve," *Monographs of the Society for Research in Child Development*, Vol. 35, No. 6 (Chicago: University of Chicago Press, 1970), 48-53.

Children acquire syntactic rules in six stages. Developmental rate rather than chronological age accounts for children's progress through the six stages. Table 7.2 summarizes syntactic development in children.

First, children (one to two years) use the *sentencelike word*, which illustrates the simplest of syntactic relationships. These early sentences reflect the combination of a word, prosodic features (such as intonation), and body movements (for instance, pointing).

In the *modification* stage, children (about two years of age) join modifiers to topic words, thereby forming the kernals of four basic sentence patterns: the declarative, the question, the negative, and the imperative.

The *structure* stage involves the transformation of the four sentence patterns into complete subject-predicate relationships. The

Table 7.2 *Six stages in children's syntactic development.*

STAGE OF DEVELOPMENT	NATURE OF DEVELOPMENT	SAMPLE UTTERANCES
1. Sentencelike word	The word is combined with nonverbal cues (gestures and inflections).	"Mommy." "Mommy!" "Mommy?"
2. Modification	Modifiers are joined to topic words to form declarative, question, negative, and imperative structures.	"Pretty baby." (declarative) "Where Daddy?" (question) "No play." (negative) "More milk!" (imperative)
3. Structure	Both a subject and predicate are included in the sentence types.	"She's a pretty baby." (declarative) "Where Daddy is?" (question) "I no can play." (negative) "I want more milk!" (imperative)
4. Operational Changes	Elements are added, embedded, and permuted within sentences.	"Read it, my book." (conjunction) "Where is Daddy?" (embedding) "I can't play." (permutation)
5. Categorization	Word classes (nouns, verbs, and prepositions) are subdivided.	"I would like *some* milk." (use of "some" with mass noun) "Take me *to* the store." (use of preposition of place)
6. Complex Structures	Complex structural distinctions made, as with "ask-tell" and "promise."	"Ask what time it is." "He promised to help her."

sentences of children from two to three years sound almost adultlike.

In the fourth stage of development, preschool children learn to make *operational changes* on the basic structures of their language. They learn to conjoin, embed, and permute elements within their sentences in order to express more complicated relationships.

During the *categorization* stage, children of early elementary-school age develop an understanding of the subcategories of the major word classes (such as nouns and verbs). For example, they learn that nouns can be categorized as singular or plural and as mass or count. Assignment of a noun to categories dictates the form of other words in a sentence. In this stage children learn to categorize verbs, prepositions, and other word classes as well.

In the sixth stage of syntactic development, children learn the *complex structures* of their language. These include the "easy-to-see," "promise," and "ask" structures. Often, children struggle with the complex structures until age ten.

SUGGESTED READINGS

DEESE, JAMES, *Psycholinguistics*, Chap. 3. Boston: Allyn and Bacon, 1970.

MCNEILL, DAVID, *The Acquisition of Language: The Study of Developmental Psycholinguistics*, Chap. 6. New York: Harper & Row, 1970.

SLOBIN, DAN, *Psycholinguistics*, Chap. 3. Glenview, Ill.: Scott, Foresman and Co., 1971.

CHAPTER
8

semantics
and the communication
of children

Children must learn to use words in relation to each other and in relation to situations. The associations between words and situations are examined in the study of semantic development. If you ask preschool children to follow these four commands with a plate and a penny, you may be surprised at how they respond.

1. Put the penny on the plate.
2. Put the plate on the penny.
3. Put the penny under the plate.
4. Put the plate under the penny.

The first two commands, which utilize the preposition, "on," are usually the easiest ones to follow. Children will manipulate the penny and the plate appropriately. The third command may result in a slight hesitancy, but they can usually perform appropriately. It's the fourth command that causes a problem, and their responses are often inappropriate. Why is this so? Semantic theorists would begin by suggesting that children probably have not acquired the meaning of "under." Although they can respond to the third command, they cannot respond to the fourth. There appears to be a weak association between the word "under" and the plate-penny situation. Studies have found that the relational term "under" is usually acquired after the term "on." Furthermore, children may think that putting a cumbersome plate under a little copper is "unnatural." If we could see how children's minds work in decoding the words in the fourth command, we would have valuable information about their understanding of meanings in language. But presently, we do not have the tools to look inside the child's mind. Instead, semantic theorists must present a theory on how the child's mind works in learning meanings, gather data to test that theory, and then try to explain how the data fit the theory. The task is often frustrating because it seems like so much guesswork. But that's the present state of semantic research.

In this chapter, we will explore the child's development of semantics in communication. Our concern is with *meaning*—the relation of words and sentences to situations and ideas; as opposed to syntax—the relation of words to each other in sentences. Actually, we launched our discussion of semantic development in Chapter 6, but in that chapter we emphasized "first words." In the present chapter we take a broader look at the child's acquisition of meaning, by extending the discussion from words to sentences.

The acquisition of semantics is a slow process. Theorists suggest that words may not have meanings that are apart from the situations in which they are used until sometime after the tenth birthday. In fact, children are unable to give dictionary-type definitions of words until they are about twelve years of age. Before this time, children understand word meanings only in the context of sentence situations. Let's consider an example. An eight-year-old may provide the following definition of *to drink:* "Drinking is to drink milk or juice or pop." Notice that the child defined drinking in terms of the liquids he drinks and not the act itself. By the way, the boy that provided this answer commented that the beverages were mentioned in an ascending order of liking—pop is best! His response never seemed to touch on the meaning of *to drink;* instead, he explored beverages and how he likes them. An older girl (age thirteen) related important features of the action, *to drink*, and responded, "To drink means to put a glass or bottle or something up to your mouth and swallow what's in it." Notice the difference between these two meanings of the verb. The younger child defines the verb only in terms of the sentence context; the focus for him is on the beverage to be consumed. The older child understands the properties of the action and relates these properties in her definition.

To understand why semantic learning is a slow and complicated process in children's development of language, let's take a look at the child's mind and how it grows.

THE CHILD'S MIND:
STAGES OF DEVELOPMENT

Let's begin by considering a classic experiment in intellectual development suggested by Jean Piaget, a noted Swiss psychologist who has studied the development of thought and language in children.[1] Piaget uses this experiment to illustrate the very important intellectual capacity (or lack of it) in five- and six-year-olds. The concept being tested is the conservation of continuous quantity. (I have substituted orange pop for water, which Piaget uses, because I have found that children are far more attentive and perform at their best when the liquid under consideration is attractive.) With the appropriate materials for the experiment (glasses of different shapes and the liquid) we are ready to go:

Tester: Here are two glasses of orange pop. Do they have the same amount of pop or are they different? (The tester and the child made sure they were the same prior to the experiment.)

Child: They're the same.

Tester: OK, now, I'm going to pour the orange pop from this glass into this glass—all of it. (The tester pours pop from the regular glass into the short, squat glass.) And now, I'll pour the orange pop from this glass into this one. (Tester pours contents of second regular glass into the tall, slim glass.) Now, I poured this pop into this glass, and that pop into that glass. Now, look at the glasses of orange pop. Do they have the same amount of orange pop or are they different?

[1] The following experiment is adapted from the discussion in Herbert Ginsburg and Sylvia Opper, *Piaget's Theory of Intellectual Development: An Introduction* (Englewood Cliffs, N.J.: Prentice-Hall, Inc., © 1969), pp. 161-66.

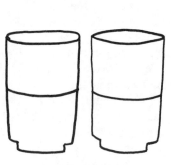

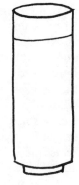

regular glasses   short, squat glass   tall, slim glass

Child: Different.

Tester: Oh! Which one has more orange pop?

Child: This one. (Child points to tall, slim glass.)

Tester: Does this glass have more orange pop than this one? (Pointing to the tall, slim glass and then to the short, squat glass.)

Child: Yes, it does.

Tester: OK. Now, I'm going to pour this pop back into this glass, and that pop back into that glass. (Tester pours orange pop into original containers.) Now, which one has more orange pop?

Child: They're the same.

Try this simple experiment with a five-year-old child; the child will consistently claim that the quantity of the orange pop in the glass is a function of the shape of the container.

In intellectual terms young children equate a one-dimensional scheme, the height of the pop, with a multi-dimensional concept, quantity. Their understanding of the terms "more," "less," and "same" is constrained by their intellectual capacity. Children's behavior in this test situation fits beautifully with what Piaget considers to be the second stage of intellectual development: *preoperational intuitive thinking* (two to seven years). Table 8.1 outlines Piaget's four stages of intellectual development in children. Notice that the third stage of development entails children's understanding of complex relationships, such as the conservation of volume and weight. This third stage, *concrete operational thought*, occurs sometime after seven years of age, so we couldn't expect a five- or six-year-old child to answer the foregoing test questions appropriately.

Children's development of language to express and understand the meaning of complex relationships can happen only as quickly (or slowly) as their minds develop. Children do not possess the capabilities for formal, propositional thinking until they are upward of eleven years. Children's semantic development—their development of word and sentence meanings—parallels their intellectual development. The four stages of intellectual development presented in Table 8.1 can be summarized in this way:

1. *Acquisition of perceptual invariants:* children are able to identify the main features in their environment. (to two years)
2. *Preoperational intuitive thinking:* children begin to understand the relationships among the features in their environment. (two to seven years)
3. *Concrete operational thinking:* children acquire an understanding of complex relationships. (seven to eleven years)

4. *Formal propositional thinking:* children are able to think logically. (eleven years and older)

Table 8.1. *Stages in children's development of thinking.*

STAGE	AGES	CHARACTERISTICS
1. Acquisition of Perceptual Invariants	to 2 years	Children are able to identify the main features in their environment. They understand that words relate to objects and their properties.
		Things in children's environments are "invariant," despite the various forms in which they appear—for instance, water is still water even though it's sometimes in a glass, a pan, or coming from a faucet.
		Meanings are related to sensory qualitites—for example, how things look, feel, touch, and taste.
2. Preoperational Intuitive Thinking	2 to 7 years	Children understand the relationships among perceptual invariants. Elementary concepts of time, space, and causality are considered.
		Children make intuitive judgments about relationships. Their judgments of conservation of volume, weight, and quantity, for example, are based on their attention to only one property of experience at a time. They are unable to see how two properties—for instance, height and width—interact with each other.
3. Concrete Operational Thinking	7 to 11 years	Children have acquired an understanding of complex relationships, such as the conservation of weight, volume, and quantity.
		Children have attained "reversible thinking"—that is, they can trace a physical operation back to its starting point and account for the transformations in its appearance.
		Children can classify objects according to a wide range of criteria related to size, shape, function, and so forth.
		Children have trouble in dealing with abstractions and events that are not visible to them.
4. Formal Propositional Thinking	11 years and older	Children can think in terms of purely logical propositions that can be stated and tested against their experiences.
		Children are capable of understanding syllogistic reasoning and are quite adept in causal reasoning.
		Children can derive hypotheses about relationships and draw inferences from appropriate data.

Remember these four stages of intellectual development as we now examine the child's meaning dictionary at successive stages of development.

THE CHILD'S MIND:
A DEVELOPING DICTIONARY

Word meanings exist in the minds of people who use words. If your meaning for the word "mother" is slightly different from mine, a dictionary could not resolve our difference in opinion. Our meanings are the result of our experiences with events and situations that the word symbolizes. In the same way, a child's meaning for a word might be totally different from our meaning for the same word. It doesn't help to suggest that the child's meaning is faulty, incomplete, or wrong from an adult standpoint. The better approach is to understand *what the basis of meaning is for the child.*

We can think of a child's mind as having its own dictionary, which changes as the child develops intellectually. The child's dictionary might change like this:

Stage 1: the child's sentence dictionary. The first dictionary in which the child stores and retrieves meanings is composed of sentences, not words. The sentences are really the sentencelike words discussed in the first stage of syntactic development (see Chapter 7). These sentencelike words accomplish a number of functions, such as to declare, to question, to exclaim, and to request. Words, per se, do not exist in the mind of the toddler. (one to two years of age)

Stage 2: the child's word dictionary—abridged. The child who is able to produce and understand sentences composed of two or three words is beginning to compile a dictionary of word meanings. Let's call this dictionary an abridged version since most of the meanings contained in it are related to *concrete actions.* Missing are word meanings for complex mental operations, such as cause-effect reasoning and concepts of volume, weight, and time. (two to seven years of age)

Stage 3: the child's word dictionary—unabridged. The child who is capable of perceiving complex operations and relationships among events and objects is developing an expanded dictionary, containing a greater number of full-fledged meanings. At this stage of develop-ment children are able to talk about complex operations and processes that they experience directly. Conversations about objects and events not directly visible to them are not as easy, however. The meanings of abstract notions and concepts are not included in this dictionary. Definitions are strongly tied to children's experiences and to the sentences in which they use the words. Dictionarylike definitions are not a part of this stage of development. (eight to eleven years)

Stage 4: the child's semantic dictionary. When the child is able to understand and talk about complex processes and events from an abstract point of view (for instance, the child can talk about events not visible), then the child's dictionary becomes a semantic dictionary. The child is able to provide adultlike definitions of words, definitions that take into account the semantic properties of the thing, event, or concept being defined. This dictionary is like the one that exists in the mind of an adult. (eleven years and over)

In terms of the child's age, these four stages of dictionary meanings match the four stages of intellectual development. This is not simply a coincidence. Piaget emphasizes that language and thought are related in a simple, straightforward manner: intellectual operations direct language meanings, rather than vice versa. Table 8.2 portrays the one-to-one correspondence between the development of the child's mind and the development of meanings.

With this basic discussion of intellectual development, we are ready to explore semantic development more fully. The topics to be considered are the following:

1. Children's development of dictionary meanings.
2. Children's understanding of relational terms, such as "more," "less," "before," and "after."
3. Children's acquisition of double-function terms, such as "cold," "sweet," and "crooked."
4. Children's comprehension of sentence meanings.

We will examine, in the light of each of these areas of semantic research, the stages of semantic development just outlined.

Table 8.2. *The child's mind and the development of meanings.*

AGE OF CHILD	THE CHILD'S MIND	THE CHILD'S DICTIONARY
to 2 years	perceptual invariants	*sentence dictionary:* meanings tied to functions that words perform
2-7 years	preoperational intuitive thinking	*word dictionary—abridged:* meanings tied to concrete actions
7-11 years	concrete operational thinking	*word dictionary—unabridged:* meanings tied to direct experiences, operations, and processes
11 years and older	formal propositional thinking	*semantic dictionary:* meanings expanded to abstract notions

THE DEVELOPMENT
OF DICTIONARY MEANINGS

To account for the meanings that could be communicated by a sixteen-month-old child, we would have to list all of the child's sentencelike words and their associated contexts. Each word or lexical item would be listed several times in this dictionary, primarily because each word takes on several functions in the sentencelike words. A segment of a young child's dictionary of meanings might look something like this:

Items	*Meanings*
1. Mommy!	Look at this, Mommy!
2. Mommy?	Mommy, will you get that for me?
3. Mommy.	I see my Mommy now.
4. Car!	Look at that car going by.
5. Car?	Is that a car?

The definition of one sentence in this child's dictionary is not clearly related to the definition of any other sentence. The child's sentence meaning is determined by listening and watching the child and from knowledge of the communication situation in which the child's utterance occurs. In moving from a sentence dictionary to a word dictionary, which is the primary focus in the child's acquisition of meanings, a dramatic change takes place in the format of a dictionary entry: a child introduces *semantic features* into word meanings.

Children do not begin to compile meanings in a word dictionary until about eighteen months to two years of age. Prior to that time, single words are the whole of their communication. When children are able to put words together to form multiple-word sentences, then we are pretty sure they have begun to acquire word meanings apart from sentence meanings. The word dictionary takes a long time to complete, however. According to research in semantic development, a person is still adding items to his word dictionary in adulthood.

The nature of the *dictionary entry*—the word and its definition—changes drastically as children age. Their first words and definitions (stage 2 of semantic development) are totally related to *concrete action*. Things, events, and ideas are defined in terms of visible actions related to them. For example, a bird is "something that flies in the sky," and a bowl is "where you eat your cereal in." According to one study, 82 percent of a six-year-old's definitions are in terms of concrete actions.[2]

[2] Heinz Werner and Bernard Kaplan, *Symbol Formation* (New York: John Wiley and Sons, Inc., 1964), p. 184.

At about eight years of age a dramatic change takes place: children no longer define words solely in terms of actions. In stage 3 of semantic development, words are defined in terms of the sentence contexts in which they are used by children. If a girl usually talks about birds in terms of how they perch on the branches of a tree in front of her house, chances are her definition of "bird" will include that fact: "Birds perch on branches on the tree in front of my house." Another eight-year-old girl (in stage 3) might define a bird in this way: "It's like an airplane except it's little and chirps." In this instance, the child's association of a bird with an airplane reveals the use of semantic features in word meanings. Both "bird" and "airplane" share semantic features—they fly, they have wings, and they are found in the sky. That the child understands the similarity between the two shows that she had begun to incorporate semantic features into her word meanings.

When children reach twelve years of age, they may be able to define birds as "warm-blooded animals that use their wings to fly." In this stage 4 definition, children associate several semantic properties in their meaning of "bird." This definition sounds almost like one you might read in a dictionary.

To better acquaint you with the stages in the child's development of dictionary meanings, read the following examples of definitions given by children of various ages:

child	definition stage	definition type	definition	
Jim (4 years)	2	action	bottle:	"Where you pour something out of."
			mother:	"She feeds me and gives me a bath."
Ann (8 years)	3	sentence context	bottle:	"It's like a can only you can see through it."
			mother:	"She has babies and takes care of them."
Ben (12 years)	4	dictionary	bottle:	"A hollow glass container that holds liquids."
			mother:	"A lady who is a parent of children."

The definitions provided by the children differ in their mention of semantic features of the word being defined. For the word, "bottle," Jim mentions only what he does with a bottle—the action of pouring something from it. Ann compares a bottle to a can: they are both containers (a semantic feature) but differ in the perceptual quality of transparency. Ben, the oldest child, is able to formulate an adultlike definition of "bottle," which includes several semantic features of the object.

Jim explains the word, "mother," in terms of the actions his mother performs for him—feeding and bathing. Ann sees mothers as having babies and taking care of them, a sentence-context definition. Ben provides a definition of mother that takes into account two semantic features: female and parent.

Studies that explore the changes in word meanings are called word-association studies. Children and adults are told, "Say the first word that comes to your mind," when the tester gives them a particular word. Such studies have been helpful in explaining the basic difference between stage 2 and stage 3 of semantic development. Results have indicated the following differences.

1. Older children (eight years and over) typically respond with a word that is of the same syntactic class as the prompt word. Opposites are often given. Here are some examples:

prompt word	response word
square	round
fast	slow
run	walk
up	down
cottage	house

In each case, the response word as of the same syntactic class as the prompt word and could be "plugged into" a similar sentence context.

2. Younger children (ages two to seven) typically give response words that are not in the same syntactic class as the prompt word but that might follow the prompt word in a sentence. Examine these examples:

prompt word	response word
square	box
fast	car
run	fast
up	there
cottage	cheese

The responses of younger children are not syntactically related to the prompt words: the only relationship is that the words "go together" in a sentence. Roger Brown and Jean Berko have called the responses given by older children and adults homogeneous *because of their linguistic likeness to the prompt word.[3] The responses of the younger children have been called* heterogeneous *because of their linguistic difference from the prompt word. The shift from heterogeneous word associations to*

[3] Roger Brown and Jean Berko, "Word Associations and the Acquisition of Grammar," *Child Development*, XXXI (1960), 1-14.

homogeneous word associations characterizes children's shift from action definitions (stage 2) to sentence-context definitions (stage 3).

Let's consider one of the words used as an example in the foregoing discussion: "square." Paula Menyuk states that this word elicits "box" most frequently from first graders and "round" most frequently from fourth graders.[4] She argues that "square box" is probably not a dictionary entry for the first graders; instead, "square" and "box" share the semantic feature or property of, say, having corners. First graders have a limited set of semantic features for any lexical item. From another perspective, younger children have a set of semantic properties that link words of different syntactic classes, based on sentence usage. Fourth graders undoubtedly understand the semantic property of shape that is associated with their meaning of "square." Because they respond with another shape—"round"—we can be fairly certain that the semantic property of shape exists in a fourth grader's dictionary.

In summary, children learn dictionary definitions of words in a step-by-step fashion. First, they acquire definitions that are strongly tied to action and function. Next, their definitions relate to the sentence contexts in which the words occur, and these words are perceived as being related to other words in terms of syntactic class. Finally, words are totally associated with semantic properties, and definitions take on an adultlike appearance. The key in distinguishing stage 2 from stage 3 is the addition to the child's dictionary of a limited number of working *semantic features* whereby the child can distinguish among words in a selective and efficient manner.

LEARNING TO COMMUNICATE IN TIME AND SPACE

When we learn a language, we learn the meanings of words that describe objects, events, and actions. We also learn words that describe relationships among objects, events, and actions. We learn that some events happen "before" or "after" other events and that one object is "in front of" or "in back of" another object. Acquisition of spatiotemporal terms has been explored in great detail by Eve Clark: in this section we shall focus on a few of these relational terms in what Clark calls the *spatiotemporal semantic field.*[5]

[4] Paula Menyuk, *The Acquisition and Development of Language* (Englewood Cliffs, N. J.: Prentice-Hall, Inc., 1971), p. 179.

[5] Eve Clark, "On the Acquisition of Antonyms in Two Semantic Fields," *Journal of Verbal Learning and Verbal Behavior*, XI (1972), 750-58.

At some point in their development, children must learn that words are related in terms of meaning. For example, do children learn that "walk" and "run" are alike because they refer to motion before they learn that they differ in the speed of motion involved? Clark suggests that *meaning relations* are learned before *distinctions in meaning* are learned. Research on the relational terms of size, time, and space supports this notion. For example, children may first understand that "big" and "little" are like "tall" and "short" before they know that *big-little* refers to the general size of an object along a potentially multidimensional space, whereas *tall-short* relates to a one-dimensional (vertical) space. Consequently, a young boy may call a book "tall," in comparison with another book, as often as he might call it "big." When he learns that *tall-short* applies basically to a one-dimensional space, he realizes that the *tall-short* distinction for a book is inappropriate, and he reserves it for forty-story buildings, six-foot-five-inch persons, rocket ships, and telephone poles.

Children may learn the meanings of spatiotemporal terms from *physical demonstrations* given by adults and older children. We show young children what "tall," "big," and "under" mean through our use of gestures and body movements. The order in which children acquire spatiotemporal terms cannot, however, be explained totally on the basis of which terms *are* and *are not* demonstrated by adults or which terms are demonstrated early as opposed to late. Children learn the meanings of spatiotemporal terms in a highly predictable order, which is based on *meaning complexity*. The following diagram outlines the general order in which children acquire the meanings of spatiotemporal terms:

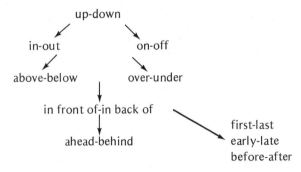

Your first glances will tell you that terms related to space are acquired earlier than terms related to time. Research on relational terms substantiates the generalization that the child is established "in space" before he understands how events fit together "in time."

The simplest space terms for young children are *up-down*, which relate an object's position on a vertical axis. A balloon is either "up" or "down." The relationship is simple and involves no reference objects.

On the other hand, if a balloon is "in" or "on" something else, that "something else" (the reference-object) has to be considered. Consequently, in the case of the balloon that is "in a box" or "on a table" the referent, "table" or "box," is necessary if the *in-out* or *on-off* terms are used. The space being considered is slightly more complex than the simple vertical space of the *up-down* terms. Thus, children learn to use *on-off* and *in-out* later than *up-down* because the space involved is more complex.

Going one step further, a balloon can be "above a table" or "over a table." In the cases of *above-below* and *over-under*, the child is concerned with more than simply an object's spatial location in a bounded space ("in") or on a line or surface ("on"). "Over" and "above" involve specification of a space between the reference object (the table) and the object being considered (the balloon). A balloon can be above the table but separated from it—in the air. A cloud can be "over" the house, but there is a space between the house and the cloud. That there is the possibility that a space exists between the object and the reference object makes the *over-under* and *above-below* terms more complex, spatially, than *in-out* and *on-off*. Children learn to use these more difficult relational terms after they learn the simpler ones.

The terms describing an object's visibility on a front-back axis are *in front of-in back of* and *ahead-behind*. For example, a dog can be playing "in front of a house" or "ahead of a child's bicycle." The bicycle is capable of moving whereas the *house* is not, so the bicycle-space is more complex than the house-space. You can say "in front of the house" but not "ahead of the house." The *ahead-behind* set of terms refers to a space that is capable of moving, whereas the *in front of-in back of* terms refer to a fixed space. Children apparently understand relational terms in a stationary space before they understand terms in a moving space.

For the same reason children learn relational terms of time, which consider events on a motion continuum, after they learn most of the spatial terms. Children first understand temporal terms relating *simultaneous* events—for example, "when" ("When the dog barked, she jumped."). Next, they understand temporal terms relating *nonsimultaneous* events: *first-last, early-late,* and *before-after.* For all three sets of terms, time has elapsed between events that are either reported or understood in the sentence. Consider the following situation:

> Jimmy's school ends at 3:00 P.M. Normally, Jimmy goes home after school. But today, he has a party to attend at 4:00 P.M. Because he has nothing to do after school, he goes directly to the party.

Sentences can express temporal relations among the events:

1. Jimmy went to school first, and then he went to a party.
2. Jimmy went to the party early.
3. Jimmy went to school before he went to the party.
(or)
    After Jimmy went to school, he went to the party.

In these sentences, time has elapsed between events. The relational terms indicate the passage of time.

Recent studies of children's acquisition of temporal terms have indicated that there is a particular order in which children acquire these terms.[6] The order is explained by the complexity of meaning involved in the terms. The least specific temporal terms, in terms of the complexity of the relationship, are *first-last*. Children learn to use this set of terms before they understand *early-late*. Finally, *early-late* is acquired sometime prior to *before-after*. Think about the specificity of time for each of these three sets of terms. In the *first-last* set, we only specify that "x" occurs first and "y" second. With *early-late*, on the other hand, we specify that someone engages in either "x" or "y" early or late. A time reference-point is established for either event in order for a person to reach "x" or "y" before or after the appropriate time. Thus, "early" and "late" are more complex than "first" and "last."

The *before-after* terms can be employed in four different sentences to illustrate the relationship of the "x" (school ends) and "y" (party starts) events:

1. Jimmy went to school before he went to the party.
2. Before Jimmy went to the party, he went to school.
3. After Jimmy went to school, he went to the party.
4. Jimmy went to the party after he went to school.

All four sentences say the same thing—they are alike in meaning. But they are not alike in terms of the ease with which children understand them. All four sentence types are usually understood by five-year-olds, but younger children have difficulty in understanding some of the *before-after* sentences. The sentences that mention the events in the order of their occurrence (order-of-mention sentences) are easier for younger children than non-order-of-mention sentences: thus, sentences 1 and 3 are easier than sentences 2 and 4. In other words, sentences that express the events in an order corresponding to their occurrence in "real time" are far easier than sentences that violate this.

[6] Eve Clark, "On the Acquisition of the Meaning of 'Before' and 'After,'" *Journal of Verbal Learning and Verbal Behavior*, X (1971), 266-75.

To complicate matters further, *after* sentences are more difficult to understand than *before* sentences. Research has indicated that the opposites in a set of relational terms are not necessarily acquired at the same time. The differential degrees of difficulty in understanding "before" and "after" is quite obvious in research with children. A four-year-old child might do the right things in the right order when told, "Make the doll jump before she sits." In response to another command, "After you make the doll jump, make her sit," the child may perform the actions in the *reverse* order. Both commands involve an order-of-mention strategy in expressing the two events in time. The only variation is that the first sentence includes "before" and the second sentence, "after." Five-year-olds understand both "before" and "after" sentences, but preschoolers have difficulty in understanding "after" sentences. The difficulty in understanding is quite apparent with very young children. Tell a young girl that she can have some ice cream after she finishes her meat and potatoes, and she will ask over and over, "Is it time for ice cream?" or "Now?" Older children know that something more than time must pass before the ice cream is theirs.

"markedness": explaining acquisition
of relational terms

Linguists have tried to explain the differential times of acquisition of the terms in a pair of antonyms (such as *before-after*) according to a semantic theory of "markedness." This theory is based on the concept that children learn semantic markings for the meanings of words and that some words are more difficult than others because they are "marked." Take the terms *more-less.*[7] "More" is *unmarked:* though it may imply a comparison, you can say "Put more milk into my glass" without really thinking about a comparison. To say "Put less milk in my glass" does not make too much sense. "Less" is *marked:* its meaning is not ambiguous, and a comparison is always implied.

To understand the differences between marked and unmarked terms, here are comparative statements provided by semantic theorists:

1. Unmarked terms are used more frequently in everyday speech; marked terms appear less frequently in our speech.

2. Unmarked terms are less complex than marked terms, from a semantic point of view.

[7] Margaret Donaldson and Roger Wales, "On the Acquisition of Some Relational Terms," in *Cognition and the Development of Language*, ed. J. Hayes (New York: John Wiley and Sons, Inc., 1970), pp. 235-68.

> *3. Unmarked terms are less meaningful than marked terms because they are potentially ambiguous.*

To elaborate, the supposed ambiguity of the unmarked term is due to the possibility that it may be used in different ways—for instance, in a comparative sense but also in an additive sense. The "more" and "less" terms constitute a good example of this type of ambiguity: more milk can be used in a comparative sense ("He has more milk than I have") or an additive sense ("I would like more milk, please"). "Less" typically refers to meaning in a comparative sense; thus the ambiguity is reduced.

Studies have suggested that three-and-a-half-year-old children do not understand the meaning of either term: they confuse both "more" and "less" in most comparisons. They understand the *additive sense* of "more"—as in "Give me more milk (than I have)"—but they do not understand that given two containers, one may have "more milk" than the other. Four-year-olds understand that one glass can have "more milk" than another one, but the implication that the other glass consequently has "less milk" baffles them. In other words, the more general term is acquired before the more specific term; thus, "more" is acquired before "less." Children of both ages (three-and-a-half and four years) have not yet acquired the meanings of antonyms. Not until their early school years do children know that "more" is the opposite of "less."

Eve Clark suggests that "before" is unmarked and "after" is marked. Although children of three years understand that certain things occur "before" other things, they often find it difficult to understand how the same events are related in terms of "after." Both terms concern time and are marked +time. In addition, the events are nonsimultaneous (−simultaneous). The terms are thus alike up to this point, according to semantic markings. But they differ when we consider the relation of the main clause (the *assertion*) to the temporal clause (for instance, "before he jumped" or "after he bent his knees"). In the case of "before" the assertion is "prior to" (+prior) or *happens first*, before the temporal clause. In the case of "after" the assertion clause is "not prior to" (−prior) or *happens last*, in relation to the temporal clause. Check these examples:

temporal clause	*assertion*	*temporal clause*	*assertion*
Before he jumped,	he bent his knees. (happens first)	After he bent his knees,	he jumped. (happens last)

The marking of *after* as −prior may help explain why children typically have more difficulty in using and understanding *after*. *Semantic markings* help us predict the order in which children learn sets of relational terms, as well as members within each set. Although discussions of semantic marking are difficult to understand—they take time to "decode"—the approach has gained considerable momentum in the study of language development.

In summary, children acquire spatial terms before they acquire temporal terms. The acquisition process is well defined in terms of the order in which the sets of relational terms are learned. Terms that relate the simpler concepts of space and time are acquired early. As the space or time becomes more complex, from the standpoint of dimensions and the passage of time, the relational terms become more difficult. Within a set of relational terms, such as *more-less* and *before-after*, children learn the unmarked member of the set (*more*, *before*) before they learn the marked member.

LEARNING THE MEANINGS OF DOUBLE-FUNCTION TERMS

An interesting way to observe children's progress in understanding meanings is to test their ability to relate double meanings of words.[8] To see if children understand that words can be used two ways, we must find out if they realize that a single word can describe both physical and personality properties. Some of the double-function terms that have been studied are: "sweet," "hard," "cold," and "crooked." These terms can describe both an object and a person. A relationship does exist between the physical term and the personality term. For example, a warm apple pie radiates heat almost like a warm, friendly person. We like to use adjectives such as "warm," "cold," and "hard" to describe personality because of the physical images they create in our mind—images related to the senses of touch, sight, and the like.

Children first learn the double-function terms in relation to objects only. Between three and six years of age children communicate physical information with the terms, understanding the terms in relation to objects and the physical appearance of people:

"The apple was cold."

"Her hands were cold."

   not

"She was a cold person."

[8] Solomon Asch and Harriet Nerlove, "The Development of Double Function Terms in Children: An Exploratory Investigation," in *Perspectives in Psychological Theory: Essays in Honor of Heinz Werner*, ed. B. Kaplan and S. Wagner (New York: International University Press, 1960), pp. 283-95.

Between seven and ten years of age children learn to understand the value of applying the physical term to the personality of a person: they understand, for instance, that a cold person is an unfriendly person. Sometime between their tenth and twelfth birthdays children are able to understand the application of the term to both objects and persons. In addition, they can verbally state the relationship between the two meanings:

> "I know why we call her a warm person—because she makes you feel warm all over, just like a fire does."

It's not until this stage of development that children see a relationship between the meanings of the physical term and the personality term. Prior to this (ages seven to ten) they give two separate and totally distinct meanings to the double-function terms.

The study of double-function terms sheds light on how children think about the complexities of meaning. If children see no relationship in the use of an adjective to describe both an apple pie and a person, then their meaning for that adjective is limited. Children's progress in learning the meanings of double-function terms is strongly tied to the stages of semantic development outlined earlier. Between the ages of three and six, children's meanings relate primarily to physical things; such meanings are like the stage 2 concrete-action definition. When they are able to see the application of the term to a personality (seven to ten years), they are probably employing a type of stage 3 sentence-context definition. In this stage children are able to relate the term to both situations, but they fail to see the relationship between the two. Finally, between ten and twelve years children are able to express the relationship between the two meanings. By this time, they are probably in the early phases of stage 4, at which point they are able to present definitions based on propositional thinking.

UNDERSTANDING SENTENCE MEANINGS

Pay close attention to Lorie's answers in the following experiment. (Hint: the tester does not tell the truth.)

Tester: Here is a picture, Lorie.

I'm going to say something about the picture and you tell me if I'm telling the truth. *The puppy is being chased by the kitten.* Am I telling the truth?

Lorie (four years):   Yes, that's right!

Tester: Now here's another picture.

I'm going to say something about the picture and you tell me if I'm telling the truth. *The boy is being carried by the frog.* Am I telling the truth?

Lorie: Ummm, say that again?

Tester: *The boy is being carried by the frog.*

Lorie: That's not right. You've got it backwards!

Why did Lorie apparently understand the meaning of the second sentence, albeit she was hesitant in her answer, but not the meaning of the first? Might there be something wrong with her perception? Actually, Lorie is a normal, intelligent little girl answering the test questions as semantic theorists would predict she would. Her "mistake" with the picture of the puppy and her correct response to the picture of the boy can be explained according to principles of semantic development. Let's take a look at the sentences as a semantic theorist would.

semantic factors:
passivity and reversibility

The two pictures used in the experiment are similar in that both portray similar events. In the first picture the puppy chases the kitten, and in the second the boy is carrying a frog. Both pictures have an *actor*—the puppy in picture 1 and the boy in picture 2—and both have a *recipient* of the action—the kitten in picture 1 and the frog in picture 2. The *actions* of chasing and carrying are simple ones. The test sentences to be judged as "true" or "false" by the child are versions of these active sentences:

Sentence 1 (active):   The dog chases the kitten.
Sentence 2 (active):   The boy carries the frog.

These active sentences would have been relatively easy for Lorie to respond to because they follow a direct expression of the actor-action-recipient format. In active sentences the actor is always first and the recipient is last. Lorie's difficulty with the test sentences is partially explained by the fact that young children have more difficulty understanding passive sentences (the test sentences are passive) than active sentences.[9]

Lorie's difficulty with the test sentences requires a more complex explanation, however. She seemed to understand the second sentence but not the first. Is there a difference between the two sentences that would explain Lorie's answers? Linguists would say no. On the other hand, semantic theorists argue yes. They call the first passive sentence *reversible* because either the puppy or the kitty could do the chasing. Reversible sentences involve an actor-recipient relationship that could go either way. The second sentence introduces a *nonreversible* relationship between actor and recipient: frogs never carry people! The action of carrying involves certain restrictions, which are based on the physical properties of the would-be actor. The verbs "carry" and "chase" have different semantic attributes. Relating these attributes to the potential actors and recipients involved in the two sentences, we can say this: puppies can chase kittens or kittens can chase puppies, but neither puppies nor kittens (nor frogs, for that matter) can carry people.

Research in semantic development has indicated that four- and five-year-olds may interpret correctly the meaning of a nonreversible

---

[9] Dan Slobin, "Grammatical Transformations and Sentence Comprehension in Childhood and Adulthood," *Journal of Verbal Learning and Verbal Behavior,* V (1966), 219-27; Elizabeth Turner and Ragnar Rommetveit, "The Acquisition of Sentence Voice and Reversibility," *Child Development,* XXXVIII (1967), 649-60.

passive sentence but may misinterpret the meaning of a reversible passive sentence. Apparently, they are advanced enough, cognitively, to perceive the clue given in the verb: "carrying" is restricted to certain physical conditions, such as the size and strength of the carrier and the entity to be carried. "Chasing" has no such restrictions. Any living being can chase any other one (with varying degrees of success) because the act of chasing does not depend on the size or the physical strength of the being. Four- and five-year-olds understand reversible active and passive sentences according to the same strategy: they assume that both are actor-action-recipient statements, even though the passive verb indicates that this strategy is inappropriate.

Considering nonreversible sentences in which only one of the participants (nouns) is capable of being an actor, the four- or five-year-old child is able to see a difference between the active and passive versions of the sentence. Lorie interpreted the nonreversible passive sentence in this manner:

1. I will assume that the first noun ("frog") is the actor and the second ("boy") is the recipient UNLESS this seems implausible. It does!

2. Since I see an implausibility factor—frogs don't carry people!—I interpret the meaning according to this strategy: recipient-action-actor.

You may recall that she hesitated slightly before arriving at the correct answer to the tester's question. Quite possibly, the implausibility factor (for nonreversible passives) was just being acquired by Lorie at the time of the experiment. Younger children, say three-year-olds, are unable to see a difference between active and passive versions of nonreversible sentences: In all cases, the first-mentioned noun is interpreted as the actor and the second-mentioned noun is the recipient—even though this may not be so. Children older than Lorie (six-year-olds, for example) are capable of interpreting both active and passive versions of both reversible and nonreversible sentences.

To understand how children acquire sentence meanings, it is important to examine both the syntactic and semantic qualities of such sentences. *Passivity* and *reversibility* affect the ease with which a young child understands what a sentence is "trying to say." If the sentence is expressed in a passive voice, chances are the child will have greater difficulty understanding what the sentence means *if* both persons, animals, or objects discussed in the sentence are capable of carrying out the action of the sentence.

additional semantic factors

Let's discuss some other factors affecting children's acquisition of sentence meanings. Try to picture a full range of more difficult reversible sentences, which vary according to the following semantic factors:

1. syntactic form: active or passive
2. verb type: affirmative or negative
3. sentence-picture match: true or false

The following eight sentences, devised according to these factors, could be used to test the child's understanding of the puppy-chasing-kitty picture (a natural reversible situation):

true sentences	*false sentences*
1. The puppy is chasing the kitty.	5. The kitty is chasing the puppy.
2. The kitty is being chased by the puppy.	6. The puppy is being chased by the kitty.
3. The cat is not chasing the puppy.	7. The puppy is not chasing the kitty.
4. The dog is not being chased by the kitty.	8. The kitty is not being chased by the dog.

You might say that the eight sentences express the same general idea but are either true or false statements about the relationship between the kitty and the puppy. In all cases the actor is the puppy, the action is chasing, and the recipient is the kitty. The sentences differ according to syntactic, semantic, and truth-value criteria, however. These differences affect children's understanding of sentence meaning. The following results are based on a study of children five to eleven years of age.[10]

First, the passive sentences—in which the actor was mentioned second—were more difficult for the children than the active sentences. The children simply did better in responding accurately to the active sentences. Thus, sentences 1, 2, 5, and 6 were easier than sentences 3, 4, 7, and 8. Second, when sentences were stated in the affirmative, judgments of truth were much easier than judgments of falsity. Likewise, when sentences were stated in the negative, judgments of falsity were easier than judgments of truth. Consequently, sentences 1 and 2 were easier than sentences 5 and 6 and sentences 7 and 8 were easier than sentences 3 and 4. Apparently,

[10] Slobin, "Grammatical Transformations," 219-27.

children find it easier to answer correctly when there is a match between the verb type (affirmative or negative) and the truth-value of the picture-sentence match. The most effective combinations are these: affirmative verb plus true match, and negative verb plus false match.

We can draw a number of generalizations from the results of this study:

> *1. Considering the fact that the children studied were between five and eleven years old, it seems obvious that school-age children are still learning the semantic features of their language. That ten-year-olds have difficulty understanding certain sentence types makes us realize why children's semantic development is not completed during their elementary-school years.*

> *2. Children learn to understand sentence meanings according to a number of semantic factors: (a) negative sentences seem to be fairly easy for children to understand; (b) reversibility is more difficult for children to understand; when a sentence contains a reversible relationship between objects or events, the sentence is easily misinterpreted.*

The general conclusion of most studies on sentence understanding is that children learn more complex strategies for understanding sentence meanings as they grow older.

The simplest strategy for understanding sentence meaning is this:

> *1. Understand all sentences as* actor-action-recipient.

This strategy is employed by preschoolers. Children in their early elementary years will continue to apply this strategy in certain instances. A second strategy is as follows:

> *2. Understand a sentence as* actor-action-recipient *unless that sentence is passive with a nonreversible verb; then understand it as* recipient-action-actor.

Older children (over ten years) understand both active and passive sentences according to a more complex strategy:

> *3. Understand active sentences as* actor-action-recipient, *but interpret all passive sentences as* recipient-action-actor.

The progression from a simple strategy for both sentence types to the use of two strategies for the two sentence types is possible because of semantic strategies mastered by children in the process of learning. In other words, their experience has told them that not all sentences follow the actor-action-recipient strategy. They are most aware of this when they realize that some action relationships are simply impossible: frogs don't carry people.

SUMMARY

Semantic development in children can be characterized by four stages, which parallel children's intellectual development. First, meanings are found in the child's *sentence dictionary*. During this stage (one to two years) the child communicates meaning in the sentencelike word. Next, the child begins to compile a *word dictionary (abridged)*. In this stage children (two to seven years) communicate with word meanings that are related primarily to concrete actions and objects. The third stage of development involves a more complex *word dictionary (unabridged)*. During this period, between the ages of eight and eleven, children are capable of communicating meanings that relate to complex operations and processes. Finally, children develop their own *semantic dictionary*. In this final stage of development children (eleven years and older) are capable of formal propositional thinking and are able to formulate statements of meaning.

Children learn the meanings of spatiotemporal terms in an order based on their complexity of meaning. Spatial terms that characterize a relatively simple physical space—*up-down*—are acquired before spatial terms that represent a more complex physical space—*in front of-in back of*. Temporal terms are acquired later than spatial terms. *First-last*, *early-late*, and *before-after* are acquired later than terms for simultaneous time, such as *when*. Semantic theorists argue that within a set of relational terms such as *more-less* and *before-after*, one term—in these instances, "less" and "after"—is always marked. Marked terms are less meaningful—because they are potentially more ambiguous—and are acquired later than their unmarked counterparts, "more" and "before."

Double-function terms—for example, "sweet" and "crooked"—are first used (from three to six years) to describe the physical properties of objects and persons. Between seven and ten years of age, children learn that the double-function term can also be used to describe a person's personality. Not until after ten years of age are children able to relate this double meaning of the term and explain why the term can be applied in both contexts.

Children first understand sentence meanings according to a basic semantic strategy: interpret all sentences as actor-action-recipient statements. When they are able to take advantage of the semantic clue provided in a passive sentence with a nonreversible verb (a verb that implies that only one of the nouns can be the actor), then they are able to interpret nonreversible passives correctly: recipient-action-actor. After children understand the notion of reversibility (at about ten years of age) they are able to interpret all active and passive sentences according to the appropriate strategy.

SUGGESTED READINGS

MCNEILL, DAVID, *The Acquisition of Language: The Study of Developmental Psycholinguistics*, Chap. 8. New York: Harper & Row, 1970.

MENYUK, PAULA, *The Acquisition and Development of Language*, Chap. 6. Englewood Cliffs, N. J.: Prentice-Hall, Inc., 1971.

THE CHILD'S
COMMUNICATION SYSTEM:
NONVERBAL DEVELOPMENT

It would be very convenient if we could employ the distinction between linguistic competence and linguistic performance in the study of children's nonverbal communication, as we did in our study of children's verbal language. Conceivably, our discussion could focus on the rules of the nonverbal system as they relate to our intuitions (and those of children) about the acceptability, grammaticality, and meaningfulness of physical and vocal behavior in communication. Such an ideal situation simply does not exist in the field of nonverbal communication at the present time. Instead, researchers struggle to find order amidst chaos in their study of the human being's use of nonverbal communication. Although theorists suggest that we follow rules in our use of nonverbal codes, they have not yet presented explicit statements of such rules. The chaos in the field can be accounted for by a number of conditions, the first being the infancy of the field as a scientific area of study.

Although language experts have suspected that nonverbal cues constitute a significant portion of a message, traditional theories have given very little importance to such cues. Often, tone of voice and body movement are discussed as cues that simply enhance or clarify the verbal message. However, recent studies argue that nonverbal language has a far more important function in communication than merely dressing up words. Scientific study in selected areas of nonverbal communication has extended over many years. Nonverbal communication of emotions through intonation patterns in the voice is certainly not a new area of study. Moreover, the examination of gestures dates back to ancient theories of speechmaking. Yet, the concerted effort to study nonverbal communication as a *system*—one that is described by sets of rules for the communication of information, attitudes, and feelings—is a product of recent years.

A second condition that helps explain the chaos in the study of nonverbal communication is the lack of an established system of coding and classifying the meaningful nonverbal units in a person's communication. Although we have numerous systems for classifying the sounds, words, and sentences of our language, established methods for classifying our "winks, blinks, and nods" are just now being developed. In essence, we are striving to find a science of nonverbal communication.

A third condition that accounts for our caution in nonverbal study is our lack of knowledge concerning the basis of nonverbal language. At the present time, experts do not agree about the nature of children's acquisition of nonverbal language. Some scientists argue that the biological endowment hypothesis works well in explaining verbal language development but falls short in accounting for nonverbal development. Is the nonverbal system a totally learned system, based on environmental conditioning? Or do infants have innate capabilities in the use of facial, vocal, and bodily cues? We know very little about the relationship of nonverbal communication to the human mind. As we begin to discover that human emotions are predictably related to neurological and physical processes, we are beginning to see new avenues for research in the physical communication of emotions. With greater understanding of the human brain and the relationship of the brain to the communication process, we will be in a better position to examine the course of nonverbal communication development in children.

With these qualifications in mind, we approach the study of nonverbal communication development in children. Chapters 9-11 are based on *what we believe to be true* about nonverbal communication in children and adults. We will explore recent theories and scientific investigations that have helped explain children's communication with their bodies, their voices, and the space around them. Although there are, as of now, no specific methods for examining the whole of nonverbal development, there are three research directions that describe the existing body of knowledge.

1. The science of kinesics, which deals with bodily communication, offers an approach that is very compatible with studies of verbal language. This approach involves the analysis of gestures, movements, and positions of the body according to a system closely akin to the verbal system; the result is an attempt to isolate "kines," "kinemes," "kinemorphs," and even a "kine-grammar." Analyses are mainly of adult communication, but a few studies do attempt to account for the emergence of nonverbal cues in infants and children.
2. Scientific study of prosody in speech has attempted to account for the relationship of features of the voice, such as pitch and loudness, to meaningful cues in our messages. Experts in the study of prosody are beginning to examine the emergence of prosodic features in the speech of young children.
3. The science of proxemics, which deals with our use of distance (and touch) in communication, offers still another direction in nonverbal language study. Based on research with adults, proxemic theorists have established norms of proxemic behavior—actually, distance "conventions" in communication. The direction of study in children's communication, then, has been to examine the emergence of such conventions in children's communication.

Part III examines children's communication through the channels of body motion, the voice, and space. Although the discussion in Chapters 9-11 is not as sophisticated as our study of verbal communication in Part II, it should provide an overall perspective of the development of children's nonverbal communication.

CHILDREN'S BODY LANGUAGE

As adults, we have been taught that first impressions are crucial in social and business interactions. A person's physical appearance, which includes his posture, bodily movements, and dress, is considered to be a most important persuasive tool in conveying positive first impressions. Apparently, we believe that initial messages sent by our bodies are more immediate than initial messages sent with words.

Going beyond first impressions, we know that the meaning underlying a person's message is often communicated with arm movements, eye blinks, and smiling faces. We include a chapter on children's body language because of its supreme importance in most communication situations. Chapter 9 discusses body language in two important contexts: the communication of emotions and the communication of gender.

THE VOICE COMMUNICATES!

One of the first channels of communication available to the infant is the voice. Infants communicate vocally and understand basic vocal messages. "Tone of voice," or prosody, is based on the pitch, loudness, pausing, and rate of a message. Children have had practice in communicating meaning vocally from the time they became social beings.

As children come closer and closer to acquiring the adult communication patterns of their cultures, they learn to vary aspects of their voice in accordance with ideas, moods, and feelings. Children learn that others will understand their tone of voice even if their verbal message seems unclear. Although it may take children longer to understand the meaning of prosodic variations in the voices of others, particularly in terms of emotional communication, the importance of such learning cannot be deemphasized simply because of its slower development.

As teachers of children, we must be very aware of vocal communication and its development in children. Chapter 10 focuses on children's development of prosody, in terms of pitch, loudness, rate, and pauses.

CHILDREN'S COMMUNICATION
IN SPACE

Edward Hall, the founder of the study of proxemics, insists that one of the most nagging barriers to effective communication between cultural groups is interpersonal spacing in communication. Hall has observed marked differences in the communication patterns of adults from different cultural and subcultural groups, such as differences in distance between speakers, shoulder orientation, eye contact, and other proxemic variables. These differences are apparently the product of cultural learning. If we are to strive for more effective communication among social and cultural groups, we must understand proxemic conventions and how they develop in children. Exploratory studies with children suggest that proxemic conventions emerge early in the child's life.

The messages we send with our bodies do not exist in a vacuum: they emerge in a personal space around us—our "communication territory." These proxemic messages are important because they indicate our feelings, likings, and judgments. We know that children are in the process of learning to act and talk in space, but we have only basic information about children's spatial behavior. The purpose of Chapter 11 is to explore children's development of proxemic communication in four distance zones outlined by Edward Hall. Proxemic differences are related to the child's sex and ethnicity.

9

the body language of children

The child's first communication experiences with other children are considered *acted conversations* by child psychologist Jean Piaget. Acted conversations are cryptic because they rely heavily on gestures and bodily demonstrations rather than words.[1] To understand what young children are talking about, you must notice their pointing, bobbing, and waving movements. The child's gestures often tell us more about what he is "really saying" than do his words. In fact, it's virtually impossible to interpret utterances such as these,

"This does that."

"That goes there."

"Make that thing do it this way."

without watching a little finger pointing to a car or a head bobbing toward the playhouse. The dialogue of an acted conversation lends that quaint character to children's speech. There is no question about it: young children talk with their bodies.

[1] Jean Piaget, *The Language and Thought of the Child*, trans. M. Gabain (New York: Meridian Books, 1955), p. 94.

181

Acted conversations depend almost totally on body language, whereas verbal conversations—which emerge later, according to Piaget—present a more balanced picture of the verbal and nonverbal channels of communication. For younger children, communication is synonymous with movement: their arms, legs, and heads seem to be in a constant state of motion as they work, play, and talk with others. Younger children depend on gestures and bodily movement for a *direct statement* of their message. With the acquisition of verbal language, gestures and movements take on the different role of *complementing the verbal message.*

How do children learn to "talk" with their arms, their faces—their entire bodies? Ray Birdwhistell, a leading scholar in *kinesics,* the study of body motion communication, insists that all children acquire a system of body motion communication as they learn their native language. In fact, membership in a social or cultural group depends on mastery of the nonverbal communication system—body motion and voice—as well as the verbal system.[2] Initially, children get to know their new friends through obviously physical contacts. A poke in the eye, a tug on the ear, and a finger in the nose are simply the child's ways of saying hello and learning more about you. Julius Fast, in *Body Language,* states that children rely heavily on their bodies in discovering the world around them.

> Children, before they are taught the inhibitions of our society, explore their world by touch. They touch their parents and cuddle into their arms, touch themselves, find joy in their genitals, security in the texture of their blankets, excitement in feeling cold things, hot things, smooth things and scratchy things.[3]

The communication of young children is also very physical. The message of a two-year-old boy might involve standing at the cookie jar, pointing, and uttering a gruntlike sound. If he gets a cookie, or even if he doesn't, for that matter, communication probably took place if someone was around. As the child becomes adept in his verbal ability, we assume he relies less and less on nonverbal communication. That the child becomes proportionately more verbal as he ages, does not and should not suggest to us that the nonverbal channels of communication become either nonexistent or unimportant. In fact, all adult speakers constantly engage in body motion communication, and although some of us may "move" more than others, all of us would be lost without it.

[2] Ray Birdwhistell, *Kinesics and Context: Essays in Body Motion Communication* (Philadelphia: University of Pennsylvania Press, 1970), p. 7.

[3] Julius Fast, *Body Language* (New York: M. Evans and Co., 1970), pp. 79-80.

CHILDREN AND MOVEMENT

Imagine yourself a parent trying to keep a two-year-old child inactive for ten days. A pediatrician gave this order to a friend of mine following her little girl's surgery. The thought of keeping an active, rambunctious child relatively motionless for such a long period of time seemed impossible—and it was. The young child understood her mother's orders to be still, but the child's compliance lasted about thirty seconds. From a child's point of view living is synonymous with moving. Restrictions in movement are frustrating for anyone, especially young children. According to psychoanalytic theory, a child's reactions to bodily restrictions reveal the human drive, based on an urge called *motility*, to be free to move at will.

"Jim Thorpe, the famous four-star athlete, is said to have imitated each move in a baby's active day. He gave out, exhausted, after four hours. The infant continued for eight or more."[4] The child moves constantly. He engages in movements that serve no visible purpose aside from the sheer experience of movement—crawling, running, bouncing, jumping, and whirling. Many of these activities are rhythmic and seem to provide the child with great satisfaction and pleasure. If the activity is blocked, the child inevitably becomes restless or angry.

Motility, the spontaneous movement of the skeletal musculature, is considered an urge in the same sense as the oral, excretory, and genital urges. Dr. Bela Mittelmann, a noted authority of psychoanalytic study of the child, explains that there are identifiable parts of the body that communicate a sense of urgency.[5] During the second and third years of life, the child experiences rapid development of motor skills. Many of the child's motor activities can be considered spontaneous releases of emotions, feelings, and reactions. The so-called urge to be bodily free is at its peak in preschool years and steadily declines after five or six years of age. After the child is ten years old, the motor urge remains at a consistent low. Dr. Mittelmann related the decline of the motor urge to the rise of children's preference for verbal activity over motor activity.

WHAT IS BODY LANGUAGE?

All of us know that a wink, a smile, or a frown may tell someone how we feel. Words are not always necessary. We can tell that

[4] T. Berry Brazelton, *Infants and Mothers: Differences in Development* (New York: Delacorte Press, 1969), p. 158.

[5] Bela Mittelmann, "Motility in Infants, Children, and Adults," *Psychoanalytic Study of the Child*, IX (1954), 154.

someone is uncomfortable by watching his fidgeting, bodily tension, and wandering eyes. Body language can be defined as any reflexive or nonreflexive movement or position used to communicate an emotional, attitudinal, or informational message to someone else. Let's explore this definition in detail.

Body movements (for instance, waving and winking) and positions (for example, hunched shoulders and wide-open eyes) are the basic categories of body language. Although any movement or position during communication is capable of message value, not all motion necessarily communicates. For example, we could conclude that our friend's wrinkled brow is a sign of her dissatisfaction with our presence, but we could be wrong. Maybe her wrinkled brow is simply the result of her attempt to keep light out of her eyes as she is talking.

Body movements and positions can be considered either *reflexive* (involuntary) or *nonreflexive* (voluntary). An involuntary motion often studied by kinesic experts is pupil dilation—the widening of the pupil in the eye. It can tell your opponent in cards that your hand is good. Research also indicates that the male's pupil dilates twice as much as normal when he is shown a picture of a nude woman. Supposedly, he is communicating his excitement. Pupil dilation has been used as a measure of students' reactions to critiques of their speeches by a video-taped critic-teacher. When the teacher made positive statements about their speeches, the students' pupils dilated. These studies suggest that the eyes communicate messages of excitement, arousal, and pleasure. Are we conscious of our pupils dilating? Probably not. Facial twitches, eye movements, and shoulder orientation are body language cues that we send involuntarily to others.

Nonreflexive movements or positions seem to be more within our control in communication; however, their interpretation is often more difficult. Because we can control our movements in communication, we can also deceive the person to whom we are talking. A smile to an employer may be well within our control: we want him to receive a positive message. Maybe our real feelings for him at that moment are not positive, but let's assume that we don't want him to see our true feelings. Instead, we put on a kind of act with our body language, hoping he will believe it. In this case, the message in body language was inconsistent with our feelings. In other instances, our controlled movements, verbal language, and thoughts can all be on the same wavelength.

The agreement of body language with our verbal language is a crucial point. When our verbal and nonverbal messages are in agreement—let's say both are very positive—then few problems arise regarding how communication should be interpreted; the task is easy. But how about the situation in which the verbal message contradicts the nonverbal message? Which message should we believe? For centuries, psychoanalysts have tried to resolve this problem. A patient seems to be saying one thing but meaning something else. Psychoanalysts approach the problem by attributing the inconsistencies (the contradictory messages) to a conflict between superficial (deceitful) feelings and true feelings. Often, the verbal channel conveys the superficial feelings and the nonverbal channel communicates the true feelings. According to nonverbal theorist Albert Mehrabian, the role of the psychiatrist, then, is "to help the client separate the wheat from the chaff."[6] This is done by analyzing the nonverbal channel to determine the person's underlying feelings and attitudes.

Verbal language can be used to communicate almost anything. In contrast, the nonverbal language of body movement appears to have a more limited range. Body language communicates feelings, emotions, preferences, and selected bits of information concerning gender, time, relationship, and so forth. Generally, body language either reinforces or contradicts the feelings and information conveyed in the verbal channel.

Body language includes movements of *a part of the body*, such as a nod of the head or a raising of the eyebrows, and movement of *the entire body*, such as overall body tension or jumping up and down. Movements and positions are usually related to emotional messages. Your pleasure in seeing someone you haven't seen in a long time may result in a visible expression of that emotion. Body motion can also communicate your attitude toward another person: how much you like him ("liking" messages) and how important you perceive him to be ("status" messages). Research has indicated, for example, that extreme bodily tension may communicate "You're a high-status person" or "I don't like you." In addition, our body language can answer questions: "How much?" (a little or a lot), "Which way?" (up or down), and "How big?" (tiny or gigantic).

To understand body language, kinesic scientists stress the importance of cultural and environmental differences. Body language is culture-bound, and a body motion may communicate two entirely different messages to members of two different cultural groups. To complicate matters, a body motion may not even convey a particular meaning. If there were always a one-to-one correspondence between *motion* and *meaning*, we could simply learn "body words" (move-

---

[6] Albert Mehrabian, "Communication Without Words," in *Communication: Concepts and Processes*, ed. Joseph DeVito (Englewood Cliffs, N. J.: Prentice-Hall, Inc., 1971), p. 108.

ments or positions always associated with a particular meaning) and a "body grammar" (patterns of movements and positions that communicate meaning in "body sentences"). According to Birdwhistell, the aim of kinesic research is to uncover the movements and combinations of movements that generally relate meanings. After decades of research, however, a *body language* has been difficult to isolate. Although we are fairly confident that we have discovered the morphology and grammar of verbal language, the morphology and grammar of body language is certainly in its infancy.

KINESICS:
THE SCIENCE OF BODY MOTION

The science of body motion communication is concerned with defining and classifying the bodily motions that serve communicative functions. Body motion communication is most easily explained in terms of *kinegraphs*, visual pictures of body movements and positions. In *Kinesics and Context*, Birdwhistell groups kinegraphs according to eight areas of the body: (1) head, (2) face, (3) trunk and shoulders, (4) shoulders, arms, and wrists, (5) hands and fingers, (6) hips, legs, and ankles, (7) feet, and (8) neck. The following kinegraphs* illustrate significant motion in the face:

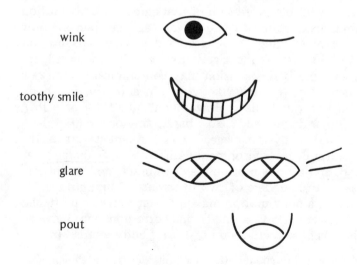

wink

toothy smile

glare

pout

*Adapted from Ray Birdwhistell, *Kinesics and Context: Essays in Body Motion Communication* (Philadelphia: University of Pennsylvania Press, 1970), p. 260.

In addition, "flared nostrils," "clenched teech," and "raised eye-brows" constitute an important part of our message. Body motion must be studied along with words, sentences, and intonation patterns.

To get an idea of the nature of kinesic research, let's take a closer look at the eyelids. It's been found that the human eye can distinguish eleven different positions of the eyelid. Only four of the eleven appear to be used by Americans in their communication: (1) "overopen" (wide-eyed), (2) "slit," (3) "closed," and (4) "squeezed." The eleven possible positions are called *kines*, and the four meaningful positions (to Americans) are called *kinemes*. Kinemes are like phonemes: they are the building blocks of nonverbal messages, just as phonemes are the building blocks of verbal messages. Kinemes are defined differently for different "speech" communities: one culture may have four kinemes of eyelid position, and another may have as many as five or six.

In addition to kines and kinemes, there are *kinemorphs* and *kinemorphemes*. Kinemorphemes are "body words," defined in terms of a movement or series of body movements where the total effect is a minimal meaning unit in body language. *Social kinesics is* the study of bodily movements that accompany spoken language and appear to convey social meaning. Research indicates, for example, that bodily movements vary when the message refers to "he" as opposed to "they," something that happened in the past versus something that will happen in the future, and something "over" rather than something "under." Our posture—specifically the carriage of the pelvis—is a dead giveaway of gender. The messages we send with our bodies are patterned and have a structure comparable to spoken language—thus, the meaningful phrase, "body language."

Body movements—gestures, facial expressions, and posture—cannot be studied apart from the words, changes in voice, and context of the message. A salute, for example, may convey a number of meanings, such as ridicule, rebellion, subversiveness, and respect. Smiles, nods, waves, and bows can also have several meanings. Studies of body language must necessarily consider the totality of communication, including the message context and the spoken words. Stated simply, then, body language is the patterned series of body movements that, along with the other channels of communication, conveys messages to other human beings.

GESTURES IN CHILDREN'S COMMUNICATION

One of the most elementary approaches to the study of children's body language examines children's gestures. In such studies, gestures are defined as self-contained communication segments and are studied in isolation. Gestures of greeting (such as indicating "hello" with a waving hand) would be considered, for example. Obviously, there are limitations to this kind of study. Most body language accompanies our verbal and vocal messages and does not stand alone as a communicator of meaning. In short, our gestures—in fact, all of our body motions—*accompany* the messages we convey in our words, our language structure, our voice, and our use of space. The study of "isolated gestures" does, however, lend some insight into how children learn what theorists have called nonverbal "emblems"—that is, nonverbal segments of communication that can stand alone and signal meaning to a listener-observer.

To study the development of gestures in children, Geraldine Michael and Frank Willis examined children's ability to transmit and interpret twelve frequently employed gestures:[7]

1. Go away.	7. How big?
2. Come here.	8. Shape: for example, round or square.
3. Yes.	9. I don't know.
4. No.	10. Goodbye.
5. Be quiet.	11. Hi.
6. How many?	12. Raised hand for attention.

These twelve gestures were selected for study on the basis of direct observation of children (four to seven years) at play and in the classroom. The gestures observed most frequently were selected for study.

The children in the study were interviewed individually. They were asked, first, to transmit each of the twelve gestures and, then, to interpret the same gestures when communicated by the interviewer. To elicit the gesture, "come here," for example, this instruction was used:

"If you had to be quiet and you were over there (pointing away) and you wanted me to come to you, what would you do?"

Children were judged on their accuracy of transmitting and interpreting the twelve gestures. The study posed the following basic questions:

1. Are older children (in this case, first graders) better in transmitting and understanding gestures than younger (preschool) children?
2. Are girls or boys better in transmitting or interpreting gestures?

[7] Geraldine Michael and Frank Willis, "The Development of Gestures as a Function of Social Class, Education, and Sex," *The Psychological Record*, XVIII (1968), 515-19.

3. Are middle-class children better in transmitting and interpreting gestures than lower-class children?

Children with one year of school (about six years of age) were better in both transmitting and interpreting the gestures than children of preschool age. The older children's longer exposure to communication in peer groups—communication that includes non-verbal messages and signals—probably explains their ability to send and receive gestural messages more accurately. The age comparison was particularly pronounced for lower-class children: first-grade children from poverty neighborhoods were significantly better in gestural communication than preschool children.

Boys scored better than girls in interpreting the gestures, but the authors could only guess why this happened. They suggested that because boys are slower to acquire verbal language (a questionable assumption), they develop nonverbal language more rapidly. Conclusions regarding sex comparisons are almost impossible to draw.

Finally, the results indicated that middle-class children were more accurate than lower-class children with the twelve gestures. In fact, a majority of the middle-class children tested (mostly boys) had perfect scores. Only a few of the older boys in the lower-class group received perfect scores. We must be careful in drawing conclusions from the social class results, however. Remember that the gestures employed in the study were taken from observations of children at play and in the classroom. The authors were not careful to account for the backgrounds of the children they observed in drawing up this list of gestures. It is possible that preliminary observations were based primarily on typical gestures of middle-class children and not lower-class children. Further, the researchers did not use informants[8] from the lower-class neighborhoods to help them in their study. It is entirely possible that the typical gestures of lower-class children were not even noticed by the researchers, or that they couldn't interpret them. Consequently, the list of gestures may have been biased toward the middle-class backgrounds of the researchers.

The study of children's gestures is an interesting one but doesn't lead us in meaningful directions. Children's development of bodily

---

[8] An "informant" in language or communication research is a person who is able to *talk about* the language or communication of his culture, social group, or geographic area. Furthermore, he is able to observe the patterns of communication in the group and verbalize a description of such patterns. Most adults can act as informants, as can older children. Usually, young children cannot talk about their own language or communication because they have not yet developed the cognitive skills to do so. Informants are very important in social class research because they provide insight into social classes and cultural groups that are different from those represented by the researchers.

communication is more appropriately studied *in context*. We cannot learn too much from the study of "Hi!" unless we study when, where, and how children communicate this message. Thus, a more productive method of examining children's body language focuses on *communication contexts*. Consequently, the major sections of this chapter center on bodily communication in two contexts: communication of emotion and communication of gender. Although we don't have volumes of data on each of these areas, we have enough information to sketch the picture of development. Our goal is to provide parents and teachers with a perspective on how children learn to communicate with their bodies.

THE BODY LANGUAGE
OF EMOTIONAL COMMUNICATION

Envision two individuals in a heated argument with their faces, heads, arms, and legs in perpetual motion. Consider in contrast the absurdity of the same two persons arguing with immobile faces and bodies in statuelike poses. Our daily experiences in communicating emotions remind us that the body plays a leading role in human interactions. This point was beautifully demonstrated to me a few years ago when I observed a teacher attempting to control a small "riot" in her class. Armed with a frog he had captured on the playground, Bobby ran from girl to girl in the classroom, poking the frog into their faces. The girls responded with screams of horror. The boys seemed to enjoy watching the show. In fact, they egged Bobby on. In the midst of the pandemonium, the teacher held up her arms and asked for silence. Prompted by her desire to show control in the uproar, and with her body completely still and no sign of emotion on her face, the teacher said, "Bobby, you make me very angry." Amazingly, her voice didn't even show her anger. Bobby, having watched and listened intently, said to her, "You don't look very angry to me, Mrs. Hanson." Bobby was certainly correct in his analysis. The teacher communicated two different messages: one with her words and quite a different one with her body and voice. Children's experience with angry people leads them to expect angry faces and voices in situations like this one. Children, and adults as well, are puzzled when individuals attempt to control the emotion they display in their bodies and voices.

The anger experienced by the teacher and the fear experienced by the little girls are normal human emotions. John Watson, the "Father of Behaviorism," believed that all emotions (including fear) are learned, and he conducted experiments designed to prove this belief.[9] Of particular interest to him was the origin of a child's alleged fear of "furry things." He presented four- and five-month-old infants with a variety of animals—cats, dogs, rats, and rabbits—and the children showed no fear. Then, he conditioned an eleven-month-old boy, Albert, to fear a white rat that he had not previously been afraid of. Watson employed a standard conditioning technique of combining a loud noise with the presence of the rat. Because Albert disliked the noise, he disliked the rat. His fear was transferred to other furry things—rabbits, muffs, human hair, and even a Santa Claus mask. Watson concluded, therefore, that the fear of furry things, if a child has it, is learned. Modern psychologists agree with Watson's conclusion that emotions are learned.

The body language of emotions cannot be explained totally on the basis of conditioning, however. Two landmark studies of nonverbal communication in bodily channels suggest that the patterns of development are so stable across cultural groups of children that aspects of body language may be preprogramed in the child's neurological system. Recall that according to Lenneberg, the basic forms of human language are likewise "wired" in the human mind (see Chapter 2). One of the two studies dealt with the most elementary body motion of communication in infants: the smile. Infant smiling was studied in various contexts. The second study concerned infants' and children's communication of basic emotions through the channels of body language and the voice. Let's examine both studies for patterns of development in and possible origins of body language in children.

the smiling baby

In some contexts smiles indicate pleasure, but in others a smile may signal humor, ridicule, friendliness, or good manners. They may even transmit doubt or subordination. But what about the "natural smile" of the happy infant? The landmark study of infant smiling was conducted by René Spitz and Katherine Wolf.[10] Their cross-cultural and cross-environmental study posed three basic questions:

1. What makes an infant smile? Is it the mother's face, or is it the smile on her face?
2. Is the stimulus for smiling different for an older infant than for a younger infant? If so, what are these differences?
3. Does the smiling response differ according to race (white, Negro, Indian) of

---

[9] John B. Watson, *Behaviorism* (New York: Norton, 1924), Chap. 15.

[10] René Spitz and Katherine Wolf, "The Smiling Response: A Contribution to the Ontogenesis of Social Relations," *Genetic Psychology Monographs*, XXXIV (1946), 57-125.

the infant? Does the smiling response differ according to the environment of the infant (nursery, foundling home, delivery clinic, Indian village)?

Infants in this study ranged from birth to one year of age.

The infant's first smiles result from changing sensory stimulation. These so-called gastric smiles can be internally induced, as when the well-fed infant dozes off, or externally induced, as when the infant's cheeks are stroked. Within two to eight weeks after birth, the *social smile* begins to appear. The human voice seems to elicit this smile. Even blind babies of this age smile as much as babies who can see. A little later, human faces become "smile producers," and babies smile at human faces even if they don't smile in return. The Spitz and Wolf experiments demonstrated the following points:

1. The configuration of the face—not the expression on the face—elicits a smile in infants of three to six months.

2. In addition, motion or movements of the head (or any of its parts) will elicit a smile from young infants.

Because their experiments were so fascinating and well conceived, let's consider them in greater detail.

In the first experiment infants were presented with smiling and nodding human faces, first in a full-face position and then in profile. Infant smiling was recorded. The investigators recorded the amount of smiling with these experimental conditions: the smiling face only and the nodding face only, each in full face and in profile. They discovered that the babies' smiles "turned off" the moment the face turned sideways. The profile view, even with movement, was no substitute for the full-face configuration. The full-face view, smiling or nodding, was the only stimulus that worked.

Then, the experimenters put on savage masks like those used in Japanese No Drama or in the ancient Greco-Roman theatre. The masks were designed to induce terror in audiences. The savagery of the masks was unmistakable—at least for adults—but, alas, not for the infants. They saw nothing menacing in the beastly masks. The infants continued to smile at their wearers—until they turned sideways! Then the babies stopped smiling, and some began to cry. Spitz and Wolf concluded that the face (whether smiling, speaking, nodding in a friendly manner, or bearing its fangs in savage rage), as seen in full and in motion, is the crucial stimulus for the infant's smiling.

The indiscriminate smiling behavior of the infants ceased,

however, when they reached their fifth or sixth month.[11] Older infants smiled only in response to the human face, smiling or nodding. Perhaps the more discriminating social smile of the older infant emerges from the "raw," undiscriminating form of smiling, which has a biological basis. The nonverbal "communication" of smiling begins with a relatively weak social meaning but gains a strong social meaning as the infant matures.

Regardless of their race or environment, children's patterns of response were similar. The development of smiling communication into its mature social form was explained by the researchers on the basis of the common experience children have with their mothers or mother-substitutes, whose faces are seen in full in both feeding and caring. Since feeding and caring constitute most of their waking hours, the visual experience children have with their mothers' faces is a strong and ever-present stimulus. In conclusion, there is little variation in the emergence of smiling behavior in infants. Regardless of the race or environment of children, evidence suggests that smiling follows a predictable sequence in their development. This predictability suggests a biological basis for the bodily communication of emotions.

the genesis of emotion in children

Another landmark study in the development of emotions in infants and children was conducted by Dr. Katherine Bridges in 1932.[12] She studied the emotional behavior of sixty-two infants (from birth to two years) by keeping detailed records of their day-to-day behavior during feeding, dressing, bathing, and sleeping. Her research procedures were surprisingly sophisticated, considering the early date of the studies. Accordingly, her studies have gained fair acceptance in child-study circles today. More recent studies have not been as comprehensive. For our purposes, we will utilize the

---

[11] A more recent study by Jerome Kagan and his research team suggests that four- to six-month-old infants could distinguish differences between human and distorted (nonhuman) faces. Using cardiac deceleration as the measure of differences, Kagan found that an infant's cardiac rate was significantly different in response to a human as compared to a nonhuman face. Although such facial differences (human face/nonhuman face) did not produce a difference in infants' smiling responses, per se, Kagan argues, as a result of the cardiac rate changes, that the infants were probably perceiving a difference between the faces. See Jerome Kagan et al., "Infants' Differential Reactions to Familiar and Distorted Faces," *Child Development*, XXXVII (1966), 519-32.

[12] Katherine Bridges, "Emotional Development in Early Infancy," *Child Development*, III (1932), 324-41. By permission of the author and The Society for Research in Child Development.

Bridges data to propose the initial stages of development in children's communication of emotions.

The basic principles of Dr. Bridges' theory can be stated quite simply:

1. *The excitement emotion appears first in all infants, regardless of their culture, home environment, or sex.*

2. *With maturation, excitement is differentiated into distress and delight; that is, the one emotion "splits" into the two different and distinct emotions, one positive and the other negative.*

3. *With age, each emotion (for instance, delight) splits further, into more specific emotions; at two years of age, the child is capable of communicating nearly a dozen different emotions.*

The process of differentiation is the key to Dr. Bridges' theory. Essentially, differentiation involves a refinement or specialization of a behavior (in this case, emotional behavior) that occurs when that behavior is replaced with two more specific behaviors.

Let's take an example. When the excitement emotion is differentiated into delight and distress, the following patterns emerge:

EXCITEMENT

Stimuli:	a variety—holding infant's arms to sides, nursing, hunger, shining light into infant's face, and so on.
Responses:	loosely organized and irregular movements; general body tension; constant crying.

DELIGHT		*DISTRESS*	
Stimuli:	nursing (or feeding), rocking, patting infant.	Stimuli:	discomfort, hunger, physical pain.
Responses:	soft vocalizations; eyes open and bright; relaxed muscles; rhythmic movement of limbs; smiling face.	Responses:	loud, high-pitch cries; eyes squeezed shut; tense muscles; jerky movements of limbs; unhappy face.

By examining the stimuli and responses, it seems clear that a kind of polarization occurs. The stimuli for delight (for instance, being fed) are almost opposite to the stimuli for distress (being hungry), as are the responses (for example, open eyes and closed eyes, respectively).

Delight and distress are further differentiated so that by twenty-four months a child is capable of communicating almost a dozen different emotions. Body motion—an emerging body language—plays a leading role in the child's messages. Figure 9.1 adapted from Dr. Bridges' study, outlines the child's development of emotions from birth to two years of age. The following discussion proposes stages of development in the child's bodily communication of emotions. The stages are based on Dr. Bridges' data but are not taken directly from her reports. We have cited hypothetical case studies with children to characterize each stage.

Stage 1: wild, irregular, jerky movements of the entire body. Tommy (one month old) seems to cry all the time. To make matters worse, he cries during the intake *and* during the expiration of air when he breathes. He never seems to rest. He flails his legs and arms in jerky, irregular patterns. Sometimes his entire body shakes and quivers. Tommy's eyes are squeezed shut and his muscles are tense. Such a picture of distress! What is a mother to do? Her only comforting thought is that Tommy cries with no tears.

A few weeks later, Tommy changes his "strategies" slightly. He takes short breaths, only to exhale long, drawn-out cries. His fists are clenched and his arms and legs flap about spasmodically. Is he hungry? Uncomfortable? Or is a diaper pin hurting him? Who knows? So his mother makes her "experienced guess" and feeds him, as mothers will do. This stage of communication is based mainly on overall body activity characterized by wild, irregular, and jerky motions. *Distress* also fits this pattern.

Stage 2: regular, rhythmic movement of the entire body. Ben (three and a half months) waves his legs and arms bilaterally as well as up and down. His movements are rhythmic and vigorous. Stand next to

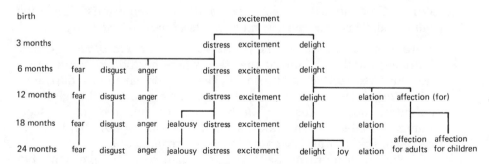

Figure 9.1. *Emotional communication: its emergence in the first two years of life. Adapted from Katherine Bridges, "Emotional Development in Early Infancy,"* Child Development, *1932, 3, p. 340. By permission of the author and The Society for Research in Child Development, Inc.*

Ben's crib (but don't pick him up) and see what happens. He communicates his *anger* with real tears, unlike Tommy. His cry leaves no reason for doubt: Ben is angry and wants to be picked up. He is beyond the stage of jerky, irregular movements, but he still uses his entire body to communicate a message.

If the circumstances are more ideal for Ben, as when someone is playing with him and stroking his face, a slightly different message may emerge. Instead of tears and crying, we can see Ben smiling and cooing with soft, rhythmic sounds. Even his legs and arms fit the pattern: the movements are rhythmical. He communicates his *delight* in response to another's attention to him.

Stage 3: specific movements—making faces, turning the head, and poking. Johnny (five months) has more refined "strategies" in his communication of emotions. Instead of relying on his entire body to do the job, his approach is more sophisticated. His head, face, and fingers may signal his feelings in much more specific ways. For example, Johnny doesn't like spinach at all, yet his mother persists in feeding him this terrible vegetable quite often. To let her know what he feels (disgust), Johnny purses his lips, frowns, and turns his head with each spoonful. "Get the picture, Mom? I don't like it!" Notice Johnny's specific body language of disgust. Compare his bodily movements with those of either Ben or Tommy, who relied on their entire body to communicate a message.

Let's take another example. Johnny, a few months older now, watches his mother attentively as she feeds him. (Thank heavens, she has dropped spinach from the menu.) While being fed, he explores her mouth with his fingers and pokes her face very gently with his hands. He smiles with a big smile that extends from ear to ear. His *affection* for her is easy to see. His pokes, smiles, and glances tell the story. Communication of two additional emotions, *fear* and *elation*, also involves specific movements of parts of the body.

Stage 4: contact movements (pokes, hits, caresses) to others. Gail is fourteen months old and at the stage where her bodily communication involves contact with others. The temper tantrum, a derivative of the *anger* emotion, was a real circus one morning, although it was definitely no fun for her mother. Gail became red in the face, stamped her feet on the floor, screamed terribly loudly, and hit her aggressor (her mother), who withheld the coveted object.

Picture a more pleasant incident. Gail loves to play with her neighbor, a little girl about her age. When Gail sees her friend, she holds her hand, kisses her, hugs her, and in general stays very close to her. Gail's communication of *affection for another child* presents a picture of body contact, including touching and caressing, which was not characteristic of previous stages in the development of body language. In addition, *jealousy, affection for adults*, and *joy* present similar patterns of contact body language in emotional communication.

Beginning with the rather primitive body language of jerky movements of the entire body, the child has progressed to more specialized and sophisticated movements directed to another person. Dr. Bridges' studies of emotional development remind us of three principles in children's development of body language:

1. By two years of age children are capable of nonverbally communicating nearly a dozen different emotions.

2. Young children communicate emotional messages primarily with their bodies.

3. Regardless of background or sex, children's development of emotional communication follows four basic stages.

Table 9.1 portrays the basic stages of development in the body language of emotions.

interpreting emotional "faces"

As children progress through their elementary-school years they become more adept in interpreting emotions communicated facially and bodily. The exact nature of this development has not been specified, but we do know that with experience children become better decoders of emotion conveyed in body language. Certain emotional messages cause young children extreme difficulty, however; we talked briefly about contradictory messages such as joking and sarcasm in Chapter 1 (pp. 14-15). Studies have indicated that elementary-school children have trouble realizing the role of a

Table 9.1. *Stages in children's development of emotional communication. Based on the data of Katherine Bridges' 1932 study.*

STAGE	AGE	CHARACTERISTICS	SAMPLE EMOTIONS
1	to 3 mos.	Wild, irregular, jerky movements of the entire body.	excitement, distress
2	3-5 mos.	Regular, rhythmic movements of the entire body.	anger, delight
3	5-14 mos.	Making faces, turning the head and poking: specific movements.	affection, fear, elation
4	14-24 mos.	Contact movements (pokes, hits, caresses) to others.	affection for child, affection for adult, jealousy, joy

smiling face in resolving a conflict message contained in joking or sarcasm. They tend to pay much greater attention to the negative intonation of the voice and judge the conflict message to be extremely negative (more negative than adults would judge).

A recent study explored the evaluative connotations of smiles in parents' communications to their children.[13] Interactions between children and their parents were video-taped in the families' homes. One purpose was to examine the positiveness of the mother's smile in comparison with the father's smile. Based on previous studies, the authors' prediction was that the fathers' smiles would be accompanied by more friendly, approving statements than the mothers' smiles. The prediction was supported: the fathers' smiles had a greater positive meaning for children, whereas the mothers' smiles were accompanied by messages that could be positive, neutral, or even negative. Apparently, Mom's smile doesn't "mean as much" as Dad's. It was suggested that mothers employ smiling as frequently as they do to soften the more negative messages they often send to their children. The result of this may be that mothers' smiles may become less meaningful to children.

A second phase of this study centered in what psychologists call the double-bind hypothesis, the thrust of which is that emotional disturbance in children may be the result of negative and conflicting messages directed to children by their parents. The emotional messages promote the emotional disturbance. The other aspect of the double bind is that the child's condition probably prompts negative messages from the parents. To obtain some evidence in this controversial area, the authors examined the smiling behavior of parents with normal and disturbed children. The disturbed children were those whom teachers and specialists claim demonstrate behavior or emotional disturbances in the classroom. To support the idea that parental smiling is correlated with the disturbance, the authors looked for a higher incidence of smiles with negative messages directed to the disturbed children, but they didn't find this.

Smiling communication differed according to the social class of the family. In fact, the incidence of smiling was limited to middle-class families because the majority of the lower-class mothers in the sample did not smile at all. Apparently, the incidence of smiling communication by middle-class mothers to their children is unreliably high, whereas that of lower-class mothers is surprisingly low. This result may be an artifact of the testing situation, however. Further studies must be conducted that eliminate the potentially

[13] Daphne Bugenthal, Leonore Love, and Robert Gianetto, "Perfidious Feminine Faces," *Journal of Personality and Social Psychology*, XVII (1971), 314-18.

negative effects of video-taping in the home, a condition that may
have prompted lower-class mothers to smile less than middle-class
mothers. Once the conditions are equalized, we may find very little
difference, according to social class, in the incidence of smiling.

What are the implications of this study for children's communication development? First, children must learn to evaluate
smiles in the communication of their mothers and fathers to them.
The task appears to be far simpler when the father smiles: Dad's
smile can be associated with a friendly, approving message. But
understanding Mom's smile may be a bit more difficult for a child.
The mother's smile may be associated with a variety of messages, not
all of them positive, friendly, or approving. The "public smile" of the
middle-class mother presents additional problems, according to the
authors. It is possible that she tries to meet middle-class expectations
of being a good mother. To soften the blow of a more critical
message, or to communicate submission or compliance, she may
smile to fit the role of the loving mother. What happens, however, is
that children may have difficulty understanding what the *real
message* is. And that's a tough job for anyone.

A second set of implications relates to how children will
perceive the facial expressions and smiles of their teachers, in the
classroom or anywhere. If children weigh the smiles of males and
females differently, assigning different meanings to them, then this
behavior could extend into the educational setting. Quite possibly,
the male teacher's smile may be a strong tool in the communication
of pleasure or satisfaction with the children's performance. On the
other hand, the female teacher may be at a disadvantage because her
smile may indicate more general meanings. Children's reactions to
encouragement provided by teachers of both sexes should be studied
more closely, to see whether there are some real and significant
differences.

COMMUNICATING GENDER

No one wants to raise a child who doesn't know what sex he or she
is. Very early in life, according to Germaine Greer in *The Female
Eunuch*, both boys and girls are taught strategies of coyness and
shyness. Eventually, these strategies are reserved for little girls; little
boys are shocked out of them. Inevitably, the little boy must "break
his umbilical cord with mother; little boys are encouraged to get out
of their mother's way, and they eventually 'want to' and are
encouraged to do this. Little girls are not."[14] According to Greer,

[14] Germaine Greer, *The Female Eunuch* (New York: McGraw-Hill, 1971),
p. 68.

little girls are punished for wandering too far from home, whereas little boys are urged to wander and to explore the unknown in groups with other little boys. Little girls must stay home like little mommies and do their household chores.

Children acquire gender behaviors in their homes. Elementary-school teachers continue parental training in the classroom by rewarding and punishing the children for their "appropriate" and "inappropriate" gender behaviors.[15]

the basis of gender role

According to Dr. Benjamin Spock, "babies in the last half of the first year discover their genitals the way they discover their fingers and toes, and handle them in the same way, too."[16] Although a one-year-old boy does not know that he is a boy, he becomes aware, long before he enters school, that he is "sexed," and he behaves accordingly.

The child's awareness of being masculine or feminine is not simply an outgrowth of being male or female. The child's sex (male or female) is an inborn variable based on physiological parameters, mainly the reproductive organs. Gender (masculine or feminine) *may* or *may not* be inborn in the child. Many psychologists consider gender a learned variable, one based on the child's experiences with parents and others he encounters. But recent studies by Harry Harlow (University of Wisconsin Primate Laboratory) dealing with chimpanzees and their acquisition of gender roles suggest that gender may be inborn. Monkeys reared with "cloth mothers" behave in typical sex-typed ways: male monkeys behave in typically boyish ways, whereas female monkeys wouldn't think of playing in such roughhouse ways. The monkeys in this study had no parental models to copy, yet they developed appropriate sex-typed behaviors. Future research with human beings is clearly necessary: we can't answer questions on the origin of human gender behavior with monkey studies. Yet such studies indicate that the previously "settled" issue of gender as a learned set of behaviors must be examined more carefully.

[15] Support for this statement can be found in Teresa Levitin and J. D. Chananie, "Responses of Female Primary School Teachers to Sex-Typed Behaviors in Male and Female Children," *Child Development*, XLIII (1972), 1309-16.

[16] Benjamin Spock, *Baby and Child Care* (New York: Pocket Books, 1968), p. 372. © 1945, 1946, 1957, 1968 by Benjamin Spock, M. D. Reprinted by permission of Simon & Schuster, Inc., Pocket Books Division and the New English Library, Ltd., England.

Medical studies conducted by Dr. John Money and his associates at Johns Hopkins University (mentioned in Chapter 2, pp. 30-31) reveal that the child's gender role is well established by his second birthday, about the time he begins to string words together. Psychologists studying the child's development of gender role have argued that "identification with model" is a primary factor in the development process. Children develop their gender role from·their second year on. Next, let's examine the factors affecting the development of gender role.

acquisition of gender role

According to Jerome Kagan, there are at least three kinds of experiences that affect the degree to which children regard themselves as masculine or feminine:[17]

1. The child's identification with mother, father, sibling, parent-surrogate, or peers.
2. The child's acquisition of bodily and verbal behaviors that define masculinity or femininity.
3. The child's perception that others regard him (her) as possessing appropriate sex-typed characteristics.

As background for the discussion of the body language of gender display, let's discuss the kinds of experiences affecting the gender communication of children.

An identification is a belief that some attributes of a model—parents, siblings, peers, and so forth—belong to the self. If a six-year-old boy identifies with his father, he believes he exhibits characteristics of his father and regards himself as masculine. A boy's motivation to identify with his father is based on his desire to command the attractive goals (such as strength and power) that are possessed by his father. The child assumes that if he possesses some of the physical characteristics of his father, such as the way he walks and carries himself, he might also possess his desirable psychological properties, such as power, respect, and love. The child behaves as if he believes in the argument that things appearing alike on the outside are alike on the inside.

Of primary importance in the child's acquisition of gender role is the ability to imitate or copy the bodily behavior of the same-sexed parent. The important "test" of the child's gender-role

[17] Jerome Kagan, "Acquisition and Significance of Sex Typing and Sex Role Identity," in *Review of Child Development Research*, ed. M. Hoffman and L. Hoffman (New York: Russell Sage Foundation, 1964), pp. 137-67.

behavior comes when the child enters social groups, particularly school. Consider the following case.

> A boy with a minimally masculine father will confront the societal standard for masculinity when he enters school. Since his overt behavior will be less sex typed than that of his peers, he will perceive a discrepancy between his actions and those of "other boys." He will be tempted to conclude that he is not masculine because his behavior does not match that of the male peer group, and because he may be the target of accusatory communications implying that he is not masculine.[18]

The result of this child's experience was that his gender role was challenged and thus weakened.

Compare the above test situation with that of a boy who had extensive practice in copying the very masculine behavior of his masculine dad. Not only had this boy identified with his father, he had also succeeded in copying the masculine behaviors of his father. When he encountered peers with similar masculine behaviors, he perceived the similarity between his behavior and that of other boys in his school. Similar test situations occur for girls. The traditional signals of feminine behavior—submissiveness with boys, inhibition of aggression, cultivation of personal attractiveness, and so on—become the bases for the girl's comparison of herself with her peers.

A primary means for communicating gender role is through a body language of gender display. Ray Birdwhistell has studied the communication of gender and has discovered gender identifiers in adults that are also present in young children. Birdwhistell's studies of gender communication in children located the emergence of gender communication at about eighteen months to two years of age—about the same period Dr. Money and his associates argue that gender is determined in children. Although the preschool child may have intellectual difficulties realizing that her gender is a constant and unalterable phenomenon of her world, her body clearly indicates that the matter of gender has been decided.

gender identifiers

Working with informants from seven different cultures throughout the world, Birdwhistell found that each culture has stereotypes of feminine and masculine behaviors, stereotypes that can be "acted out." Bodily movements and positions are an important part of this "act." Birdwhistell's investigations pointed out that young children mature into gender behaviors and that as people grow older, they mature "out of them."

[18] Ibid., pp. 147-48.

The gender display of Americans was found to be accomplished through three gender cues, two derived from posture and one from facial expression:[19]

1. In sitting, males tend to cross their legs with the thighs at a ten- to fifteen-degree angle apart, whereas females tend to cross their legs with the thighs, legs, and feet together. Similarly, men tend to stand with their arms alongside their trunk at a ten- to fifteen-degree angle; women stand with their arms directly beside their trunk. This distinction is called the *intrafemoral angle and arm-body angle.*
2. Females carry their pelvis rolled forward (bottom pulled forward) in what is called an anterior roll, whereas males roll their pelvis back in a posterior roll. This distinction is called the *flexibility of the pelvic spinal complex.*
3. Males open and close their eyelids in a relatively continuous fashion; female eyelid movements are much more variable. Unless there are accompanying signs of sleepiness or drowsiness, men are judged as "effeminate" if they disobey this "rule" of *eyelid movement.*

These three gender identifiers constitute the basic cues with which Americans communicate gender. Such bodily cues may differ from culture to culture, but these three supposedly remain constant for most Americans.

the child's acquisition of gender identifiers

There have been few studies of the child's stage-by-stage acquisition of the body language of gender communication. Probably the most revealing of such studies have involved analysis of films of young children. In one of his filmed studies (discussed in Chapter 2, pp. 31-32), Birdwhistell slowed the film to study the existence of gender identifiers in infants and children. He concluded that children begin to display gender identifiers in their second year of life. For example, a female of fifteen months had learned to communicate, bodily, that she was a Southern, upper-middle-class female. She held her pelvis in an anterior roll and kept her arms alongside her trunk. A twenty-two-month-old boy in the same study was filmed in a spread-legged position and rolled his pelvis posteriorly. On the basis of this study and other slow-motion-film analyses of infants and children, Birdwhistell located the emergence of the body language of gender as early as the second year. He insists, however, that further research is necessary if the acquisition process is to be described in detail.

[19] Birdwhistell, *Kinesics and Context*, pp. 43-44.

gender communication: changing identities?

Birdwhistell suggests that children in today's society have some difficulty in learning gender behaviors, primarily because of the sexual revolution. He finds no evidence that men in Western European society are becoming weaker or that women are becoming stronger. Other observers maintain that children are not having difficulty in acquiring their gender role; rather, they are acquiring gender roles that are not defined as specifically as before. One writer notes that "countless parents, confronted by their daughters in blue jeans and old Army shirts and sons with hair that curls well below the seventh vertebra, are struggling mightily to overcome the cultural shock of the so-called 'unisex' revolution."[20] What may trouble parents is whether this "blurring" of genders is merely a fad their children are going through or a permanent state of affairs.

Further study of the body language of gender communication may reveal a shift from traditional gender cues to a more modern set of cues in children's communication. One implication of children's development of gender communication is this: teachers must understand the process of development in children as well as the "norms" of the community. Teachers' reactions to children's gender messages must not be confined to the more traditional conception of gender roles.

SUMMARY

Young children communicate in a very physical manner. They may point, poke, and wave in an effort to be understood. Often, their body language is a direct statement of their messages. As children develop verbal skills, the bodily channel of communication becomes more entwined in the total communication process. Body language includes all reflexive and nonreflexive movements and positions of the body that communicate emotional, attitudinal, and informational messages. Just as children must learn the phonology, morphology, and syntactic rules of their language, they must also learn the patterns of bodily movements that communicate messages to others.

Kinesics, the science of body motion, involves the study of bodily movements in communication. Birdwhistell has studied body motion cross-culturally and has derived a notation system for recording bodily behavior in communication. He stresses, however, that elements of a body language, such as "body words" and a "body grammar," are yet to be defined.

[20] "Changing Identities," *Newsweek*, Sept. 6, 1971, 44-45.

Studies of children's development of gestures in communication have examined *isolated* body motions and their meanings. Sterile gestures, such as "waving hello" and "be quiet," are learned by children in their preschool and early elementary years. One study found that boys interpreted gestures more accurately than girls, and that children with one year of school were better in transmitting and interpreting gestures than preschool-aged children. Apparently, children "pick up" these nonverbal emblems early in life. Yet, such isolated, context-free body motions represent only a small portion of all body motion communication that takes place. Most body language occurs in *context*. Our nonverbal messages are part of a communication setting and accompany verbal messages. We examined children's body language in two communication contexts: (1) the communication of emotion and (2) the communication of gender.

In our study of children's communication of emotion, we examined smiling as an early, significant form of bodily movement. Regardless of their race or environment, children's development of smiling is similar: infants younger than five months smile in response to any facial configuration, smiling or nodding, if that face is presented in a full-face position; older infants smile only in response to the human face.

To characterize children's early development in the communication of emotions, we examined Bridges' landmark study. In this study, Bridges observed infants between birth and two years of age. Nearly a dozen different emotions were communicated through nonverbal means. There appear to be four distinct stages in the infants' development of the body language of emotions:

Stage 1. Children communicate with wild, irregular, and jerky movements of the entire body.

Stage 2. Emotions are communicated with regular, rhythmic movements of the entire body.

Stage 3. To communicate emotion, children make faces, turn their heads, and poke; they employ specific movements of parts of their bodies in communicating.

Stage 4. Contact movements (pokes, hits, caresses) toward others constitute the body messages of emotion.

Studies involving older children indicate that the interpretation of emotions communicated by others is sometimes difficult, particularly if the message is a contradictory one: verbal and nonverbal channels do not agree as to the positive or negative value of the message. The learning process is further hampered by the fact that children must learn to interpret the smiles of their mother and father differently.

The body language of gender communication in children also suggests an early learning process. Both medical studies and communication studies suggest that children have learned to communicate their gender by the time they use language—that is, around their second birthday. Communication of gender by Americans is accomplished through posture, eye behavior, and the angle of arms and legs to the body. Two-year-olds have acquired some of the bodily cues related to gender, and during their preschool years they practice the body language of gender display. In the elementary-school years, the child matches his or her gender display against that of peers.

SUGGESTED READINGS

BIRDWHISTELL, RAY, *Kinesics and Context: Essays in Body Motion Communication*, Chap. 1. Philadelphia: University of Pennsylvania Press, 1970.

MEHRABIAN, ALBERT, "Communication Without Words," in *Communication: Concepts and Processes*, ed. Joseph DeVito. Englewood Cliffs, N. J.: Prentice-Hall, Inc., 1971.

WOOD, BARBARA, "The Body Language of Children," *Illinois Speech and Theatre Journal*, XXV (1971), 17-24.

CHAPTER

10

the child's voice
communicates

The voice is a powerful channel for communicating ideas, feelings, and attitudes, both obvious and subtle. We demonstrated this generalization dramatically in a modest experiment with fifth-grade children. The children sat in front of a television monitor and watched a "TV teacher." The teacher delivered short messages to them, and after each one the children told us what the teacher was "really saying." Some of the messages constructed for the children's viewing were contradictory messages in which the verbal (words), vocal (voice), and bodily (face) channels were not saying the same thing. In one instance the teacher said, "You did a real good job, children!" with a big smile on her face but with a negative, sarcastic voice. How would the children resolve a conflict message such as this one?

The children studied the TV teacher carefully, their eyes opened wide and their bodies motionless. When she finished her sarcastic message, and before we had the chance to ask the children what they thought of it, they gave away their feelings about it. The children stuck out their tongues at the television monitor. The teacher's smiling face didn't help to ease the pain of the message. Incidentally, adults probably focus some attention on the positive facial and verbal channels in resolving a sarcastic message; adults' reactions to sarcasm are significantly less negative (although still negative, per se) than young children's reactions. The teacher's voice was an extremely powerful element in the children's interpretation of her words: her voice was negative, the children heard this, and they didn't like it. "Her voice was nasty," said some of the children, and so they interpreted the message to be a nasty one. What better way is there to strike back at a nasty message than to stick out your tongue at its sender?

Children pay close attention to the voices they hear. In terms of content the voice communicates a lot to children, even very young children. This is not surprising because children understand and convey meanings and attitudes in the voice before they understand and convey meanings and attitudes verbally. In our discussion of phonology (Chapter 5), we explored the relevance of babbling in the child's first year of life to the emergence of phonemes in speech. We concluded that babbling is not a practice period for the child's acquisition of phonemes; it is simply a period in which the infant exercises her vocal apparatus, making sounds for the sake of making sounds. The infant is not "careful" to make only those sounds that occur in the speech of adults around her. Instead, she produces a variety of sounds, many of which are totally foreign to her native language. The adult speech she hears has little to do with the *content* (sounds) of her babbling, but it has a great deal of bearing on the *form* of that babbling.

It is during the period of babbling that children begin to experiment with the intonation of their language. Sometime between six and twelve months, children learn to ask questions, express anger, and communicate excitement—not with words but with gobbledy-gook. Infants communicate their needs and feelings by means of the intonation patterns in their voice. A nine-month-old boy who babbles a question, complete with a rising intonation contour, deserves an answer. He is experimenting with the communication of meaning by the prosodic features of the voice. According to Phillip Lieberman, the child's crying and babbling contain the same signals that serve the linguistic function of intonation in adult speech.[1] Apparently, infants first develop the *form* of human speech by acquiring the prosodic features of speech. Then, they "plug in" the *content* when they acquire verbal language. They use both aspects of

[1] Phillip Lieberman, *Intonation, Perception and Language* (Cambridge, Mass.: M. I. T. Press, 1966), p. 41.

their language—form and content—to communicate meaning to others. Just as an eighteen-month-old girl can communicate her needs with sentencelike words, the nine-month-old boy communicates his needs with rising and falling pitch patterns in his crying and babbling. The speech of a three-year-old child shows almost total mastery of the form of human speech: the child's speech contains the elements of pitch, pause, loudness, and tempo that characterize adult speech.

An account of children's development of communication would be incomplete without a discussion of the voice—how children use their voices to send messages and how children interpret the vocal messages of others. Before we explore these issues, we must define the key terms used in the study of the voice. We will focus on the prosodic features of language: pitch, pause, loudness, and tempo.

PROSODIC FEATURES

Prosody, sometimes called the "music of our speech," is the earliest dimension of language to be used and understood by young children. "From infancy to old age it will continue to be the critical marking that makes one's speech peculiarly his own."[2] The prosody of our speech is flexible, varying with our moods, thoughts, and feelings. The elements of prosody—pitch, pause, loudness, and tempo—are varied to produce meaningful signals in our messages. Because these elements interact with each other in intricate ways, the vocal channel in communication is exceedingly complex.

To place prosody in its proper perspective in the vocal system, let's compare three types of vocal signals:[3]

1. rising pitch at the end of a question (prosodic feature)
2. whisper or giggle (paralinguistic feature)
3. yawn or cough (nonlinguistic feature)

These three signals all originate in the vocal channel; they differ mainly in their degree of linkage to the verbal channels. Prosodic features, such as the rising pitch pattern at the end of a sentence, are tied directly to words and sentences. In a sense, intonation is "nested in" the verbal channel. The paralinguistic features, such as giggles and whispers, are linked more loosely to the verbal channels. Often, such features are totally separate from the content of our speech. The

[2] Mildred F. Berry, *Language Disorders in Children* (New York: Appleton-Century-Crofts, 1969), p. 128.

[3] David Crystal, *Prosodic Systems and Intonation in English* (Cambridge: Cambridge University Press, 1969), pp. 128-31.

nonlinguistic features are even more removed. The linkage of coughs, sneezes, and throatiness to the verbal channel is minimal. Figure 10.1 illustrates the three-part division of voice characteristics. In brief, the three aspects of voice can be defined as follows:

1. *Prosodic features:* the pitch, pause, loudness, and tempo of our voice during communication; these features interact to produce variations in "melody" that are related to meaning.
2. *Paralinguistic features:* the manipulations of the voice, such as giggling or breathiness, that are a part of the stream of speech and that may signal our "mood."
3. *Nonlinguistic features:* voice quality (determined in part by characteristics that act as a background for speech) and vocal reflexes (for example, sneezing and yawning).

STRONG   1. *Prosodic Features*

     a. pitch: the direction of tone change (rising or falling) and range of tone (high to low) in the voice

     b. pause: the filled hesitations ("um," "ah," repeats) and silences in our speech

     c. loudness: the overall volume in the voice, as well as changes in volume (stress)

     d. tempo: the overall rate in speech, as well as internal changes in rate (speeding or slowing down within phrases, sentences, and messages)

2. *Paralinguistic Features*

     a. vocal qualifiers: whisper, breathiness, falsetto, resonant

     b. vocal qualifications: laugh, giggle, sob, cry

3. *Nonlinguistic Features*

     a. voice quality: the permanent background characteristics of the voice that help identify a person's voice (for instance, as harsh or throaty)

     b. vocal reflexes: uncontrollable sneezes, coughs, yawns, and snores

WEAK

degree of linkage to verbal channels

Figure 10.1. *Aspects of the voice: prosodic, paralinguistic, and nonlinguistic features.*

This chapter considers the first set of features in the network of the voice: prosodic features. Our primary concern is with *variations in the voice* that contribute to the meaning of our messages. The prosodic features are the features linked most directly to the verbal message, and, consequently, they vary more than paralinguistic features and nonlinguistic features. For example, a person may have a raspy voice (a nonlinguistic feature) that characterizes his speech. As a permanent background characteristic, his raspiness doesn't really communicate a message. When voice quality is considered as permanent, then it is clear that variation is not employed. Paralinguistic features involve some degree of variation in the voice, especially for vocal qualifiers. Whispered speech or breathy speech helps communicate a feeling or mood, but these features are applied more generally to our messages. Variation within messages is not characteristic of paralinguistic features.

Variations in the prosodic features of a child's message can help shape the meaning in his message, a characteristic of adult communication. Consequently, we must take a careful look at children's communication in terms of children's production and comprehension of prosodic variations. We don't have a comprehensive statement of how children acquire the prosody of their language. We do have some evidence that the more grammatical aspects of prosody, such as the pitch contour at the ends of sentences, seem to come naturally to children. Children learning English typically employ downward pitch contours at the ends of sentences.

Phillip Lieberman's research with infants' cries attempts to show that the falling pitch contour is innate. He begins his argument by citing studies that measure the respiration, pressure, intensity, and frequency of the infants' cries after they have been pinched. The measurements for pinch-elicited cries were strikingly similar for all infants:

1. The pressure (referred to as *subglottal pressure*) gradually rose from the start of phonation to a high level or "plateau"; the pressure fell abruptly prior to inspiration. (It's as if the infants were catching their breath for the next cry.)
2. The shape of the fundamental frequency curves were very similar to the shape of the pressure curves. Following the gradual increase in fundamental frequency (result: a more piercing and high-pitched sound), the frequency dropped abruptly at the end of the cry.

Phillip Lieberman relates this crying pattern to an "innate breathgroup," a pattern of physiological events that is automatically tied to acoustic events. In essence, infants' cries give them practice in the intonation contours of sentences. The interesting and still debatable aspect of the subject is whether or not the relatively automatic responses in crying carry over to sentences.

What about those aspects of prosody that are related more closely to the communication of nongrammatical information on how we think, feel, and believe? Research in this area is quite limited, even for adults. Most studies simply describe the voice patterns in children's and adults' speech. For example, pitch changes in children's voices have been studied very thoroughly. We can also read detailed accounts of how adults use pauses in speech. But theories that explain *why* we pause when we do are sketchy. Other topics, such as how children learn to use pauses to emphasize an idea, are sorely neglected. In this chapter we will discuss the information that is currently available on the aspects of the child's voice during communication. The result is a rather tentative picture of vocal communication and its emergence. After defining the four major prosodic features of the human voice—pitch, pause, loudness, and tempo—we will explore how they are involved in the development of the child's voice. Finally, we will examine the communicative potential of prosodic features from the standpoint of children's understanding of emotions communicated vocally.

pitch

The pitch of a person's voice is mainly the product of the vowel sounds in speech. Pitch is a psychological entity, dependent on the fundamental frequency of vocal-fold vibration in a vowel sound. In their cries, babbling, and eventually their first words, the pitch of children's voices depends primarily on the vocalic (a nonconsonantal feature) component of these vocalizations. Just as a musical note played on a clarinet has a fundamental frequency and distinguishing overtones, the human voice producing a vowel has a fundamental frequency and distinguishing overtones called *formants*. The perception of pitch in a human voice is based on the fundamental frequency of the sound, whereas the perception of different vowel sounds as in /ī/ as opposed to /ū/, is based on the formant frequencies of the sound.

pause

It is perfectly normal, for a number of reasons, for a person's speech to be interrupted. At the end of a phrase or sentence, we pause to signal the end of an idea for our listener. Often, we pause to make a person wait for the important word(s) forthcoming or to stress the importance of words just spoken. In other instances, we pause to select just the right word. During these pauses, we might remain silent, we might use "ah" or "um" to fill the pause, or we might repeat a phrase or word and then continue.

Most of the studies on pauses in speech have been from the speaker's viewpoint; little attention has been devoted to the effects of pauses on listeners. Consequently, pauses are categorized according to their characteristics from an encoding standpoint. Pauses are usually placed in two major categories:

1. *Unfilled pauses* are silences in the stream of speech; they are not filled with any type of verbal activity. They occur at *normal junctures* in a message (such as at the end of a sentence) and at *decision points* in a message (for instance, before a new idea or a difficult word).
2. *Filled pauses* are those portions of our speech filled with "excess" verbalizations: (a) an elongated vowel ("ah," "um," or "eh"); (b) the repeat (saying a syllable, word, or group of words again within an utterance); and (c) the false start (starting a phrase or sentence over again by repeating an initial syllable, word, or group of words).

Research on pauses in speech (or *hesitation phenomena*) has attempted to link each type of pause with a particular mental or emotional activity. For example, the silence perhaps reflects deep thinking or a decision, and the repeat or "um" may reflect a speaker's anxiety in communicating. Clear-cut correlations of this type have not emerged from the investigations. Many researchers conclude that hesitations are *predictable* in one sense—at the end of phrases and sentences—but are highly unpredictable in another sense: placed in a difficult communication situation, some persons use repeats, others use elongated vowels, and still others simply remain silent. The demands of a situation may be the same for all of them, but the manner in which anxiety or thinking is communicated by hesitations seems to vary with the individual.

loudness

Loudness is the psychological correlate of the intensity (or amplitude) of our speech. The loudness of a person's voice is primarily the product of the intensity of the voiced stream of air in vowel production. Psychoacoustic research has indicated that the perception of loudness is also based on the frequency and the duration of a sound; but generally speaking, the greater the intensity of the sound, the greater its loudness.

Loudness in speech can be considered from two points of view. One is the overall *loudness level* in a person's message. Often, we find ourselves talking very loudly to another person. This may happen when we're excited or angry, for example. In these instances, our voice is loud in relation to our level of loudness in normal conversations. At other times, we may use a soft voice throughout a conversation. The softness may communicate a sense of urgency, for

example. In both cases, we are talking about the overall loudness
level we select for a message. From a more detailed point of view,
loudness can be varied within a phrase, a sentence, or a message to
communicate meaning. We usually call this type of loudness variation
stress. We may stress certain words by uttering them louder or softer
than the words surrounding them, thus placing some degree of
emphasis on those words. In short, loudness has two prosodic
dimensions: the general loudness level we select for our utterances
and the variations in loudness within our utterances.

tempo

The tempo of our speech has two dimensions, as does loudness.
The first and more general dimension is the overall *rate* of our
speech. Rate is measured most easily as the number of words spoken
per time segment. The second dimension of tempo is an internal one:
the speeding up or slowing down of rate within phrases or sentences.
The most important consideration of tempo, of course, is whether
conventions in speech rate correlate with different meanings. Not
much is known, however, about internal variation in speech

Table 10.1. *Stages in children's development of prosody.*

STAGE	AGE	PROCESS	CHARACTERISTICS
1	4 months	general discrimination	Children "hear" a message in the prosodic features of another person's voice. They are able to obtain meaningful clues in the pitch, pause, tempo, and loudness of voices in communication.
2	18 months	heavy emphasis in early sentences	Children rely heavily on prosody in the early stages of syntactic development to communicate meaning, particularly in stage 1 (sentencelike word) and stage 2 (modification).
3	$2\frac{1}{2}$ years	complementary role in communication	The vocal channel (prosodic features) stands in a more complementary relationship to the verbal channels (morphology and syntax) in children's speech.
4	3-12 years	emotional distinctions	Children are able to produce and understand fine distinctions in emotions communicated vocally.
5	12 years and older	resolution of conflict messages	Children are able to resolve a conflict message, in which the vocal, verbal, and visual channels are in disagreement; they can assign the appropriate meaning-role to the prosodic (vocal) features in decoding the contradictory message.

rate—that is, how we speed up and slow down our rate within phrases, sentences, and oral paragraphs and how such internal changes in rate affect the communication of meaning.

The foregoing descriptions of pitch, pause, loudness, and tempo serve as background information for our discussion of the prosodic characteristics of children's speech. Our next task is to explore children's development of prosodic features in speech. Our discussion suggests that development can be characterized by five general stages of development. These stages are drawn from the available information on prosody and are proposed simply to give you a general idea of the course of development. Table 10.1 outlines the stages in the child's development of prosody. We will discuss children's acquisition of prosodic features in this sequence:

1. First, we will explore each of the four prosodic features from the standpoint of development in the early stages (1-3).
2. Next, we will discuss stage 4, which involves children's perception of emotions communicated vocally.
3. Finally, we will explore how children resolve conflict messages (stage 5).

THE DEVELOPMENT
OF PITCH IN CHILDREN'S SPEECH

Phillip Lieberman presents an experiment to confirm infants' early communication by means of pitch.[4] A ten-month-old boy and a thirteen-month-old girl were observed as "they conversed" with one parent and then the other. Their babbling was recorded and electronically analyzed. Each child sat in the lap of the mother and then the father and played with a pet—the boy with a dog and the girl with a cat. Using the fundamental frequency of the child's conversation as the measured variable, it was found that the infant's pitch varied with the sex of the parent he or she was talking to. With the mother, the infant's pitch was higher than with the father. Further, the pitch levels the infants used in their conversations with parents were lower than the pitch levels they used in solitary babbling or when they were crying. He concluded that infants are able to "control" pitch because of their acute perception of the fundamental-frequency differences in the voices of their parents. Since both children in this study were not yet communicating verbally, it seems that vocal communication (specifically, pitch) emerged first.

[4] Phillip Lieberman, *Intonation, Perception, and Language*, p. 45.

Lieberman's study strongly supports the importance of stage 1 in the child's development of prosody: *general discrimination.* Not only did the two children apparently make a discrimination on the basis of voice ("Mom's voice is pitched higher than Dad's voice"), they were also able to "mimic" this distinction in their babbling. Shortly before the child's second birthday, pitch takes on a more linguistic function. In our discussion of sentencelike words (Chapter 7) we emphasized the importance of prosodic features in conveying the meaning of the utterance. The message communicated by the sentencelike word rests heavily in the intonation patterns in the child's voice. This phenomenon suggests the appearance of stage 2 in the child's development of prosody: *heavy emphasis in early sentences.* Intonation patterns, which are primarily the result of pitch changes, reveal a bulk of the meaning in the early stages of syntactic development. They tell us, for example, whether the child is asking a question, making a statement, or delivering a command.

Let's consider children's development of pitch by examining the first three stages of prosodic development, as outlined in Table 10.1.

Stage 1. *General discrimination:* Children first learn to discriminate, in a very broad sense, among the different pitch patterns in the voices of others. They may be able to distinguish between happiness and sadness in their parents' voices, primarily on the basis of pitch variation. Children may hear their mother's voice as higher than their father's voice, and they may adapt their own pitch level to the voice of the parent with whom they are "talking."

Stage 2. *Heavy emphasis in early sentences:* Children combine words and intonation to communicate ideas in their early sentences. Often, the intonation (pitch changes) carry the bulk of meaning in children's utterances. Recall that in the development of questions, pitch was the primary signal.

Stage 3. *Complementary role in communication:* When children are able to use multiple-word sentences, intonation does not have to carry the burden in the communication of meaning. Words, syntactic patterns, and prosodic features operate simultaneously to communicate their messages. In stage 2 children signal questions only through inflection, but now syntactic word ordering can accomplish the same function. Their channels of communication, of which prosody is one, are now working together. Prosody thus plays a complementary role in communication.

In terms of pitch variation in sentences, the speech patterns of three- or four-year-old children are very much like those adults use. It seems that as the children master the basic syntactic structures of their language, they simultaneously master the intonation features that accompany these structures. The major difference between the pitches of a three-year-old's voice and an adult's voice is in general pitch level, not in variations within utterances.

pitch changes in children's voices

A number of changes take place between birth and puberty, the most dramatic being an overall lowering in pitch. Research with children has indicated, however, that the pitch of a child's voice does not simply decrease in a steady fashion from birth to puberty. Although a child's voice between about two and twelve years of age does exhibit a gradual decrease in pitch, the changes that take place in the first few years of life and at the onset of puberty are by far the most dramatic and complex. The trends in pitch change during these two periods and are more difficult to explain.

A study of infants from birth to five months of age revealed a rather complex trend in pitch change, as measured by the fundamental frequency of the voice.[5] Sheppard and Lane recorded crying and vocalizing of infants in controlled settings. Fundamental-frequency recordings were made by complicated electronic equipment attached to a plexiglass "air crib" installed in the infants' homes. The results of the study indicated that during the infant's first month of life, the fundamental frequency of his voice lowered steadily. Beginning in the second month, the pitch changed direction and rose steadily until about four months, where it leveled off.

Both the initial drop in pitch and the secondary increase in pitch after the first month were explained first by the physiological development of the infant and acoustical principles related to such development. During the first month, because of infant growth, the vocal folds increase in area, thickness, and length. These physiological changes explain the initial drop in pitch of the infants' cries. Pitch change shortly after their first month is apparently explained by the increase in subglottal pressure children can develop. These terms are simply a fancy way of saying that children can cry louder and with greater force. It's not as easy to tune out the piercing cry of a two-and-a-half-month-old infant. Because their physical and respiratory strength has increased drastically, the fundamental frequency of their vocalizations increases as well. Both of these factors—the change in vocal folds and the build-up of subglottal pressure—account for the pitch trends in early infancy.

The pitch trends of the first five months can also be explained by the different functions vocalizations serve at different ages. Infants' first cries are reflexive and are related to their needs for sleep, food, comfort, and activity. As infants approach three months of age, they have greater control over their vocalizations and cries.

[5] W. C. Sheppard and H. L. Lane, "Development of the Prosodic Features of Infant Vocalizing," *Journal of Speech and Hearing Research*, XI (1968), 94-108.

Now they can signal, to some extent, their needs and feelings for others. Researchers have called these later vocalizations *motivated vocalizations*. The change in function, then, from reflex to motivation, might help explain the dramatic change in pitch of the vocalizations.

In the child's second year of life, the pitch of the voice is only slightly lower than the pitch of an infant's voice.[6] Once children begin to use sentences in communication, however, their pitch begins to drop in a slow and steady fashion. There is a downward pitch trend through infancy and early childhood years. A short time before puberty, one begins to notice the second period of dramatic change in pitch of children's voices. At this time, boys go through the period commonly called the "change of voice." At this point, and for the first time in children's development, boys' and girls' voices begin to take on characteristic differences. The pitch of girls' voices drops slightly, but the change is not as noticeable as it is with boys.

The pitch range of children's voices has also been studied. The total range of frequencies for a newborn is about five tones—a very restricted range. The range expands in the child's preschool and early elementary years, so that by seven years of age it has doubled to about ten tones. During the early teens, the pitch range increases to eleven tones, a range only slightly greater than that of a seven-year-old's voice. Consequently, children's pitch range is relatively stable by the end of early elementary-school years.

We know a great deal more about the pitch of children's voices as they age than we know about how children learn to use pitch variations in communication of meaning. Most explanations of the pitch of children's voices assume that, starting from the babbling period, infants are able to use pitch variation to signal their needs and feelings. After children have acquired the basic syntactic structures of their language (around three to four years of age) they have also acquired the ability to use pitch variations along with these structures. Their progress in the use of pitch to communicate meanings is a relatively unexplored area in children's speech development. We know that pitch variation plays a major role in conveying whether a sentence is a question, an exclamation, or a statement, but we have little information on the role of pitch in communicating more subtle meanings within utterances.

PAUSES IN CHILDREN'S SPEECH

The study of children's use of pauses or hesitations has been largely confined to the observation of children who are in their later

[6] Robert McGlone, "Vocal Pitch Characteristics of Children Aged One to Two Years," *Speech Monographs*, XXXIII (1966), 178-81.

elementary-school years. Findings reveal that children's pauses (both filled and unfilled) are quite adultlike by this time. Apparently, children acquire pause as a prosodic feature in their speech during their preschool years. With the information that is available on pauses in speech, let's outline the basic stages of development.

In stage 1 (see Table 10.1), the process of general discrimination operates. Infants are able to pick up meaningful clues in the pauses and durational characteristics of adults' messages. According to Lieberman's notion of the innate breath-group (see p. 211), infants babble and cry in sound patterns that contain pausal features of language. Further, the babbling stage illustrates infants' early command of the pausal features of language. Although the content of their utterances is not meaningful, their babbling appears to contain pauses within and at the end of utterances. We know that children who don't yet use words and sentences are very aware of the importance of pauses in communication.

When children are able to string words together, as in the modification stage (stage 2) of syntactic development, they are also able to vary the durational characteristics of their utterances. Stage 2 in children's development of prosody (heavy emphasis in early sentences) occurs in a rather pronounced fashion when they use multiple-word sentences. Children's reliance on pauses to communicate can be seen as they approach the structure stage of syntactic development. Let's examine two sentences that characterize children's struggle for structure (stage 3 of syntactic development):

intermediate sentence	*structure sentence*
That * big boat.	That's a big boat.
Mommy * see toy?	Do you see the toy, Mommy?

The pauses (*) in the intermediate sentences may help children convey the meaning of the sentences. It has been suggested that children who are just beginning to adopt full-fledged structures in their sentences first employ pauses to signal where the structure "should appear." Consequently, the pauses in those transitional sentences between the simple two-word modification sentences and the multiple-word structure sentences signal to a listener that structure should "be there."

With the appearance of structure and operational changes in the syntax of children's sentences, pauses take on a more complementary role in conveying meanings. Stage 3 (complementary role in communication) in children's acquisition of pauses in speech occurs sometime after two-and-a-half years of age, when their sentences are complete with structure. In preschool years, as children learn the syntax of their language, they master the pausal features of speech that accompany those syntactic structures.

By the time children reach school age, their speech contains pausal features that are almost adultlike. Further, their pausal patterns are fairly well set. To illustrate these generalizations, let's review a hestiation study with children.

children's hesitations

Research with adults has indicated a strong relationship between the type of speaking activity (description versus interpretation) and the frequency of pauses or hesitations. When adults were given a cartoon from the *New Yorker*, for example, and asked to describe and interpret the cartoon, there were more hesitations in the interpretation condition. When our speech is somewhat automatic, as in description, we make little use of hesitations, except for the ones that are necessary to indicate grammatical information (for instance, the end of a sentence). But when our speech requires thought, as in interpreting the meaning of a cartoon, then pauses of various types (both filled and unfilled) increase in number and frequency.[7] It has been suggested that pauses of this nature reflect decision points within our speech.

Levin and his research team investigated pauses in children's speech during two different conditions: children were shown three physical demonstrations and asked to *describe what they saw* and *explain why it happened.* Levin predicted that pauses would be greater in the condition of explanation, as studies with adults had indicated. The children ranged in age from five to twelve years. The study found that the number and duration of pauses was greater in the explanation condition than in the description condition, as predicted.[8] The children hesitated with many more filled pauses (such as "ah," "um," and repeats) and silences when they were trying to explain why something happened. Let's take one example. The children were shown two balloons of different sizes and colors. One was filled with air and the other with helium. The researcher released both, and, of course, the helium balloon rose to the ceiling while the air-filled balloon landed on the floor. The researcher asked "Why do you think that happened?" after the children described the event. Children's answers were like these:

[7] Frieda Goldman-Eisler, "The Semantic Determination of Pauses and Spontaneity," (Ch. 3), *Psycholinguistics: Experiments in Spontaneous Speech* (New York: Academic Press, 1968), pp. 50-59.

[8] Harry Levin, Irene Silverman, and Boyce Ford, "Hesitations in Children's Speech During Explanation and Description," *Journal of Verbal Learning and Verbal Behavior,* VI (1967), 560-64.

"The red one goes up." (color answer)

"The small one goes up and the big one falls down." (size answer)

"The one that goes up is lighter than air." (scientific answer)

Regardless of the child's answer (correct or incorrect) to the "why" question, hesitations were greater in these answers than in the description condition.

The research team also examined children's development of pause as a prosodic feature. They compared pausal patterns in the speech of children five to twelve years of age and found no significant differences. This finding supports our generalization that children's pauses are well established by the time they enter school.

Studies investigating the communicative uses of pause (such as to emphasize a point) are greatly needed, in order that prosodic development may be more fully explained. Experience in listening to children tells us that from the time children use multiple-word sentences, they use pauses that are characteristic of adult speech. Young children may simply imitate the filled pause, "um," in about the same way they imitate a new word. It almost appears as if children feel grown-up when they engage in that pensive "ah" or "um" before they answer our questions. Ask a four-year-old boy to help with a chore, and he may pause, wrinkle his brow, and respond just like an adult: "Well, um, I guess I could help." Obviously he has heard that hesitation pattern before.

pausal problems in children's speech: nonfluency

Parents and teachers are rarely concerned when children use filled pauses infrequently in their speech. But we are concerned when children speak with frequent repetitions of sounds and syllables. We know there is a problem called stuttering and we dread considering what we are hearing.

Recent advice from speech pathologists has helped clarify the problems of nonfluency and stuttering. First, most experts agree that most children go through a period (or periods) of nonfluency, during which their speech includes repetitions and pauses. The result is often disturbing to adults' ears because we like to hear "fluent" speech, especially from our own children. Given the fact that most children go through periods of nonfluency, how can we spot the problem that deserves professional attention? Here is where the advice of speech pathologists becomes invaluable for parents and teachers.[9] The majority of beginning stutterers show excessive

[9] Our discussion of nonfluency in young children is based primarily on the approach of Joseph Sheehan in *Stuttering: Research and Therapy* (New York: Harper & Row, 1970). Another presentation that might be helpful in understanding beginning stuttering is Charles Van Riper's *The Treatment of Stuttering* (Englewood Cliffs, N. J.: Prentice-Hall, Inc., 1973), Chap. 14.

syllabic repetitions; some even employ blockages (complete stops in speech in an effort to "get a word out"). The problem is cyclic in nature: periods of complete fluency alternate with periods when speech is so filled with repetitions that communication is hindered and we become concerned. Young children showing these symptoms usually do not realize what they are doing. They are not aware of their nonfluency, and so they do not worry about it or react to it. As you will see in our guidelines for helping the child with nonfluencies, this lack of awareness is a "plus" for recovery.

The problem. It is important to realize that the problem does not reside within the child. Although the child's speech reveals the problem, the members of the family constitute the major portion of the problem. According to a noted expert in stuttering therapy, "The stuttering child is the parents' symptom. . . . He is a statement about them—and they are quite correct in regarding it as unflattering."[10] Although such parents may behave no differently from another set of parents with a child who is fluent, the fact remains that their behavior has precipitated the nonfluency problem. Children with nonfluencies are products of their environment. If pressures and expectations are unreasonably high, they may respond with nonfluency. Consider this perspective analogy and its conclusion.

> Putting the pressure on a child is like driving across a railroad crossing without looking. Most of the time you can get away with it. But the gain is not worth the risk. The parents of stutterers were probably not behaving conspicuously worse than others. They just got caught at it.[11]

The traditional advice to parents and teachers is this: "Ignore the problem and it will go away." This advice is based on the fact that most children who go through periods of nonfluency "recover" without professional assistance. (The number of such children is estimated to be eighty percent.) This advice works for the majority of children. But what about the unlucky 20 percent? According to Sheehan, the best advice is this: "Leave the child alone and treat the parents." "Leave the child alone" is advice quite different from "ignore the problem." Most experts in speech pathology today suggest that the best approach is to treat the parents of children with nonfluencies.

Treatment. The age of onset of stuttering or nonfluency in young children falls principally between two and seven years, with peaks at three years and five years of age. About 80 percent of these children

[10] Sheehan, p. 304.
[11] Ibid.

recover spontaneously, but 20 percent do not. Our suggestion to teachers and parents is that we not play the odds. If a child demonstrates the symptoms of beginning stuttering, the parents should be counseled by a speech and language clinician. The therapist may suggest a number of changes; one might be to make a hectic household a more relaxed one. The thrust of treatment is this: *reduce parental pressures on the child.* The following suggestions (for parents and others concerned with helping the child who is nonfluent) are some of those given in an approach employed at Northwestern University.[12]

1. Reduce pressures on the child at home and at school. Evaluate expectations for performance in view of the child's age and abilities. Avoid imposing too many pressures to perform. The pressures experienced by a given child may not be obvious at first. Look for events that seem to precipitate frustration or uncertainty in the child.
2. "Quiet down" your speech with the child. Speak at a slower rate, talk more softly, and avoid complicated language.
3. Don't demand a lot of speaking from the child. Avoid creating an atmosphere that includes pressure to talk. It's often helpful for each parent to create a "special time" with the child where the child knows he has their attention. A short period of time, one with each parent, seems to relieve the need for constant attention.
4. Be consistent in your discipline. All who care for the child must make some decisions about what limits are tolerable (for instance, at mealtime, bedtime, playtime, and in getting dressed). *The Magic Years: Understanding and Handling the Problems of Early Childhood* by Selma Fraiberg (Charles Scribner's Sons) should help parents decide what limits and goals are reasonable.
5. Avoid rushing or hurrying the child. Make certain that enough time elapses between activities and that you are not rushing from place to place. When the child's fluency increases, time demands can be increased in small proportions.
6. Treat the child normally in most respects. Try not to give the child the impression that she is "special" or "different" from other children. For example, if the child's misbehavior requires discipline, respond in a calm but firm way so that additional pressure is not imposed. If class activities require talking in front of the class or reading aloud, don't exclude the nonfluent child. Rather, be sure that the child has ample time and that others do not interrupt. In general, help relieve pressures but without being obvious.
7. Never call attention to the child's speech. When speech is nonfluent, don't comment on the nonfluency and don't tell the child to slow down, think about his speech, or say it again. When the child's speech is fluent, don't praise the fluency. In a word, avoid any comments on the child's speech whatsoever.
8. Don't call the young child with nonfluencies a "stutterer." It is most likely

[12] Diane Hill, Director of the Primary Stuttering Program in the Speech and Language Clinic at Northwestern University, offered these suggestions.

an inappropriate label. Often, when neighbors and peers hear this label, they talk about it, possibly in the child's presence. Calling attention to the problem through such a label can be very detrimental to the child's fluency. After all, the child is usually unaware of the nonfluencies, and this label could cause concern and harm a young child's normal process of developing fluency.

These eight suggestions can help parents and teachers begin to understand the problem of nonfluencies in children's speech.

Our discussion of nonfluencies in children's speech has clearly indicated a problem deeper than the prosody of the child's voice. On the surface, the nonfluencies of the beginning stutterer appear to be prosodic problems. Further investigation has revealed that what we previously called "pausal problems" are not simply that. Sheehan urges us to consider stuttering a role-conflict problem and not a voice problem. Our discussion has thus taken Sheehan's perspective in a context (this chapter on voice) that is not very appropriate.

TEMPO AND LOUDNESS
IN CHILDREN'S VOICES

Albert Murphy has made the following statement about children's development of prosodic features in communication:

> By the age of four or five years, the child is communicating with the use of his entire being. His manner of speaking, loudness level, inflections, quality of voice, rate of utterance, talkativeness or taciturnity, attitudes, and vocal spontaneity or inhibitions all combine to give an impression of his developing personality.[13]

The prosodic features of tempo and loudness are well established in children's vocal patterns by the time they enter kindergarten. Let's follow the development of these features.

In the first stage of prosodic development (general discrimination), infants are able to discriminate between soft and loud and between fast and slow. The combination of fast and loud sounds prompts jerky, excited responses from infants. Conversely, soft and slow sounds prompt more rhythmic, peaceful responses. Evidence for the infant's ability to discriminate tempo and loudness is contained in our discussion of the four stages of emotional development in infants (Chapter 9), based on the Bridges study.

With the emergence of syntactic structures in children's speech, tempo and loudness assume an important role in speech production. For example, loudness combined with a sentencelike word can alter

[13] Albert T. Murphy, *Functional Voice Disorders* (Englewood Cliffs, N. J.: Prentice-Hall, Inc., 1964), p. 33.

the meaning of that word: "Mommy" said loudly can mean something entirely different from "Mommy" said very softly. In this instance (stage 2: heavy emphasis in early sentences), the prosodic feature of loudness plays a major role in communication. With the emergence of multiple-word sentences, complete with structure, children are capable of varying tempo as well. As with pitch and pause, when children employ utterances complete with structure and operational changes, the features of tempo and loudness take on a more complementary role in the communication of meaning (stage 3 of prosodic development). When children are four or five years of age, their speech patterns show that tempo and loudness are also related to the type of speech activity in which they are engaged. The Levin study of hesitations (discussed earlier in this chapter) examined the tempo and loudness in children's voices during description and interpretation conditions. It was found that when children were explaining the events in response to the "why" question, the tempo of their speech was significantly slower. Apparently, children recognize that reasons are required in their message, and they take the time to communicate these reasons.

CHILDREN'S PERCEPTION
OF EMOTION IN THE VOICE

Thus far, our discussion of children's development of prosody has concerned the first three stages of development, which occur in their preschool years. During children's elementary-school years, they learn to make fine discriminations among emotional messages that vary in their prosodic features (stage 4 of prosodic development). Studies have indicated a strong correlation between the type of emotion communicated vocally and the objective and subjective assessment of the prosodic features of the voice. George Huttar studied the vocal characteristics of voices communicating these emotions:[14]

1. sad versus happy
2. afraid versus bold
3. timid versus confident
4. bored versus interested
5. passive versus active

He found that the vocal emotions of "happy," "bold," "interested," and "active" were associated with acoustic features as follows:

[14] George Huttar, "Relations Between Prosodic Variables and Emotions in Normal American English Utterances," *Journal of Speech and Hearing Research*, XI (1968), 481-87.

1. The fundamental frequency (and pitch) of the voice was higher.
2. The intensity of the voice (loudness) was greater.

Further, these four vocal expressions were judged (subjectively) as having a higher pitch, greater loudness, and faster tempo. In short, there appears to be a striking relationship between emotional states and objective and subjective judgments of prosodic features.

Let's extend our discussion to children's perception of emotions. In Chapter 9 we found that by two years of age, children are capable of communicating nearly a dozen different emotions nonverbally (that is, with their voices and bodies). Further, young children are able to interpret emotions communicated by others; in doing this, children normally have the benefit of multiple channels: words, syntax, body, and voice. But what happens when the emotional message is contained only in the voice and children can neither see the person nor hear any words? Studies that eliminated the bodily and linguistic channels from the communication of emotions found that a vocal message of emotion is far more difficult for children to understand than a message communicated bodily or verbally.

In a study of children from five to twelve years of age, Lilly Dimitrovsky found a steady increase with age in children's ability to identify various emotions communicated by the voice.[15] In a sample of 224 children of both sexes, Dimitrovsky found that the more negative emotions, such as "sad" and "angry," are more easily understood by children than the more positive emotions, such as "happy" and "loving." The children tended to assign negative labels to all emotions. They gave negative names ("sad" or "unhappy") to emotions that adults judged as positive ("happy" or "pleasant"). Dimitrovsky suggests that this finding is related to a "negative set" in children's perception of emotions communicated vocally. Further, she suggests that girls generally do better than boys in correctly identifying the various emotions in the voice.

Fenster and Goldstein conducted a similar study but reached slightly different conclusions regarding the "negative set" that children supposedly employ in interpreting emotions.[16] Their study found quite the opposite to be true: children provided *no more* negative labels for emotions than did adults. To explain the

[15] Lilly Dimitrovsky, "The Ability to Identify the Emotional Meaning of Vocal Expression at Successive Age Levels," in *The Communication of Emotional Meaning*, ed. J. R. Davitz (New York: McGraw-Hill, 1964), pp. 69-86.

[16] Abraham Fenster and Alan M. Goldstein, "The Emotional World of Children 'Vis A Vis' the Emotional World of Adults: An Examination of Vocal Communication," *The Journal of Communication*, XXI (1971), 353-62.

discrepancy between their findings and those of Dimitrovsky, they proposed a social-class explanation. One basic difference between the children in the two studies was their social class. The Dimitrovsky study included working-class children, whereas Fenster and Goldstein studied children from middle-class backgrounds. Fenster and Goldstein suggest that Dimitrovsky's "negative set" might be a social-class phenomenon, or at least related to social class in some way. Either children from lower social classes "expect" more negative messages, especially in a testing situation, or the rather sterile conditions of experimental testing prompted these children to make negative "readings." Admittedly, this line of reasoning needs further study; it is purely speculative at this point.

The Fenster-Goldstein study employed six different emotions, four being direct copies of those used in Dimitrovsky's study (the copies are indicated with an asterisk): anger,* content, fear, happy,* love,* and sad.* Children improved with age in their ability to interpret correctly the emotion being communicated vocally. The rate of development, in terms of understanding, was about the same for all of the emotions studied.

For our purposes, the major implication of these two studies is that when prosodic features are varied to produce different emotions (keeping the content of speech "neutral," as did both studies), children simply become better at interpreting the emotional message as they become older. We know that children are capable of vocally communicating a number of different emotions from a very young age. These two studies indicate, however, that understanding the prosodic features involved in emotional communications by others takes a far longer time. Through the elementary-school years, children become more aware of the importance a voice plays in the communication of emotions (stage 5 of prosodic development: emotional distinctions).

CHILDREN'S INTERPRETATION OF CONFLICT MESSAGES

When adults are given conflict messages—that is, messages in which the vocal, visual, and verbal channels are not in agreement, which channel is most important in resolving the conflict? For example, adults watching and listening to this message,

"You're a real winner!" (words)
smiling face   (visual)
sarcastic voice   (vocal)

would agree that the message is one of pleasant sarcasm and not one of extreme criticism. The adult is capable of understanding the important role of the visual channel (the smile), based on experience in resolving sarcastic messages.

Children are unable to let the smiling face resolve the conflict in the direction of some degree of pleasantness. Research with adults has indicated that *visual cues*—facial changes and position—are of extreme importance in the interpretation of emotional messages, whether those messages involve channels that agree or channels that disagree (conflict messages). The face seems to tell a little more (predict total judgment better) than the voice or the verbal channel. Children, on the other hand, pay closer attention to the verbal and vocal channels in attempting to resolve conflict messages. Like sarcasm, joking is not adequately interpreted by children. When joking is done with either a positive or negative voice (but always with a smile) and negative words, children find the "joke" to be a negative statement. The words and possibly the tone of voice predict children's interpretation. If the words are negative, the statement is interpreted as negative, even in light of a positive face and maybe a positive tone of voice.

Apparently, children do not learn to interpret conflict messages correctly until they are well into their teens.[17] The simpler, nonconflict messages of emotion are far easier to understand than those involving conflict. Visual cues do not help children resolve conflict messages, whereas for adults they are extremely valuable in resolving all messages. In the final stage of prosodic development (stage 5), children learn to resolve conflict messages, in which prosodic features are in disagreement with the verbal and visual features.

SUMMARY

Prosody, the music of our speech, is the earliest dimension of language to be employed and understood by infants. The elements of prosody—pitch, pause, loudness, and tempo—vary with our moods, thoughts, and feelings and with the information in our utterances. Infants begin to experiment with intonation during the babbling period. Their babbled utterances contain the prosodic features of the full-fledged sentences that adults use.

To follow the development of prosody in children, we proposed five basic stages of acquisition.

[17]Daphne Bugenthal et al., "Perception of Contradictory Meanings Conveyed by Verbal and Nonverbal Channels," *Journal of Personality and Social Psychology*, XVI (1970), 617-55.

Stage 1: general discrimination. Children "hear" the prosodic features in the speech of others, and make general distinctions (for instance, happy versus sad) in meaning on this basis. In addition, infants' babbling contains evidence that prosody is beginning to emerge. (four months on)

Stage 2: heavy emphasis in early sentences. When children begin to use words, their early sentences rely heavily on prosodic features for the communication of meaning. For example, modification sentences require children to vary pitch and loudness in order to distinguish among sentence intentions: negative, question, exclamation, or statement. (eighteen months and older)

Stage 3: complementary role in communication. When children's sentences contain the structure and operational changes of syntactic development, prosody assumes a more complementary role in communication. Children's sentences begin to sound like adult sentences, from a prosodic viewpoint. (two and a half years and older)

Stage 4: emotional distinctions. During children's elementary-school years, the focus of development changes from production to understanding. Between five and twelve years of age, children learn to identify emotions communicated vocally. Since prosodic features (intonation, pause, loudness, and tempo) play a major role in distinguishing emotional messages, the child must learn to respond appropriately to these cues. Studies characterize the process of interpreting emotions communicated vocally as a slow and steady struggle. (preschool through twelve years of age)

Stage 5: resolution of conflict messages. Probably the most difficult communication task for children, in terms of prosody, is the resolution of *conflict messages*—that is, messages in which the prosody of the voice does not agree with the content and bodily aspects of the message. Children are able to resolve conflict messages after twelve years of age. Sarcasm and joking are difficult types of communication for children younger than twelve years to understand. Children under twelve years resolve the message in an extremely negative fashion.

SUGGESTED READINGS

BERRY, MILDRED F., *Language Disorders in Children*, pp. 128-35. New York: Appleton-Century-Crofts, 1969.

MENYUK, PAULA, *The Acquisition and Development of Language*, pp. 54-64. Englewood Cliffs, N. J.: Prentice-Hall, Inc., 1971.

CHAPTER
11

children and communication through space

The following discussion took place in a second-grade classroom after the teacher had presented some pictures and information on animals' spacing patterns.

Teacher: Animals are fun to watch. Have you ever noticed what an animal does when you come very close to him? Sometimes, if you try to get too close to an animal, he might run away or get angry and snap at you. Has this ever happened to you?

Terry: My cat runs away whenever I get close to her—I don't think she likes it when I sneak up on her.

Kenneth: If I go near my neighbor's dog, he growls at me. He scares me, so I don't get too close to him.

Carol: I can get real close to my dog—he never seems to move. All he does is curl up in the corner of our kitchen and sleep. If I yell at him, then he'll bark a little.

Teacher: The reason why animals run away, growl, or bark at you is because maybe you've done something to them that bothers them. You know, an animal has a "bubble of space" around him. If you get inside this bubble, the animal reacts. He might run away, bark or try to attack.

230

Children: (Verbal and nonverbal signs of understanding)

Teacher: Do you think that *you* have little bubbles of space around yourselves?

Children: (giggles)

Teacher: Of course you wouldn't bark or growl at someone, but you might react in another way. Do you think that if someone came very close to you—came inside your bubble—that you would like it?

Kenneth: If my sister comes too close to me I just pop her one![1]

The teacher was trying to discuss principles of proxemics—interpersonal spacing in communication—with her second-grade class. The aim of the discussion was understanding that humans as well as animals have "territories" that they defend in their day-to-day encounters with others. The teacher was attempting to draw a correlation between the territorial behavior of animals, which the children could easily observe, and territorial behavior in human beings, probably a more difficult observation for seven-year-olds. After the lesson, the teacher admitted in an interview that her children didn't seem to understand the proxemic concept very well. Apparently, the entire lesson produced more giggles than fruitful discussion.

Because the teacher was familiar with *proxemic study*, which is concerned with our use of space in our day-to-day encounters with others, she was aware that both humans and animals have a personal space surrounding them. Territoriality is a characteristic of people, as well as animals, based on recent anthropological findings. The teacher was interested in discovering whether children realized that humans exhibited territoriality, a notion easily understood by adults. Her conclusion was that the concept of human territoriality was somewhat difficult for young children to understand.

The children commented after the lesson that they thought the topic was silly. They said it was silly to compare themselves to their dogs or cats and they could only laugh at such thoughts. The teacher perceived the children's reaction to the lesson, and so she shifted the discussion to another proxemic principle:

Teacher: Sometimes we have a space or place we call our own. We might have a special chair at the kitchen table that we like to sit in, and so we call it "our chair." If anyone else sits in it, we remind him it's ours—that he shouldn't sit there. Or, we might have a special place in our house or our

---

[1] This and the following discussion between a teacher and students in her second-grade class is based on a study conducted by Linda Schiff, for which I was the thesis director: "A Study of Proxemics for Elementary Education," (Master's thesis, University of Illinois at Chicago Circle, 1973).

apartment that's "our place." Do you have a territory—a space or place—that you call yours?

Kenneth: I have my own room, where I can sleep and play.

Teacher: Good! That's a good example.

Kenneth: And I don't let my brother and sister come into my room either—unless I give them permission.

Children: (giggles)

Teacher: How about your own chair at the dinner table? Do any of you have your own special chair?

Children: (laughter)

Teacher: Think about it for a minute. Don't you usually sit in the same place for your meals, or do you sit in a different chair each time?

Bob: I do. I always sit in a chair closest to the back door, so that when I'm done eating, I can run right out the back door.

Children: (laughter)

Teacher: Is that chair "your territory"?

Bob: I guess so. (children giggle)

Teacher: What would you do, Leslie, if you walked into our classroom one morning and someone else was sitting in your desk?

Leslie: (indignant) I'd tell him to move—he's in the wrong desk!

Children: (giggles)

Teacher: What if he didn't get up right away? Would you tell him it was "your desk"—that he invaded your territory?

Leslie: Yeh, and if he didn't move, I'd kick him out!

Children: (uproarious laughter)

The teacher obtained much better results when she asked the children to talk about their territories in terms of physical objects. They seemed to understand the proxemic principle better in relation to objects and places, such as a chair or a room, than in relation to their own bodies.

THE STUDY OF PROXEMICS

The teacher and her second-grade class were discussing principles of proxemics. More specifically, proxemics has been defined by its major theorist, Edward T. Hall, as

> the study of how man unconsciously structures microspace—the distance between men in conduct of daily transactions, the organization of space in his houses and buildings, and ultimately the layout of his towns.[2]

[2] Edward T. Hall, "A System for the Notation of Proxemic Behavior," *American Anthropologist*, LXV (1963), 1003-26.

Hall has written two revolutionary books on proxemics—*The Hidden Dimension* and *The Silent Language.* As his definition implies, the study of proxemics encompasses more than what we might call "interpersonal spacing"—how people position and space themselves when they talk to one another. In fact, proxemics includes spacing in our homes, offices, neighborhoods, and cities. Proxemics concerns a broad range of topics, from how we use interpersonal space to communicate our trust in a friend to how city planners use spacing in houses, streets, and natural resources to communicate a feeling of peace and tranquility in a city.

Our concern in this chapter, as was the teacher's concern in the classroom discussions cited earlier, is with the human use of space in interpersonal communication. The teacher was attempting to make her children aware of the crucial proxemic principle that human beings are territorial beings. Each of us has a personal space bubble that surrounds us, according to Hall; when someone unexpectedly invades this space, we react in a number of different ways, depending on how well we know that person, the circumstances of the "invasion," and several other important factors. Certainly, we don't growl, bark, or bite another person who invades our territory. But we do react to territorial invasion in rather interesting and observable ways. We might show signs of tension, our eyes might open wide or look up, we might squirm a little, or we may even move away. All of these reactions illustrate the discomfort we feel when someone simply gets "too close" to us.

Hall's research demonstrates that all animals have a protective sphere or "bubble" that they keep around themselves. Enter that bubble and the animal will either flee or attack. Some animals have smaller bubbles than others, usually because of the animal's size and his relative power in an "animal world." For example, a smaller animal, such as a lizard, has a smaller bubble than a larger animal, such as a bear. The powerful lion has a bubble far larger than his size would indicate, primarily because of the lion's power in the jungle.[3] In addition, Hall found that animals exhibit different spacing patterns among themselves, depending on their particular activity. He found predictable distance patterns for different kinds of animal activities.

In attempting to correlate this kind of animal behavior with human communication behavior, Hall found strikingly similar findings. Human beings, like animals, have a personal space they defend in their day-to-day encounters. If another person comes too close, a person will react in some manner, probably a visible one. If someone stands too close to you on a relatively empty bus, you may pull

[3] Edward T. Hall, *The Hidden Dimension* (New York: Doubleday, 1969), pp. 10-15.

away, wondering if that person had a motive. If a stranger sits very close to you in a church, you might move away, hoping the person doesn't notice what you have done. In some instances there's not much you can do. In a crowded elevator someone may be right on top of you, and because the person is a stranger you don't like the invasion. But since there's nowhere to go in a crowded elevator, you employ other proxemic techniques to alleviate your discomfort: you look up or down, you stare at the floor lights in the elevator, or you even pull your arms close to your body.

If given some type of instruction on the subject, adults can recognize their territoriality. Children acquire territoriality at some point in their development of communication. Young children are typically considered as cuddly, close little people. Do children have to learn spacing patterns? Why do children find the notion of territoriality so amusing when it relates to themselves?

Hall argues that the conventions of proxemic space in communication with others are learned at a very early age. Children learn to use space in their communication much in the same way they learn to use words. Recent research in proxemics suggests that young children display some of the proxemic patterns in communication that are typical of adults from a comparable ethnic background. For example, children as young as six years of age maintain about the same distance between themselves and others that adults do, and they use different spacing patterns for communicating with males than with females—again, an adult pattern. Just as a child's grammar and vocabulary increase in size and complexity through the first years of life, so does the child's proxemic communication become increasingly more complex, adapted to situations and other persons.

Before we examine the available information on children's development of proxemic communication, it is important that we examine proxemic research with adults. In other words, our starting point will be the interpersonal spacing patterns of adults, both male and female, of several ethnic backgrounds and social-class groups. Our "communication territory" is divided into four zones, each serving a particular function and regulated by a specific set of rules. We will discuss these zones as well as interpersonal spacing differences attributable to sex and cultural group. Following a brief summary of the results obtained with adults in each area of investigation, we will examine these results in light of studies with children. However, there are very few studies dealing with children's interpersonal spacing patterns. Consequently, our generalizations regarding children's development of proxemic communication patterns are tentative and must be examined in greater detail by more extensive research.

OUR ZONES OF TERRITORY

Edward Hall has described four distance zones (the *zones of territory*) that constitute the space in which people communicate under a number of circumstances.[4] Hall proposed these zones following observations of middle-class adults, mainly natives of the northeastern seaboard of the United States, a high percentage of them with professional backgrounds. His studies indicate that adults communicate in four proxemic zones, each containing a "near" and "far" phase:

1. *The intimate zone:* In the near phase of the intimate zone (zero to six inches), another's presence is overwhelming. This is the distance for love-making, wrestling, comforting, and protecting. In the far phase of the intimate distance (six to eighteen inches), the head appears very large and some features appear distorted. Within this distance, people converse intimately with each other.
2. *The personal zone:* In the near phase of the personal distance (one and a half to two and a half feet), physical features are very apparent. Holding hands is done in this zone. In the far phase of the personal zone (two and a half to four feet), physical contact is not easily engaged in, but the vision of another person is clear. People might discuss personal problems in this zone.
3. *The social zone:* In the near phase of the social zone (four to seven feet), touching is not possible. Personal business and social gatherings are characteristic of this zone. The far phase of the social zone (seven to twelve feet) allows total vision of the other person's body. Formal business is typical of communication in this zone.
4. *The public zone:* In the near phase of the public zone (twelve to twenty-five feet), the body of another person is visible, but details of the face are not. Formal styles of language are appropriate. A speaker addressing an audience is an example of communication in this distance. In the far phase of the public zone (over twenty-five feet), details of facial and bodily movement are extremely difficult to see. This distance occurs between an important public figure (for instance, a political personality) and an audience.

Those who write about proxemics have argued that the zones of territory cannot be generalized to all segments of our society. They stress the fact that the classification system was based on a limited sample of the population, a sample certainly not representative of all human beings. Omitted were the young, lower social-economic groups, nonprofessionals, and many other groups. Yet, studies presenting distance standards appropriate for these groups are not available. In fact, few studies have been conducted to test the validity of Hall's zones of territory for other social, cultural, age, and economic groups.

[4] Ibid., Chap. 10.

When told about the zones of territory, many students today argue that the zones are not appropriate for their own communication. They suggest that the distance zones prescribed by Hall are far too large for their own communication. For example, at social gatherings they prefer to communicate within much closer distances than Hall's scheme provides. When discussing personal issues with another person, they suggest that a distance over three feet does not seem right. Yet, research to support a different set of distance standards for younger communicators has not been reported. A study conducted on our campus did indicate the need for further research with different age groups. Our study placed college students in an interview situation in which the topics were of a personal nature.[5] We predicted, based on Hall's scheme, that a personal interview in the intimate distance zone would be a "failure." Interviews were conducted in both the personal and intimate zones.

The results indicated that although students fidgeted more in the intimate-distance interview, they did not object to such a distance nor did they evaluate the interviewer negatively—even though she sat nose to nose with them. The results surprised us. We predicted that the extremely close interview (six to eighteen inches) would be perceived by students (eighteen to twenty-five years of age) as an invasion of their personal space. Yet, students said they liked it, they were not uncomfortable, and they didn't think something was wrong. Although their physical behavior (for instance, in turning away, twisting their shoulders, and becoming tense) gave away the fact that they were at least unconsciously uncomfortable, they didn't seem to mind the close proximity. In fact, many of the students suggested that interviews should become more intimate communication situations in which desks, tables, and distance do not separate the two persons involved.

This study suggests further examination of the zones of territory as applied to different age groups in our society. It might be the case that with age comes more "distant" communication. It might also be true that with today's emphasis on close and truthful communication, a territorial description of man will be fashioned that differs drastically from Hall's scheme, derived some years ago. Of great importance in any case is an answer to the question of how children acquire the distance conventions of a social group. Research with children should hold the key to a better understanding of interpersonal spacing behavior.

[5] Diane Shore, "The Effects of Close Proximity in a Dyadic Interview Situation" (Master's thesis, University of Illinois at Chicago Circle, 1971).

HOW CHILDREN LEARN
THE ZONES OF TERRITORY

Little information about the zones of territory for adults is available, but even less information is available regarding children. One study that we conducted in a Chicago suburban school dealt with principles of proxemics and elementary education.[6] The study examined second-grade children's awareness of the four zones of territory outlined by Edward Hall. Two methods were employed:

1. Children were shown a series of "absurd pictures" in which communication was taking place at an inappropriate distance. For example, a girl was telling a secret in the personal zone instead of the intimate zone, or two people were talking intimately from a social distance. The children were told that there was something "silly" about the picture and were asked to identify what it was.
2. Children were presented groups of three pictures, each group containing pictures of similar communication situations. Two of the three pictures were alike in terms of proxemic distance, and one was different in comparison. Other features of the pictures (such as the persons included, their dress, and their bodily positions) were held constant. The children were asked to find the picture that was different, much in the same way that *Sesame Street* asks children to play the "same-different" game.

The results of our study indicated that seven-year-old children were aware of proxemic absurdities in both the intimate and personal zones (they said that "distance was silly"). In addition, they were fairly good at isolating the "different" picture in a set of three, when the pictures illustrated the intimate and personal zones. However, the pictures illustrating the social and public zones caused difficulties for second graders. Our study also reported a three-day instructional program and its results. In this program researchers attempted to see whether children would benefit from proxemic instruction, part of which focused on explanations and role playing of communication activities in the four zones. After three days of instruction, children still experienced difficulties with the social- and public-distance questions. Although their overall test scores were significantly better following the instruction, the children found the intimate and personal distances easier to talk about than the social and public distances.

To explain why the second graders had difficulty with the social and public zones, we presented a number of possible explanations, including the following major ones:

[6] Schiff, "A Study of Proxemics for Elementary Education."

238 The Child's Communication System: Nonverbal Development

1. Children talk with other children and adults in much closer proximity than adults do. Children hug, cuddle, and generally stay close to others when they communicate. Since their communication typically occurs in the closer zones, children would be more aware of deviations from these norms, as in pictures with a "distance absurdity."
2. Children have more experience with activities and situations that occur in the closer proxemic zones than in the far-distance zones (social and public). For example, they tell secrets, talk with friends, and play close to another child, but they do not often attend social gatherings or present talks in front of large audiences. The closer zones were reasoned to be more relevant to their experiences than the far-distance zones. Experience, then, may explain the differences in awareness.

Our results provide some data for speculation on children's acquisition of the zones of territory. First, our study suggested that children may learn the "rules" for the zones of territory in a step-by-step fashion. They may become aware of human distance behavior in the intimate zone first, because from infancy they are most closely involved with touching, close proximity, and activities related to the intimate zone. Next, children become aware of the personal zone, when they begin to socialize, attend school, and engage in personal activities with their peers. Communication in the intimate and personal zones is probably well developed in the early elementary-school years. As children gain new experiences, such as working in groups, they begin to experience social situations of a more organized nature, in which proxemic rules of the social zone would begin to form. Finally, with experience in formal settings, as in talking to an audience, children would develop an awareness of distance in public communication.

A zone-by-zone explanation of children's acquisition of communication space seems to make much sense. Although this explanation is speculative, the entire body of research in child development would support the personal-to-social explanation of children's proxemic behavior. Based on the few developmental data gathered so far, we can propose four tentative stages of proxemic development in children, which are based on the four territorial zones. Table 11.1 outlines these stages.

In addition to learning the proxemic zones, children must also learn proxemic "conventions" typical of adult communication. Further study of children's interpersonal spacing has taken three directions:

1. The comparison of children from different culture groups regarding proxemic conventions.
2. The comparison of boys and girls in their interpersonal spacing patterns in communication.

Table 11.1. *Children's acquisition of territorial zones: a tentative proposal.*

AGE	ZONE*	EXPLANATION
birth to 3 years	Intimate	Children learn the closeness of communication with their mothers, other members of their family, and caretakers. They engage in touch, desire hugging, and profit from "close" communication.
3 to 7 years	Personal	With their acquisition of language, children become full-fledged communicators. They talk to others, usually on a personal basis. Much of their activity is self-centered (egocentric), and they have not acquired an understanding of socialization to any great extent.
7 years and older	Social	When children become more social, as opposed to egocentric, they form strong social relationships. They learn how to behave in social settings, and they can understand social relationships.
7 years and older	Public	Older children acquire an awareness of a "public" type of communication, particularly if the school setting offers the opportunity for performing in a public situation.

If proxemic zones are acquired in a zone-by-zone fashion, then we might assume that the zones learned first are retained while further learning takes place.

3. The comparison of elementary-school children of different ages (usually, first graders through fifth graders) regarding their proxemic communication.

The focus on *comparisons*, such as those on the basis of age and sex, stems from the abundance of research with adults along these lines. Research with adults has indicated that proxemic patterns vary according to sex and cultural group. In fact, the impetus for such research has come from Hall's writings, in which he argues that cultural groups differ so radically in their interpersonal spacing patterns that such differences cause misunderstandings between cultural groups. Further, Hall claims that males communicate less directly (at a greater distance and with less direct shoulder orientation) than females. Several studies have been conducted to gain experimental support for these generalizations. Although all of these studies do not agree in their findings and conclusions, we are able to draw a number of generalizations. Some support Hall's theory and others do not.

SEX DIFFERENCES
IN PROXEMIC PATTERNS

In studies of interpersonal spacing with adults it has been found that almost without exception, males differ from females in their *directness* (shoulder orientation) in communication. Two important focal points for studying interpersonal spacing in communication are:

1. The distance (in feet and inches) between the participants.
2. The shoulder orientation (the *proxemic axis*) between the participants. Axis measurements are usually based on the "clock position" of the shoulders— for example, 12:00 indicates parallel shoulders in face-to-face communication. The following diagrams outline three axis positions (shoulders are represented by the hands on the clock):

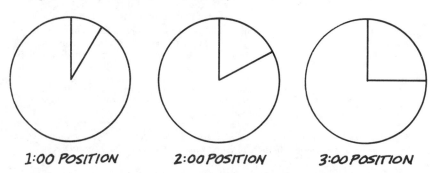

1:00 POSITION   2:00 POSITION   3:00 POSITION

Stanley Jones found that the interpersonal spacing of blacks, Puerto Ricans, Chinese, and Italians demonstrated sex differences that were consistent across these subcultural groups in New York City.[7] In all cases, males communicated with a less direct shoulder orientation than females. In other words, women faced each other more directly than males did in their communication. Perhaps the difference stems from females having greater affiliational needs, more desire for emotional involvement, and a higher degree of interest in nonverbal feedback, or a combination of these factors. Other studies have supported the finding that females communicate more directly to each other than males. However, differences in proxemic distance between males and females have not been found.

interpersonal spacing of children:
sex differences

Stanley Jones and John Aiello conducted two studies focusing on the interpersonal spacing patterns of young children, hoping to draw generalizations regarding acquisition of the proxemic conventions found in research with adults. In a study with first- and

[7] Stanley Jones, "A Comparative Proxemics Analysis of Dyadic Interaction in Selected Subcultures of New York City," *Journal of Social Psychology*, LXXXIV (1971), 35-44.

second-grade children from three cultural groups—Puerto Rican, black, and white—they found that white boys stood farther apart than white girls but that this difference did not occur with the Puerto Ricans and blacks.[8] In short, the white middle-class boys and girls in the study communicated at different distances. Sex differences in communication distance may be acquired at an early age by white middle-class children because of the greater emphasis placed on appropriate gender roles in the home. The shoulder-orientation results were not as easy to interpret, however. In fact, the results were inconsistent with adult norms: girls exhibited less direct shoulder orientation than boys.

In a second study conducted by Jones and Aiello, this time with first-, third-, and fifth-grade children (blacks and whites), they found that boys were less direct than girls in shoulder orientation.[9] These results fit the adult norms rather well. Sex differences in interpersonal spacing begin to emerge sometime after the first grade and are most obvious around the fifth grade. Differences in shoulder orientation between boys and girls are more pronounced with fifth graders than with either first or third graders. The directness of communication by fifth-grade children is comparable in terms of shoulder orientation with norms exhibited by adults. When communication distance between children is measured, there are no clear-cut differences based totally on sex.

sex differences in children's communication:
what do they mean?

That very young white middle-class children "learn" sex differences in communication, as demonstrated in their proxemic patterns, may illustrate the greater emphasis placed on gender display by this culture. Further, results indicate that proxemic conventions typical of adults within any cultural group are exemplified by young children belonging to that social group sometime in their early elementary-school years. In comparing boys and girls, the major difference in interpersonal spacing rests with communication axis, or the "directness" of communication. Sometime in the child's early elementary years, he will demonstrate proxemic patterns of communication typical of adults in his cultural group. As Edward Hall

[8] John Aiello and Stanley Jones, "Field Study of the Proxemic Behavior of Young School Children in Three Subcultural Groups," *Journal of Personality and Social Psychology*, XIX (1971), 351-56.

[9] Stanley Jones and John Aiello, "Proxemic Behavior of Black and White First-, Third-, and Fifth-Grade Children," *Journal of Personality and Social Psychology*, XXV (1973), 21-27.

suggests, these patterns emerge early. Deviations from these interpersonal spacing patterns might cause difficulties for a child. Teachers must be aware of developmental trends in proxemics in order to cope with these potential difficulties.

CULTURAL DIFFERENCES
IN PROXEMIC PATTERNS

In *The Silent Language* and *The Hidden Dimension*, Hall has suggested that the way people position themselves when they talk may cause misunderstanding, particularly when the participants are of different cultural or subcultural groups. What may seem an appropriate distance or orientation for one cultural group might be too close for another cultural group. Put members of different cultural groups together, and misunderstandings due to interpersonal spacing may easily arise. The insistence of a person from one cultural group for close proximity might be interpreted by someone from another cultural group as a hostile or pushy gesture. The proxemic differences in communication, as between blacks and whites, are acquired early in life. According to Hall, these proxemic conventions are rather permanent barriers to effective intercultural communication.

Studies comparing cultural groups in terms of interpersonal spacing have in many instances supported Hall's generalizations.[10] For example, Arabs interact more closely than Americans, and Mediterranean cultures interact more closely than North European cultures. In other instances experimental support has not been obtained, as in a study comparing the interpersonal spacing of Latin Americans with that of North Americans. Since most of these studies were conducted in very controlled laboratory conditions, however, the results must not be taken too seriously. "Native" cultural behavior patterns don't happen as naturally when a person from another country is being recorded, observed, and measured from all angles.

The Jones study comparing Italians, blacks, Chinese, and Puerto Ricans was conducted on the streets of New York City. Jones found

---

[10]The following studies compare cultural groups: R. Forston and C. Larson, "The Dynamics of Space," *Journal of Communication*, XVIII (1968), 109-16 (Latin Americans versus North Americans); K. B. Little, "Cultural Variations in Social Schemata," *Journal of Personality and Social Psychology*, X (1968), 1-7 (Mediterranean versus North European cultures); and O. Watson and T. Graves, "Quantitative Research in Proxemic Behavior," *American Anthropologist*, LXVIII (1966), 971-85 (Arabs versus Americans).

no significant differences among the subcultural groups in terms of communication distance or communication axis, although he predicted such differences, based on Hall's writings. Since his study was conducted in natural conditions of poverty neighborhoods in New York City, Jones suggested that his lack of support for Hall's generalizations may have been due to the overriding factor of poverty, not culture. In other words, a "culture of poverty" might be a more important factor in explaining proxemic patterns than the specific cultural origin of the persons communicating.

Hall's writings have suggested that lower-class blacks and middle-class whites differ in communication distance, primarily because blacks seem to become more "involved" with one another than do whites. Research studies comparing blacks and whites have produced mixed results, however: in one case Hall's predicted difference was supported, and in another case the opposite was true. In terms of shoulder orientation, results are more consistent: blacks exhibit a less direct shoulder orientation in communication than whites.[11]

children's interpersonal spacing:
cultural differences

Studies comparing children of various cultural groups have produced varying results, as well. For example, some studies have found that black children interact more closely than white children,[12] but others have found that distance only distinguishes black and white children's communication in earlier years (for instance, in first-grade years but not in fifth-grade years).[13] As we mentioned earlier, Hall argues that cultural differences in interpersonal spacing are acquired early in a child's life, and that these patterns remain with children as they grow older. For example, the studies conducted by Jones and Aiello support Hall's generalization that children exhibit proxemic differences from an early age. In fact, a study comparing black (upper-lower-class) with white (middle-class) children revealed the following differences:

[11] Albert Scheflen, "Non-language Behavior in Communication" (Paper presented at the annual meeting of the New York Chapter of the American Academy of Pediatrics, Elmsford, N.Y., Oct., 1969.

[12] J.C. Baxter, "Interpersonal Spacing in Natural Settings," *Sociometry*, XXXIII (1970), 444-56; and F. N. Willis, "Initial Speaking Distance as a Function of the Speaker's Relationship," *Psychonomic Science*, V (1966), 221-22.

[13] Jones and Aiello, "Proxemic Behavior"; and Aiello and Jones, "Field Study of Proxemic Behavior."

1. Black children faced each other less directly than white children, especially in the earlier grades.
2. Black children stood closer to one another, especially in the earlier grades.
3. By the fifth grade, interpersonal spacing of black children and white children differed only in terms of shoulder orientation, not in distance: black children were less direct in shoulder orientation than white children.

Clearly, we need further studies of proxemic differences based on cultural background. Understanding the roles that communication distance and axis might play in differentiating children's communication will affect how we understand the communication problems of children and adults from different cultural backgrounds.

cultural differences in children's communication: implications

Once we are able to isolate the proxemic differences in children's communication that appear to be due to cultural learning, we will be in a far better position to assist students in effective communication with members of other cultural groups. The few proxemic studies reported to date have revealed rather striking differences in children's communication. According to the Jones-Aiello study, the major cultural difference between black and white children is in the directness of shoulder orientation (*communication axis*). In communicating, black children face each other less directly than white children. The distinctive patterns of communication behavior reflected in this difference are acquired as early as the first grade, and they seem to remain beyond that level. Thus, communication axis may be a persistent barrier to effective communication among blacks and whites from childhood to adulthood.

SUMMARY

The study of human territoriality is in its infancy. How people communicate in space is a relatively new science of human behavior. There are many unanswered questions concerning adult proxemic behavior, and new studies must be designed to answer these questions. Of even greater importance is how children learn or otherwise acquire the rules of communication in space. When we understand more about a child's acquisition of proxemic behavior, our understanding of adult norms will be more meaningful: the standards and conventions employed by adults will then have a developmental basis.

The few studies that have been conducted with children indicate that certain patterns of proxemic behavior are learned in the early elementary grades. Considering the four zones of territory proposed by Edward Hall to explain adult proxemic behavior, it appears that young children (for instance, second graders) are most aware of distance in communication in the "closer" zones—the intimate and personal zones. Their understanding of communication conventions in the social and public zones may depend on social and public communication experiences in their elementary-school years. It seems likely that children acquire spacing behavior in a zone-by-zone fashion, beginning with the intimate and personal zones.

Studies comparing the proxemic behavior of elementary-school children from various ethnic backgrounds have indicated that certain proxemic patterns are well established by the first grade. For example, sex distinctions related to shoulder orientation are evident in the communication of white middle-class first graders. For black and Puerto Rican children, sex differences are slower to emerge. This difference might be explained by the greater emphasis placed on appropriate gender display in white, middle-class homes.

Another important finding related to children's communication concerns ethnic differences in interpersonal spacing. For example, a number of proxemic patterns distinguish blacks' and whites' communication in early elementary-school years, yet the only proxemic difference to remain beyond the fifth grade in the communication of black and white children is communication axis. We suggested that the "directness" variable may stand as a barrier to effective communication between the groups, a difference that seems to begin in childhood and remain through adult years. Table 11.2 outlines the

Table 11.2. *Children's development of communication in space (proxemics).*

PROXEMIC NOTION ACQUIRED	AGE ACQUIRED
communication in the intimate zone (0 to 18 inches)	birth to 2 or 3 years
communication in the personal zone (18 inches to 4 feet)	3 to 7 years
communication in the social zone (4 to 12 feet)	7 years and older
communication in the public zone (12 feet and greater)	7 years and older
sex differences in the proxemics of communication (male communication axis greater than female axis)	10 years and older, but younger (maybe 6 years of age) for middle-class white children

child's development of proxemic communication, taking into account territorial zones and sex differences.

SUGGESTED READINGS

BAXTER, J. C., "Interpersonal Spacing in Natural Settings," *Sociometry*, XXXIII (1970), 444-56.

JONES, STANLEY, and JOHN AIELLO, "Proxemic Behavior of Black and White First-, Third-, and Fifth-Grade Children," *Journal of Personality and Social Psychology*, XXV (1973), 21-27.

part
IV

COMMUNICATION DEVELOPMENT

Part IV offers an approach to learning that can help children become more effective communicators. Chapters 12-15 reflect an integration of verbal and nonverbal aspects of communication into a model of instruction that centers on the *communication situation*. Thus far, we have discussed children's communication in three areas:

1. the forces affecting communication development (Part I)
2. the stage-by-stage development of phonology, morphology, syntax, and semantics in children's communication (Part II)
3. children's development of body language, voice, and proxemics in communication (Part III)

The final part of this text suggests a classroom approach to communication instruction that aims to foster effective communication in day-to-day situations. To place Chapters 12-15 in perspective, let's begin by introducing the approach to be used ("Where Should We Go?") and the activities involved ("How Can We Get There?").

247

"WHERE SHOULD WE GO?"

Studies in children's language development have been extremely helpful in explaining why a child's language develops as it does. We can trace the stages of development in any channel of communication, whether we are talking about syntax or body language. We know that children acquire the basic rules of their language before they enter kindergarten. But the rules of language are not all that children must acquire in order to communicate effectively. Children must also learn that language is a tool that, when used creatively and appropriately, can serve them well. Consider the example of the eight-year-old boy who always waits until his dad has eaten dinner and is relaxing with the newspaper before he pops the question for permission. Or how about the child who waits until Grandma is around (she can't refuse her grandchild anything) to ask for a new toy? These children have learned something about language that has little to do with phonemes or syntactic patterns. Instead, they have acquired rules or strategies for dealing with communication situations.

"Children learn when to speak, when to be silent, when to use ritual language, when to use baby talk, when to use polite forms and when to shift language in a multilingual community."[1] While children are in the process of mastering the grammatical rules of their language, they are also in the process of learning usage rules—rules applying to the communication situation at hand. Courtney Cazden suggests that when you consider the relationship between language structure and language use, for purposes of instruction, you might see a paradox.[2] To resolve the paradox, she cites a quotation from the Duchess in *Alice in Wonderland:* "And the moral of all that is—'Take care of the sense, and the sounds will take care of themselves.' " Cazden suggests that a variant of the Duchess's moral applies here: take care of the *use* and the structure will take care of itself. In other words, if instruction centers on how children can use language effectively in a variety of communication situations, the children will easily develop the more complicated aspects of language structure. Consequently, Part IV focuses on the communication situation and offers instruction on verbal and nonverbal strategies children must acquire so that they can be effective in their interpersonal relationships.

[1] Dan Slobin, ed. *A Field Manual for Cross-Cultural Study of the Acquisition of Communicative Competence* (Berkeley: University of California Bookstore, 1967), p. 10.

[2] Courtney Cazden, "Two Paradoxes in the Acquisition of Language Structure and Functions" (Paper presented at the Conference of Developmental Sciences, CIBA Foundation, London, January, 1972), p. 5.

Often, the effectiveness of a communicator is not related to the use of an extensive vocabulary, careful articulation of speech sounds, or perfect grammatical phrasing. Instead, effectiveness is based on the *appropriateness* of what we say. The message must be appropriate to the person, the setting (time and place), the topic being discussed, and the task at hand. The competent communicator carefully weighs the *factors of the communication situation:*

1. *participants:* the person(s) involved in communication
2. *setting:* the time and place of the communication event
3. *topic:* the subject matter of communication
4. *task:* the goal or purpose of communication

Because the competent communicator weighs the factors of the situation well, she can *bargain:*

> "Mommy, if you let me have one more cookie, I promise I'll eat all my vegetables for dinner!"

The competent communicator can *manipulate:*

> "You're the best Dad in the whole world . . . Can I stay up late and watch TV with you, Dad?"

The competent communicator can *comfort:*

> "I'm sorry you don't feel good, Mom. Why don't you rest for a while on the couch? You've been working too hard. I'll be real quiet. OK?"

The competent communicator certainly knows the rules of language structure, but, more important, he knows how to use language as a tool in everyday situations.

Given the rationale for communication instruction just outlined, the first two chapters in Part IV will center on the following information.

Chapter 12: *The Communication Situation.* Since effective communication should be the product of practice in dealing with various situations of importance to children, we must first define the parameters of the communication situation: participants, setting, topic, and task.

Chapter 13: *Communication Instruction.* To correctly gear instruction for the communication situation to the needs, ages, and backgrounds of children, this chapter offers a communication guide with which teachers can determine what the *critical communication situations* are. Situations that are important from the children's perspective become the focus of instruction.

"HOW CAN WE GET THERE?"

The goal of communication instruction is to *increase the child's repertoire of communication strategies for dealing with critical communication situations.* The final two chapters of the text offer tools to reach this goal, tools in the form of classroom activities. Once the teacher has established the critical communication situations faced by children in the classroom, through the use of the *Guide,* instruction can begin.

Chapter 14: *Communication Analysis: A Children's Approach.* One method of increasing children's awareness of the options available to them in various situations is to analyze such situations and talk about them. This chapter presents activities that offer opportunities for talking about communication events that can be adapted to children's needs.

Chapter 15: *Participation in Communication Situations.* In this chapter, children are encouraged to participate in a number of previously arranged communication events. Practice in communication is the focus of these activities, and the options available to children are stressed.

In short, to increase the child's repertoire of strategies in critical communication situations, the child must be given guidance in talking about the situation and options available to him. Further, the child must be given guidance in participating in communication events that call for appropriate language choices.

12

the communication situation

A Child's Play

by A.M.A.F.C.*

*(*An average mother of an average four-year-old child)*

Cast of Characters:

Mommy .... the mother
Jimmy .... the four-year-old son

PROLOGUE: (Act I, Scene 1)

Mommy is a little irritable today. Last night she had some friends over for dinner, and Jimmy, her four-year-old son, was particularly fussy and annoying. He refused to go to bed, and when he was finally carried off to the bedroom, he played the "water game." Every fifteen minutes or so, he yelled that he was thirsty, in fact, "dying of thirst." Asking for the water (to stay up late) does not usually work with Jimmy's mom. But when company is over, she gets flustered and runs back and forth to his room to quiet him down. She is very embarrassed to have her son acting up *in front of company*. She has said this many times to her son.

Consulting Author: Royce Rodnick Gardner

Anyway, today is a shopping day, and Jimmy and his mother are going downtown. She tried to get a baby sitter but none was available. As they pass through the toy department, which isn't too smart of Mommy, Jimmy spots a shiny red truck that looks interesting. He informs Mommy that he wants it. She informs him that he'll have to wait until he deserves a new toy. Jimmy peruses the store and notes that there are many grown-ups in the immediate vicinity and decides to use the usually successful strategy of "throwing a tantrum in front of strangers" to persuade his mother to buy him the truck. He cries, he whines, and he tugs at his mother's sleeve and falls to the floor, refusing to leave. Mommy is becoming increasingly nervous. All the other mothers are looking at her (critically?) and at Jimmy (sympathetically?). What else can she do but relent and buy Jimmy the truck? She does so and Jimmy's crying subsides. He's a happy little boy because he won the battle. He decides to be especially good for the rest of the day so that by the time they get home, Mommy will have forgotten the incident. She always does.

This scene is not an unusual example of a child's shrewd analysis of a communication situation. Jimmy knows his mother pretty well. He can predict her behavior, based on his past experiences with her, and he can manipulate his own behavior (as in making a fuss in public) to accomplish a particular goal (getting a new toy). Sometimes his strategies work and sometimes they don't. In either case, the child, through success and failure, is learning a great deal about how to act in important communication situations.

Jimmy has made some sound decisions about the parameters of the communication situation:

1. *Participant(s):* His mother does not wish to have a nagging child embarrass her in front of others, and he knows this.
2. *Setting:* The daytime, public situation involves many onlookers who will notice his distress.
3. *Topic:* The desired truck, the subject matter of his communication, is in full view; everyone in the toy department can see it and can see how much Jimmy wants it.
4. *Task:* The strong desire Jimmy has for the truck is both obvious (his message is clearly stated) and understandable (a boy needs a truck, doesn't he?).

If we study Jimmy's communication from the standpoint of his verbal and nonverbal language choices, we find an absence of verbal structures (Jimmy didn't use any sentences) and an abundance of not-so-subtle nonverbal choices—a tantrum, whining, tugging, and crying. The linguistic picture looks empty: there is little evidence of linguistic mastery. However, if we view Jimmy's situational choices, which he based on the people, setting, topic, and task, we can see that he has acquired communication strategies for this situation. The communication picture is sharp, reflecting a fairly high level of communication mastery. It is from the viewpoint of the *communication situation* that verbal and nonverbal choices become meaningful and relevant.

The thrust of this chapter is a discussion of the nature and importance of the communication situation. Each situation "asks us" to make certain language choices, verbal and nonverbal, that are appropriate to the situation. These choices are called *communication strategies.* Consequently, this chapter presents two major topics: (1) the communication situation discussed from three basic perspectives; and (2) communication strategies and their relation to communication power.

THE COMMUNICATION SITUATION

There are a number of ways to define a communication situation. We can gain greater insight by viewing all approaches, since each allows us to see the situation from a slightly different perspective. The three approaches we will take are:

1. *The dramatic view of the communication situation:* the communication event is pictured in "performance" terms.
2. *The categorical view of communication events:* situations are classified according to types of language that are appropriate.
3. *The parameters of the communication situation:* the variables of participants, setting, topic, and task are specified.

a dramatic performance

Ervin Goffman, a contemporary social psychologist, suggests that we can interpret all social behavior as if it were a dramatic performance.[1] He finds that most of us have a highly developed ability to play successfully the roles demanded of us at any moment. Although most of us do not have the tools of the professional actor at our command, we do acquire "acting techniques" that allow us to cope with others. We rarely have a script that indicates what we should say. And we don't have the rehearsal time to practice the most effective tone of voice or bodily movement. Further, the setting of the scene is not always one we are familiar with or comfortable in. Although we might know the roles of the charac-

[1] Ervin Goffman, *Presentation of Self in Everyday Life* (New York: Doubleday Company, Inc., 1959).

ters—for example, mother, child, teacher—we cannot always predict the best way to deal with those roles or the persons behind them.

Yet, as we saw in our play, four-year-old Jimmy has already begun the process of discriminating among the acting techniques available to him, such as crying, asking for water, and throwing a tantrum. He has mastered a few roles, such as the "good boy" and the "bad boy," and he has some knowledge of the appropriate setting in which to play these roles. If he were home alone with Mommy, the tantrum technique and its associated "bad-boy" role might not have worked. But even without the tools of the professional actor, Jimmy possesses, as do most children, a very powerful tool: the use of both verbal and nonverbal language, which aids him in coping with the communication situations he encounters.

A child's ability to role-play is often uncanny. Many times, a mother is left wondering where her child picked up a certain expression, a particular body movement, or a strangely familiar tone of voice. She may think it's cute or she may shudder at the thought that the child is imitating her. Early in life, a child realizes that individuals are different and have different roles. Consider Maria's awareness of roles. Her learning begins with her observations of her immediate family. For example, she realizes that her father expresses his love differently than her mother does. To be tossed into the air and caught with a hug is Daddy's way. Mommy shows her love by worrying about whether she's eating her vegetables and by making certain that she's dressed warmly enough. Maria knows that Grandma never scolds her, but her older sister sure knows how to yell when she accidentally spills milk on her schoolbooks. She observes that different persons react differently to her. Perhaps she also learns that she responds differently to different persons. Her messages of hunger, anger, and illness are reserved for her mother. She saves the exciting story about the jet airplane she saw flying right over her house for Daddy's ears alone. Maria allows Grandpa to hug and kiss her, but her older brother better not try it. Children must learn how to use their language in real situations with real people. Different persons have different roles, and children's communication must be adapted to these roles. Maria, a five-year-old girl, has a good start in learning about the importance of roles in communication.

Whereas professional actors must use their abilities to portray *other* persons, our young social actors must use their abilities to learn about other persons so that they can portray *themselves* in the most successful and rewarding ways. This requires that children be given opportunities to observe other individuals and talk about how they function within their roles. Children must be encouraged to experiment with their language and analyze the results. The end product of their efforts is a repertoire of language strategies that enables them to deal successfully with characters and scenes they encounter in day-to-day communication "performances."

appropriateness categories

We can view the communication situation in the same manner in which we examined grammatical structures. Just as we reviewed the child's development of grammatical categories (Part II), we can study the child's communication development according to categories of usage. The goal of communication learning is communicative competence. Communicative competence refers to the way in which a child "perceives and categorizes the social situations of his world and differentiates his way of speaking accordingly."[2] Communicative competence, like linguistic competence, may involve a categorization process in acquisition. Just as children learn syntactic rules that tell them how to categorize and order words in sentences, they acquire a knowledge of how and when to use such sentences to express feelings and ideas in their interpersonal relationships.

Children learn about the various categories into which communication events can fit. For example, a child may have a category of "be quiet" situations—those times and places when she knows she must be silent. A child may have a category of "polite" situations, in which she finds it more advantageous to be the "good girl" rather than the "bad girl." Situational categories might look something like this:

Category: "Be quiet."

1. Mom has a headache.
2. Mom doesn't realize that it's past my bedtime.
3. I don't want the teacher to call on me in class.
4. I am being scolded by my father.
5. My friend has told me a secret.
6. I am in church.

Category: "Be polite."

1. I talk to an older person.
2. I am asking for a favor.
3. Someone has given me a gift.
4. We are eating dinner.
5. I am talking to my teacher.
6. I am asking for permission to do something.

The child forms such situational categories as "be quiet" and "be polite" because she is able to perceive similarities and differences in others' reactions to her behavior. Through a trial-and-error procedure the child is able to build mental labels for situations that are alike

---

[2] Dell Hymes, "On Communicative Competence," in *The Mechanisms of Language Development*, eds. R. Huxley and E. Ingram (London: CIBA Foundation, 1970), p. 84.

and require an appropriate type of behavior from her to insure a pleasant outcome. Consequently, categories emerge: e.g.,

"Be forceful."   (when I'm sure my idea is a good one; when I'm encouraging a friend to do something)

"Be careful."   (when I talk to my teacher about schoolwork; when I'm giving directions)

"Be concerned." (when my friend has a problem; when something is accidentally broken)

Situational categories help steer the child in an appropriate direction of behavior. New situations are added to a category as the child encounters them and classifies them. The child can generalize what he knows about a category already developed—"be polite" (to persons in high authority, such as the doctor or my teacher)— to new situations—"be polite" (to the principal of my school).

Appropriateness, a key term in the study of communication situations, is determined by (1) the culture of the child and (2) the parameters of the situation. A culture will dictate norms that a child must learn in order to become an "exemplary member" of that culture. Further, the communication situation is defined by four parameters (participants, setting, topic, task) that should have a strong bearing on the child's verbal and nonverbal language choices. We can define *communicative competence* as

> *the mastery of an underlying set of appropriateness rules—which are determined by* culture *and* situation—*that affect the verbal and nonverbal choices in communication events.*

For any one communication situation the number of possible language choices (options) could be many. Children, as well as adults, could have a few options or many options for that situation. The more options available to the person, the more likely the choice will best fit the demands of the situation. The verbal and nonverbal options selected for use in the situation can be called *communication strategies.* Ideally, the strategies selected (for example, speaking or acting in a particular way) correspond with the appropriateness demands of the culture and the situation (for instance, "be quiet," "be forceful," or "be polite").

The third view of the communication situation focuses specifically on the four parameters of the communication situation. Before explaining these parameters, let's momentarily examine the role of a culture on a person's communication behavior. Most anthropologists assume that an individual who is a member of a culture must operate by the norms of that culture. At the core of this assumption are the premises that (1) all behavior is rule-governed and (2) the culture determines the appropriateness of various behaviors by establishing certain rules of behavior for its members. In their attempt to become members of their culture, children must learn their culture's rules of communication appropriateness. Through exposure to accepted practices in their culture, children generalize rules for appropriate behavior in a multitude of situations, such as playing and talking. Sports may be the most important play activity for children in one culture, and music or games may be highly valued in another culture. Rules about children's behavior in communication situations (for instance, "Never talk to someone you don't know") also vary from culture to culture.

A young child of the dominant culture in America, for example, is taught that it is polite to address a person by his name—and in some cases a title—Mr., Mrs., Dr. Further, it is socially acceptable to inquire about a name: "Whom were you named after?" A Navajo child, on the other hand, would not dare ask about somebody's name or make a comment about it. Anthropologist Edward Hall warns us that in Navajo culture this would be a rude and unacceptable procedure.[3]

Because cultural norms are so important in determining what is appropriate communication behavior, it is imperative that teachers become familiar with the cultural norms and practices of his or her students. The task is not too difficult if the teacher and students share basic cultural values. But if the teacher is a young white woman from a middle-class, Protestant background and her students are from a different background, she must learn about the cultural practices that are important to her students.

parameters of the situation

Those who have stressed the importance of studying the communication situation agree that the basic units of analysis are the participants, setting, topic, and task. These four parameters *define* the communication situation, and help determine the appropriateness of verbal and nonverbal language. Let's discuss the four parameters and illustrate them with examples.

Participants are those persons engaged in the communication event. We can describe the participants according to age, sex, culture, education, status, or any other attribute made relevant in a particular culture. There are far simpler ways to talk about the participants in a

[3] Edward T. Hall, *The Silent Language* (Greenwich, Conn.: Fawcett Publications, 1959), p. 24.

conversation. Instead of perceiving a person's sociological attributes, we often perceive people in this way:

"He's my father." (Better watch out.)
"She's my best friend." (Anything goes.)
"He's my teacher." (Be careful.)

Children's perceptions of another person (participant) are based on their perception of that person's role in their lives. Children may speak differently with their teacher, a high-authority person, than they do with their brothers or sisters. This is probably because children see a teacher as a person continually in the process of evaluating them, making judgments, and affecting their school "careers." With a brother or sister, however, there is less fear of negative evaluation or any kind of evaluation, for that matter. Such perceptions play an important role in how children talk to others.

Children's self-images, their feelings about themselves, also affect their communication choices. If children feel pretty good about themselves, or, conversely, if they have doubts about themselves, this will probably be reflected in their verbal and nonverbal language. Furthermore, children use language differently when speaking to someone they believe thinks highly of them (their best buddies, for example) than they do when they are sure they are perceived negatively (by the principal who just last week warned them that their behavior in class had better improve).

The place and/or time of the communication event is the *setting.* Children must learn that the setting involves rules that govern the type of language that can be used. Upon entering school, children quickly learn that all sorts of things that were taken for granted at home cannot be done at school. What mother ever made her children raise their hands before asking a question? Imagine the frustration children must feel at being told to sit up straight and fold their hands instead of being able to talk and play freely with other children. Many children have been warned by a teacher, "Save that type of language for home—we don't speak that way in school!"

Timing can also be an important consideration for language usage. Most children have heard rules such as, "There will be no crying at the dinner table—save it for after dinner" or, "Don't bother Daddy until after he's read the newspaper—then he'll play with you." Timing is also involved in an occasion such as a funeral or a birthday party. There are certain conventions of behavior and communication that are appropriate in such occasions. For example, we know that silence is often the best form of communication at a funeral. On the other hand, children know they should communicate their birthday greetings to a friend when attending his party.

The *topic* is the subject matter or referent of speech. The familiarity, potency, and degree of interest the topic has to someone will affect his language choices in a situation. If you were called upon to give a spontaneous lecture on children's communication development and another lecture on computing square roots, your two lectures would probably exhibit drastic differences in your use of language. Although you would certainly be fairly articulate, confident, and secure discussing the former topic, you might appear inept as you mumbled what little you could recall about how to compute a square root. From your standpoint, children's communication is a far more familiar topic.

Sex is a potent topic in many cultures. Some cultures dictate that children should not be exposed to a topic that has any sexual overtones. After all, "the superego of the child might be affected." Yet, if it is much too early to send the children to bed and the juicy gossip can't wait, the adults might use euphemistic expressions in talking about the topic. They may spell certain words or names, or perhaps whisper or lower their voices.

A perceptive teacher will discover that her students' language gives pretty good clues as to how interested they are in a particular subject. Falling asleep, doodling, and inattention are, of course, obvious signs of boredom or confusion. Asking questions, alertness, smiles, and frowns are usually positive signs of students taking an interest in a topic. Clues that tell us the degree of interest others have in our topic will affect—should affect—how we talk about that topic.

Task refers to the reason or objective for an individual's communication. If we are analyzing children's speech, we must ask this question: What are they trying to accomplish in communicating? When children are termed "poorly behaved," teachers or parents often tend to assume that their children's objective is to annoy them. If they were to evaluate the situations more carefully, perhaps they would realize that "poorly behaved" children may be communicating a need for extra attention and that their goal in behaving poorly is to have someone notice them, even if the strategy is a negative one.

Frequently, teachers—any adults—are criticized for integrating the slang expressions of the times into their speech. They are accused of trying to be "with it" but failing miserably. Perhaps this is an unfair accusation. Their task might be a desire to show they are willing and anxious to communicate with their children, but their strategy might not be the most effective one for accomplishing this particular task.

A frequent objective of both younger and older children's communication is to avoid the bedtime hour, a task for which they may have many strategies. Toddlers use the familiar strategy of throwing a special toy out of the crib, only to cry for someone to come in and pick it up. There is also the popular "I'm thirsty" routine, which most mothers know only too well. Older children often use the excuse of "just remembering" that there is homework left unfinished or that their teacher made an assignment that required an extra hour of TV watching!

In summary, the parameters of the communication situation are the participants, the setting (time and place), the topic, and the task. Children must be aware of these parameters if they are to adapt their messages to the elements of the situation. When children learn that there are rules that operate in social situations and that their language must reflect an awareness of these rules, they are able to make appropriate language choices. Awareness of the rules of "speaking appropriately" leads to more creative and successful communication strategies. This leads us to the second major topic of this chapter, a topic that grows out of the situation: the communication strategies that represent the verbal and nonverbal language choices appropriate to the situation.

COMMUNICATION STRATEGIES

The language choices children make, based on their awareness of the communication situation, are influenced heavily by their past experiences in similar communication situations. In addition, the strategies at their command *change* as they develop. From the standpoint of communication effectiveness, the more strategies a person has for a particular situation, the more likely it is that she has just the right one to employ. Our discussion of communication strategies concerns three topics:

1. The origin of communication strategies.
2. Children's development of communication strategies.
3. Communication strategies affect communication power.

the origin of communication strategies

A communication strategy can begin with random, nonintentional behavior on the part of the child. Picture little Matt (only five months old), lying in bed, rhythmically banging his head against the headboard. He's not hurting himself. In fact, he seems to be enjoying the rhythm of his head moving back and forth.[4] His mother

---

[4] Head banging is thought to be a normal form of early rhythmic behavior in infants; see Benjamin Spock, *Baby and Child Care*, rev. ed. (New York: Pocket Books, 1971), pp. 227-28.

hears the banging and enters the room, very upset to see and hear Matt engaging in this potentially harmful behavior. She picks him up to comfort him, certain that he might hurt himself. Matt, not understanding his mother's concern, continues to bang his head the next day. After all, it feels pretty good. His mother comes running into his room again. About a week later Matt is in bed, feeling a bit uncomfortable and fussy. His mother has not given him the attention he wanted all day. Crying has not worked. Matt begins knocking his head, not so innocently this time. He moves harder and louder than he ever did when it was for his own enjoyment. Predictably, Matt's mother comes to his rescue with the much-wanted attention. A communication strategy has been discovered.

Communication strategies can also be the result of calculated behavior by the child. Such strategies are often discovered through the trial-and-error process. Susie knows that she doesn't want to eat the spinach her mother thinks is so good for her, but she also knows that she usually won't allow her to leave the table until she finished all her food. Susie must think of a strategy—a way to get her mother to see the light. She knows that if she cries she'll be called a baby, and a five-year-old certainly is not a baby. She knows she had better not talk sensibly about it either. After all, spinach probably *is* good for her and she can't find the words with which to tell her mother that it causes her a severe digestive upset just looking at the stuff. So Susie resorts to the emotional pitch. She looks at her mother with big sad eyes while she bravely puts a forkful of spinach into her quivering little mouth. Then, with the courage of a soldier in battle she swallows the spinach. But something happens to our little soldier: she begins to choke (an act), her eyes water, her face turns red (she's really holding her breath), and she uses the handy expression, "Mommy, it went down the wrong way. I need some Coca Cola quick!" In the ensuing panic to relieve the choking spell the spinach is forgotten. If this seems a rather elaborate strategy, stop for a moment and try to remember what you thought of that bowl of spinach, as a child. It wasn't very appealing, was it?

Whether a strategy is discovered through random behavior or whether it originates through shrewd, calculated thought, it represents a perceptive and creative use of language in communication situations. What is the nature of these strategies? Do children acquire a greater number of communication strategies as they grow older? We attempted to answer these questions by conducting a study.[5]

[5] Royce Rodnick and Barbara Wood, "The Communication Strategies of Children," *The Speech Teacher*, XXII (1973), 114-24.

children's development
of communication strategies

Our study was designed to gather information in an interview setting regarding communication strategies employed by children of various ages. To provide a common frame of reference for the interviews, we chose situations that children and their mothers shared. We called these shared situations *behavioral universals*—that is, behavioral contexts that we believe occur for all children, regardless of their cultural background, age, or sex. The contexts we chose were eating, sleeping, and playing.

The major question of our study was this: What kinds of communication strategies do children employ, given the contexts of eating, sleeping, and playing? Because of our interest in children's development of strategies, we posed a secondary question: Do the kinds of communication strategies employed by children, in the contexts of the behavioral universals, vary as a function of the age of the child? We reasoned that older children would have a greater repertoire of strategies than younger children. Our prediction was based on the idea that older children have had more opportunities to discover strategies than younger children. Further, older children have more complex grammatical structures and a more comprehensive vocabulary from which to choose the language most appropriate for the situation. Our interviews were based on children from four age groups:

Group 1: 1-2 years
Group 2: 3-4 years
Group 3: 5-6 years
Group 4: 7-11 years

We hoped to describe the communication strategies typical of each age group and then compare the types of strategies they used. We asked each mother to talk about her child's communication strategies in three different contexts:

1. *The bedtime hour:* the child doesn't want to go to bed, and wishes to extend the bedtime hour.
2. *Eating time:* the child doesn't like "the menu," or wishes to have a between-meal snack.
3. *Playtime:* the child wants to go outside, has a great idea about what to do, or wants to play with someone who doesn't wish to play at that time.

The children in group 1 resorted to attention-getting tactics—such as making noise, whining, crying, and nagging—in the three contexts. Incidentally, most mothers claimed that the whining strategy rarely worked because it was so annoying. (We wondered how true this was.) Most of the strategies for this group were nonverbal: pulling, banging, and affectionate behavior.

One boy in Group 1, after being bathed and dressed for bed, would play quietly by himself in a corner, out of Mommy's immediate view, in the hope of being "forgotten." If he were accidentally noticed, he would smile sweetly and lovingly and continue to play. The mother reported that this strategy did not usually work with her, but her husband, on the other hand, might insist on letting the child stay up another half hour. After all, "he's being such a good little boy!" The mother figured out that this was a strategy because her son never played quietly by himself during the day. Another mother said her young daughter would continually throw her unwanted food on the floor. The mother would pick it up and insist that the child continue eating. The daughter would again throw the food around the kitchen. This would continue until, eventually, the mother would give up. The mother claims that she's "wise" to the strategy now. After the first throw, she excuses her daughter from the table. One mother reported that when her young boy wanted to go outside and play, he would pull her over to wherever his coat was and point outside. If his mother refused, he would then go to his room and begin banging all his toys together. (This mother hated loud noises because they made her nervous.) When his mother would come into his room to investigate, the child would again point outside, indicating his choice of locale. The refusing and banging would continue until either the child or the mother relented. Unfortunately, the mother said, her child could go on banging all day.

The children in group 2 had a better command of verbal language and used it to their advantage. Although they still employed some of the strategies of the toddlers in group 1, their strategies were generally more sophisticated. They would withdraw affection or use "fear appeals" if the going was tough. One child tried to avoid the bedtime hour by reporting that there were hidden monsters in the bedroom. Another child used a threat, stating that she (the daughter) would tell Daddy if Mommy made her eat the vegetables. You see, Daddy doesn't like vegetables either. Mothers were often cast as the villains in the lives of three- and four-year-olds; the fathers were the heroes because they were more "cooperative." Remember, of course, that such statements are based on the mothers' reports and not the fathers'. Another interesting strategy employed by the group 2 children was to talk about how lonely they were when they wanted their mother or father to play with them.

Mothers of the five-and six-year-olds in group 3 found it difficult to discuss the strategies that their children used. They were uncertain as to whether their children's behavior in the three contexts could be considered strategies. They preferred to think of their child's communication in these situations as reasonable, based on common sense. One mother, a professor of oral interpretation, said that her child would tell her what a beautiful reading voice she had when he wanted her to read him a bedtime story. This particular mother was not sure, however, if this was a strategy or simply an expression of truth.

According to the mothers of children in group 4, their children had few strategies for dealing with the behavioral contexts we suggested. Apparently, the contexts of eating, sleeping, and playing were too limited or irrelevant for older children.

We considered the finding that older children apparently employed fewer strategies than younger children to be a major discovery of our study. It seemed reasonable to suggest, initially, that this result was due to the lack of relevancy of the behavioral universals to older children. Most of the mothers we interviewed were working mothers, away from their children for a portion of the day. Therefore, the older children may have been more independent and more in control of their daily behavior. A variety of strategies would not be necessary if the mothers allowed them relative freedom in their daily activities. The independence explanation seemed too obvious and possibly inaccurate, however. Might it be the case that older children *do* have strategies for the behavioral universals studied, namely, eating, sleeping, and playing? Perhaps the older children, because of their many years of experience in dealing with their mothers, do not have to *experiment* with strategies, as do the younger children, who must keep on trying until they hit the strategies that work. A twelve-year-old girl does not have to be told it is bedtime. She can look at the clock and see for herself. If she does not wish to go to bed, she can probably present a convincing case that she's not tired and that she has some homework to do, or she might be able to bargain for an extension—for instance, she might take out the garbage or offer to wash dishes tomorrow. Are these strategies? You bet they are. But because older children have had so much experience in achieving their goals or because they are simply subtle in their approach, mothers may not pay much attention to their use of language, verbal and nonverbal, in these important situations.

A final explanation we considered was that older children may have a vast number of communication strategies that apply to different behavioral universals. In other words, situations children perceive as "critical" (important and often difficult) change as they age. Accordingly, the situations that are critical for the four-year-old are probably quite different from the situations deemed critical by an eight-year-old. To observe best the older child experimenting with communication strategies, we might have selected behavioral universals or *critical communication situations* more appropriate to the lives of older children. For example, older children probably experiment with a wealth of strategies related to boy-girl relationships—that is, strategies for attracting the attention of a favorite boy or girl at school.

It is important to remember that mothers, not children, were the source of information in our study, and that they were relating their own perceptions of their children's strategies. There were several reasons why we selected mothers as the source of our information in such an exploratory study, however. First, the mother spends a great deal of time with the child. In fact, the mother is often the victim of her child's communication strategies. In addition, mothers are usually quite willing to discuss their own children, especially those aspects that highlight their children's intelligence and creativity. On the other hand, consider the topic of the interviews: we were talking about children's abilities to persuade, to get what they want. This might have presented some problems for the mothers. Their responses may have revealed a sort of image conflict: Should I reveal myself as *I really am* or as *I would like to be*? Does the mother dare admit she often allows her child to break the bedtime hour rule—because her child is so adorable at night and she hates to put the child to bed? Does she feel she must justify her own behavior rather than simply describe it? Another possibility is that the mothers were characterizing their children's communication strategies as they thought they should have occurred, from their knowledge of child-rearing practices, rather than as they actually occurred. For instance, will a mother say a whining strategy rarely works because she knows it should not?

Fully aware of the possible disadvantages of employing mothers as our source of information, we designed the interviews so that they would compensate for their disadvantages, to some extent. We shared oral and written statements with the mothers that stressed how *creative* a child can be in the use of communication strategies. Next, we tried to get each mother to admit that she was often the victim of her child's communication strategies. We encouraged them to discuss the subject freely, not as a problem but as an interesting behavior that both pleased and displeased them. Our primary concern, interpersonally, was to create an atmosphere that would prompt the mothers to answer openly, and honestly, even though their responses might reflect negative impressions of themselves. On the basis of mothers' comments following the interview, and from our review of the interview tapes, we reasoned that the interviews were quite successful in eliciting responses that could be called realistic.

The study clearly makes one important point about children's communication strategies: before they enter school, children have already mastered many communication strategies. No doubt, they have the potential for acquiring many more. If a teacher's concern is to help students in their relations with others important to them, then the study of the communication situation and associated strategies should be the focus of classroom instruction. The goal of communication instruction is to increase the child's repertoire of communication strategies for dealing with critical communication situations. This leads us to a discussion of the relationship between communication strategies and communication power.

communication strategies affect
communication power

A power philosophy of education is concerned with moving a child from a powerless position in society to one of power.[6] Our particular concern is with what can be called "communication power." Communication power can be defined as the ability to select from among options the ones best suited for accomplishing a particular objective. An approach that aims to increase the number of available options meets directly the prerequisites of a power philosophy. We can discuss communication power in two ways: as an internal or *felt* power and as an *expressive* power. A felt power is one that gives children a feeling of confidence and competence in dealing with important situations—for example, walking into a new school the first day, *curious* about the new friends they will meet instead of worried about making friends. Expressive power enables children to experience success through their use of language—as when children's suggestions are accepted by their friends, or when children call attention to themselves when they need it. Both kinds of power should be important considerations of an educational program concerned with a child's total development.

The goal of communication instruction is to provide learning experiences that will help children develop the communication tools they need in their power move. To accomplish this goal, children should be given opportunities to participate in communication situations that allow them to enhance their language performance skills through a wide variety of activities. These activities should be

---

[6] Beverly L. Hendricks, "The Move to Power: A Philosophy of Speech Education," *The Speech Teacher*, XIX (1970), 151.

based on the realistic and sometimes difficult situations children face in their struggle to make sense of themselves, the world, and others. A program of communication instruction should strive to increase children's repertoire of communication strategies so that when they are faced with a new and difficult situation, they can choose from available options the most strategic route to effective communication.

Effective communication: a co-orientational approach.   In our discussion of communication strategies thus far, it may appear that children's effective communication means that they get their own way. We certainly are not implying that educators should plan units on "How to Raise Your Allowance" or "How to Get Out of Household Chores." Admittedly, these might be attractive goals for many children, but our approach is not quite so child-centered. Our concern is not only with an individual's *success*, but also with the nature of the *interactive process* by which the goal is accomplished.

Many of us consider effective communication to be the successful accomplishment of our goal in communicating. If a girl's communication goal is to gain sympathy from her friend, and this goal is consistent with her friend's motives for communicating, few problems arise in considering "success" in accomplishing her goal as a measure of effective communication. The problems arise, however, when the persons engaged in communication have different motives and, consequently, inconsistent goals. If the girl seeking sympathy is met by a friend who wishes to give no sympathy, her communication goal is not compatible with that of her friend. When situations of this nature arise, as they often do, a co-orientational approach is necessary for judging communication effectiveness.

A co-orientational approach to communication effectiveness requires cooperation in the identification of a joint goal. Both participants reveal their initial goals in their expressions of the communication task. But when the participants discover the conflicting goals, attention must be paid to this difference. If a child's goal is to obtain permission to go to a friend's house to play and the mother's goal is to have the child help in caring for a younger sister, we have a clear mismatch of goals. The co-orientational view of communication we adopt is that both parties—the mother and the child—weigh their initial goals in terms of several factors:

1. Their degree of *compatibility*. (Can they both happen at once, or can they occur one after the other?)
2. Their *importance* to the needs of each participant. (Is one goal more strongly tied to an individual's needs than the other?)
3. Their relationship to the *ground rules* of the family. (Have there been prior agreements about the care of siblings?)

All of these factors have to be weighed in resolving the conflicting goals and producing a joint goal of communication. A judgment of communication effectiveness for either participant, the mother or the child, must be expressed in terms of the joint goal, not the conflicting initial goals. Consequently, when we discuss children's communication power, we are not talking about their ability to get their own way. Instead, we are talking about children's ability to communicate their needs and desires as they coincide with those of the person(s) involved in the situation.

Let's "turn it on"! Children are not completely powerless when they enter school. As we learned from the study of children's communication strategies, very young children are able to use language successfully to deal with the "problems" of their very narrow world. As children grow older, however, the situations they must face represent a wider world, and the problems are in many ways more difficult than those of preschool days. Children are now expected to function with ease in almost every social situation, yet their training has done little to provide them with communication tools for social situations that are often complex. It is up to the school, then, to activate children's power potential: the school must provide an open environment in which children can test and discover alternative communication strategies that they can use in the everyday situations they encounter. In other words, schools must help to develop children's communicative competence—their ability to perceive and categorize social situations and act accordingly.

Children must feel a sense of confidence in their own abilities as communicators (felt power). They must also be able to use language successfully and creatively in their everyday encounters with various persons, settings, topics, and tasks of conversation (expressive power). Communication strategies give children opportunities to achieve both kinds of power. The classroom must become an accepting environment in which children are allowed to experiment with communication strategies that could be of critical importance in their everyday communication encounters.

As children grow older, they learn how the factors of a situation make certain kinds of talking more appropriate than others. They learn which factors of the communication situation place demands upon *what can be said* and *how it should be said*. To "turn on the power," using the phrase of the children's television program, *The Electric Company*, let's take a closer look at the four parameters of the communication situation in terms of communication power.

Participants. In trying to understand children's communication, it can be extremely important to ask this question: To whom was the child speaking? Conversely, when looking at how a child responds to another person's speech, it is important to inquire about the other person, the person's status in relation to the child, and the control or power the person has in the eyes of the child. These participant-related factors might explain the nature of the child's response better than any other parameter of the situation.

Children with communication power know that they must gear their style of language to the person with whom they are talking. They must be able to recall past experiences with that person and draw on personal information that may be relevant to the present encounter. A young boy with communication power knows that his interview with the principal is likely to be about the incident in which he swore at his teacher in class. He also knows that the principal is a man who does not tolerate excuses but is impressed with neat appearances and good manners. Armed with this information and the task of trying to get off the hook, he is better able to plan his communication strategies. Perhaps a simple explanation of why he was so angry and an apology for swearing (which he now knows is wrong) will suffice. Then again, maybe he should just appear in his best clothes and wear a sad face.

Setting. Different settings provide different atmospheres for communication. A setting can refer to a physical locale—such as a schoolroom or a grocery store—or to a time or an occasion—such as when father returns home from work, or during a math exam. It is often said about children's communication that their motives are worthwhile but their timing is horrid. They ask their father for that new football just as he walks into the house after a tough day's work. They wait to obtain permission to go someplace at the very time when they must be at that place. The child with communication power knows how to weigh the factor of communication setting—the time and place of a conversation. The child with a basic understanding of timing and places knows that it's better to ask for that football after Dad relaxes and has eaten dinner. And permission is far easier to receive when the child plans ahead instead of waiting until that last tense minute.

Topic. Children want to be able to discuss matters that touch on their interests in some way. Children rarely need to be taught to be interested in something. All children turn their natural curiosity in some direction. It is often necessary to expose children to a variety of topics, giving them experience in discussing and listening to various approaches that can be taken in a conversation or discussion. Children become more powerful communicators as they develop a greater number of topic options, or subjects that they can talk about. Of greater importance, however, is that children know the "rules" concerning how and when a subject can be discussed. In other

words, not only do children with communication power have a
wealth of options related to the topics they can discuss, but more
important, they know which options to select in a particular
communication situation. If an eight-year-old girl is attempting to
discuss with her parents the fact that she is old enough to stay up an
hour later at night, it might be wise for her to avoid crying or name
calling as a means of "discussing" the topic of her maturity. It might
also be beneficial for her to avoid this same subject after complaining
that she was too tired to clean up her room or do her homework.

Task. It is often helpful in understanding children to ask this
question: What is the child's real objective in communication? Too
often, more attention is paid to how children are expressing
themselves in terms of grammar and pronunciation, than to what
they are trying to communicate. Children should be exposed to the
variety of ways in which language can be used to accomplish
communicative tasks. Children may benefit by seeing and hearing
others in the act of apologizing, asking questions, begging, and
persuading. These communication acts or tasks are important in
children's everyday experiences with others. Yet, each task cannot be
associated with a prescribed set of "how-to-do-it" rules. Instead,
there are various methods of accomplishing the same task, and the
success of any one method is relative only to the factors of the
communication event: the participants, the setting, and the topic. A
six-year-old boy may find that the best way to "talk" his mother out
of punishment is to lock himself in a room, bang a few things
around, and then remain perfectly silent, refusing to eat. This
method may work for this child but may prove to be a disastrously
hungry experience for other children. Another young boy may have
discovered that the best way to make up with his mother after an
argument is simply to apologize with a kiss and say an "I love you."
The child with communication power has more than one option or
method to accomplish the same objective.

The four parameters of the communication situation form the
dynamics of the communication event. A teacher can discover the
critical communication situations facing her students, the object of
Chapter 13. Children should be given opportunities to discuss and
participate in such situations in the classroom setting. By hearing and
observing how their peers handle critical communication situations
and by listening to ideas given by the teacher, children can learn
about novel approaches to a communication situation and can
experiment with new strategies.

SUMMARY

When children's language is viewed from the standpoint of the communication situation, the full impact of verbal and nonverbal language choices is understood. One way to understand the communication situation is by casting the event in a *dramatic* framework, in which each participant is an actor or actress with a script, assuming the role of the character. The entire performance takes place in a scene. Second, the communication situation can be viewed in terms of *categories* of usage. Situations are categorized in terms of the appropriate communication behavior required—for instance, "be polite" or "be quiet." The third view of the communication situation, and the most fruitful one for instruction, is based on communication *parameters:* the participants, the setting (time and place of the event), the topic, and the communication task.

Communicative competence is the mastery of appropriateness rules, based on cultural and situational norms, that affect the verbal and nonverbal choices in a communication situation. The verbal and nonverbal options that are selected in a situation can be called communication strategies. These strategies may result from random behavior, in which the option selected just happened to be the appropriate one, or from a more planned approach. Children acquire communication strategies in their day-to-day social experiences. The strategies at a child's disposal change in number and nature as he ages. Early strategies are typically nonverbal and quite obvious. Strategies of older children are more verbal and often subtle to others.

The purpose of communication instruction should be to increase the child's repertoire of communication strategies for critical communication situations. So that children can select the strategies most suitable for a particular situation, they must have a number of strategies available to them. A vast repertoire of strategies can increase children's communication power: an internal or felt power that gives them confidence in talking, and an external or expressive power that allows the children to experience "success" in day-to-day communication situations.

Effective communication does not involve simply the children's ability to get their own way; rather, it involves their ability to see their communication goals from a co-orientational perspective. When the goals of participants are alike, effectiveness is easily visible. But when individual goals are inconsistent, a joint goal must be created by the participants.

The aim of communication instruction should be to provide children with classroom experiences that increase their repertoire of communication strategies. Teachers can help children achieve some measure of power in their interpersonal relations. Instead of feeling relatively helpless in a multitude of communication situations, children can feel confident and optimistic—because they have an understanding of critical communication situations.

EPILOGUE

A poem was given to us by one of the mothers we interviewed for the study of children's communication strategies. The poem, "Recognition," by Barbara Burrow, illustrates how a mother gains insight into her own role as a mother from a role-playing performance by her daughter.

> "I don't want to hear another word!"
> I hear my daughter scold.
> "Dear me!" I think, "She's awfully strict
> for a playful three-year-old!"
> She rolls her big eyes heavenward
> And sighs with great disdain.
> "What am I going to do with you?"
> Her dolls hear her complain.
> "Sit down! Be still! Hold out your hands!
> Do you have to walk so slow?
> Pick up your toys! Go brush your teeth!
> Eat all your carrots! Blow!"
> I start to tell her how gentle
> A mother ought to be
> When blushingly I realize
> She's imitating me!

As we are studying children, it appears as if they are studying us.

SUGGESTED READINGS

CAZDEN, COURTNEY, "The Neglected Situation in Child Language Research and Education," pp. 81-101 in *Language and Poverty: Perspectives on a Theme*, ed. F. Williams. Chicago: Markham, 1970.
RODNICK, ROYCE, and BARBARA WOOD, "The Communication Strategies of Children," *The Speech Teacher*, XXII (1973), 114-24.

CHAPTER

13

communication instruction

The following dialogue represents a thirteen-year-old boy's attempt to describe a critical communication situation to an interviewer.

Interviewer: Think of a tough time you had talking to your Mom recently—a time that was important to you. Tell me about it.

Andrew: Well my science teacher picks on us, and when he picked on me the other day, he told my sister that I was a brat, or something like that. Then my sister told my mother and my mother asked me why I was, you know, a brat—or something like that.

Interviewer: Why was it such a hard time for you to talk to her then?

Andrew: 'Cause I couldn't think of any good reasons. I tried to tell her that it was the teacher's fault because he picks on me.

Interviewer: What did your Mom say?

Andrew: That I shouldn't be a brat.

Andrew found it difficult to convince his mother that his behavior in science class wasn't that bad. After all, from his point of view, the teacher (who picks on children) is partly to blame. According to

273

Andrew's comments in the remainder of the interview, no one really seems to understand why he does the things he does. His attempts to explain his own behavior are often difficult to handle but are very important to him: they are *critical communication situations.*

This chapter offers a *Communication Guide* to assist teachers in isolating critical communication situations encountered by the students. Since communication instruction must be adapted to the ages, backgrounds, and needs of the children in the class, communication information must be gathered prior to the actual classroom activities. Then, by giving children experience in observing and participating in communication situations that are important to them, the teacher will be helping to build their repertoire of communication strategies, verbal and nonverbal, for dealing with critical communication situations. The hub of instruction includes the goals of critical communication situations. Let's define these terms.

1. *Goal of communication:* what the child hopes to accomplish, generally, in the communication situation—for instance, information, sympathy, understanding, affection, attention, a course of action, praise.
2. *Critical communication situation:* the communication events that the child encounters (often with difficulty) and believes important in his interpersonal relationships with others.

It is important to remember that critical communication situations are child-defined: they are not prescribed by teachers, textbooks, or parents. If seven-year-old boys believe that impressing their friends with their collection of marbles is a critical communication situation, then this situation might be a focus for classroom study. Situations defined by parents or teachers can be considered critical communication situations if children agree that they are supremely important in their communication with others.

Figure 13.1 presents a model of communication instruction that serves as the basis for our situational approach. One component of the model contains the goals of critical communication situations given by children. These situations can be defined by the four parameters of a communication event. The other component includes the range of communication strategies—successful and unsuccessful—employed by children, based on the channels of communication.

The model accomplishes two important goals for communication instruction:

1. The model places in perspective all the aspects of the child's communication we have discussed in previous chapters. The channels of communication, such as voice, body, syntax, and meaning, are tied to the communication situation.

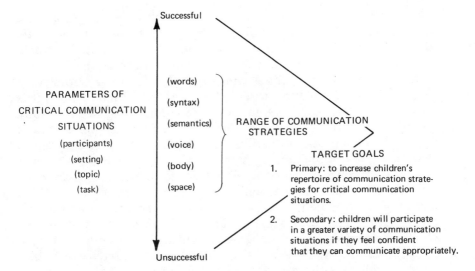

Figure 13.1.   *Children's communication: the instructional model.*

2. The model allows the teacher to visualize the various components of communication instruction as they relate to one another and to the goals of communication instruction.

The primary goal is this: *to increase the child's repertoire of communication strategies for critical communication situations.*
The greater the number of strategies children have at their command, the greater is their communication power. If children have a sizable repertoire of strategies for a situation, they will be able to *select* from among the available strategies the most appropriate and effective one(s) to deal with the situation. Further, a secondary goal of a situational approach is one of expansion: *children will participate in a greater variety of communication situations if they feel confident that they can communicate appropriately.*
        The remainder of this chapter explores the two areas presented in the communication model:

1. Discovering the critical communication situations encountered by children.
2. Designing a profile of children's repertoire of communication strategies.

Throughout our discussion we will utilize sample situations drawn from interviews with children.

DISCOVERING CRITICAL COMMUNICATION SITUATIONS

To tailor instruction to the class, the teacher should be willing to discover the critical communication situations children encounter in their relationships with others. This textbook does not prescribe a series of situations to be studied, although examples are frequently given. Instead, the text offers a *Communication Guide* that can help the teacher discover what situations should serve as the basis for instruction. Since the abilities and needs of children vary from grade to grade, from geographic area to area, and from time to time, it is virtually impossible to present an instructional plan that is fully equipped with the content for a series of communication activities. Critical communication situations must be defined by the children so that instruction is relevant to their everyday needs. When the teacher attempts, through classroom activities, to build a repertoire of strategies for real situations children encounter (primary goal), then, and only then, can children experience an inner sense of power (felt power) in coping with these situations. Then, and only then, can children exercise a certain degree of control in the outcome of the communication event (expressive power). The consequence is that children will have the necessary confidence to participate in a wider variety of communication situations (secondary goal).

To obtain a battery of critical communication situations to be adapted for classroom exercises in communication, *The Communication Guide* should be administered by the teacher to each student in the class. The administration of the questionnaire can be done in one of three ways, depending on the grade-level of the children, and the time available to the teacher.

1. *Oral interview:* The teacher interviews each child in the class on an individual basis. The time necessary for each child is approximately 20 minutes.
2. *Written method:* Particularly for older children able to write, the teacher can print forms of the questionnaire for children to answer in writing. The written procedure should be conducted in three phases, however: one phase (separate session) for each of the three persons the children are asked to talk about.
3. *Written and oral method:* Children can complete, in writing, Questions 1-7 in three sessions for each of the three participants to be discussed. A fourth session, in response to Questions 8 and 9, might involve an oral interview, so that children can discuss a difficult communication situation in greater detail than a written session would allow.

Obviously, children in their early elementary-school years must be given the oral interview method, while children in the higher grades can be given one of the two written forms. *The Communication Guide* is administered at the beginning of the school year and provides an opportunity for the teacher to get to know his or her students in a far more personal way than is usually possible. The initial commitment is heavy—there's no question about that. It takes time to talk with all the children, individually, or read their responses to the written questionnaire. The time is certainly well spent when you consider the advantages of the individualized instruction that it allows.

The interview session encourages children to discuss freely their communication experiences with persons important to them. The questions take a focus on the participant—that is, they ask children to talk about critical communication situations with three "important" persons.

The Communication Guide is entitled "People I Talk To" and is presented in the Appendix. The following are examples of some of the basic questions that are asked about each of the three important persons the child talks to:

> What's your favorite time and place to talk to __(name)__? This would be the time and place that's easiest for you to talk to __(name)__.
>
> Think about the subjects that are tough for you and __(name)__ to talk about. Name the subject that's really tough.

The first question deals with the communication setting and the second with the topic of communication. The teacher should adapt the specific questions of *The Communication Guide* to the age level and language abilities of the class.

understanding children's answers

Each section of *The Communication Guide* is explained below with the hope of providing teachers with a way to interpret children's responses. In most cases, categories for analysis are provided.

Introductory materials. Whether the oral interview, written, or written and oral method is employed, the introductory materials must be given orally. During the introduction to the interview it is important that the teacher establish an atmosphere that is both enjoyable and serious. Stress the idea that the subject is one that the child enjoys—his friends, his family, and the individuals he talks to every day. Because the contents of the interview are of a personal nature, it is important that the *privacy* of each interview is maintained. Specific situations and problems that a child talks about cannot be topics for discussion in the classroom. Since this might be the child's first experience with an interview, capitalize on the experience in follow-up discussion.

Participants. Children, like adults, talk to many people in the course of their days. To understand children's communication, the teacher should have some idea of the range of persons children talk to.

Often, we are familiar with just one segment of this range of persons—the child's school friends. Rarely do children talk to their teacher about their nonschool conversations with friends, parents, and siblings. Yet, it is often just these kinds of communication events, events that take place away from school, that are most important to the child. A good way to get to know a student is to understand something about his nonschool conversations. The first question in *The Communication Guide* asks for the names of three "special people" the child talks to frequently. Although the question does not insist that the child mention one friend, one sister, and one parent, for example, it does encourage the child to name persons other than his three best friends.

What can children's answers to the participant question tell us about their communication experiences? First, it tells us who the "special people" are that they talk to most frequently. Their answers give us a pretty good indication of the social range of their communication encounters. Second, their answers may tell us something even more important about their communication, in terms of the persons that are not mentioned. The "omission" of a parent, a sibling, or a particular classmate can sometimes tell us a great deal about the child's communication experiences. It might be worthwhile for the teacher to explore children's selection of "special people" in order to find out the reasons children employed in selecting each person.

Communication settings.   There are times and places in which we find it easy or difficult to talk to someone. The questions on setting allow the child an opportunity to mention these times and places. Setting involves the *physical location* of communication:

1. *School places:* in the classroom, in the hallway, on the playground.
2. *Home places:* in my room, in our yard, in the kitchen.
3. *Community places:* at the park, on the playground, at the beach, at someone's house.
4. *Public places:* in the grocery store, at church, at the movie theater.

Setting also involves the *temporal location* of communication:

1. *Clock times:* in the morning, in the evening, during the noon hour.
2. *Event times:* after school, when Dad comes home, when I eat, before I go to bed.
3. *Situational times:* when we're alone, when "X" isn't with us, when we're playing.

Times and places are necessary in the definition of a communication event. Communication does not take place in a physical and temporal vacuum. Of primary importance in studying children's communication is an understanding of what settings cause them difficulty when they talk to a person and in what settings they find themselves comfortable when talking to someone.

A discussion of communication settings will encourage children to talk about the times and places at which they talk with their three special persons. Answers to these questions may at times be difficult to interpret. For example, a child may make a very general answer to the *place* question: "It's easy to talk to Susan anywhere—I can't think of a place that's tough to talk to her." After some prompting, if the child doesn't change the answer accept the one provided. Another possibility is that a child may suggest a *time* that doesn't fit neatly into one of the three categories mentioned above. For example, the child may reply, "The only time it's tough to talk to my mother is when she's mad about something." The answer is an acceptable one and is probably related most closely to what we have called "situational times."

Topics of communication. The topic of communication is often called the subject matter of a conversation. The topic might concern an object, an event, a person, or an idea. The following are examples of each of these categories:

1. *Objects:* airplanes, dolls, bicycles, tools, books, pictures.
2. *Events:* baseball games, picnics, what happened in school, a trip or vacation, a party.
3. *People:* the child (self), sisters and brothers, parents, friends, strangers, the teacher.
4. *Ideas:* playing fair, happiness, cheating, loving, growing up, hurting.

It is important to know which topics are easy and which are difficult for children to talk about. Both kinds of information are helpful in designing classroom activities. Difficult topics can be discussed in order to find out what vital information the children lack about the subject. Since our knowledge of a subject affects the ease with which we can talk about it, communication activities that provide children with vital information on a critical topic will assist the child in communicating about that topic. Knowing which topics are relatively easy for children to talk about is important, too. These topics can be used in communication activities in which the instructional focus is on other communication problems.

Communication tasks. Asking children to talk about communication tasks is probably the most difficult "task" in the interview. Synonyms such as "mission" or "job,"terms that most children seem to understand, have been employed in the *Guide.* Yet, the concept of a communication task is not an easy one, especially for younger children. The key to discovering the communication task is contained in the verb phrase surrounding the child's description of a difficult communication situation.

1. *telling* Beth to try it "my way"
2. *asking* mother why I can't go
3. *requesting permission* to eat candy or cookies
4. *impressing* my father with "how good I was"
5. *giving an excuse* to my mother
6. *making* Johnny laugh

Each of these tasks can be related to an overall goal of the child's communication.

Remember that we defined a communication goal as what the child hopes to accomplish, generally, in the communication situation. Typical goals are the following: information, sympathy, understanding, affection, attention, a course of action, and praise. For example, "telling Beth to do it my way" has the goal of *a course of action*. "Asking mother why I can't go" seeks *information* but maybe more. If the mother doesn't produce a valid reason from the child's point of view, then his goal might be *sympathy* or *a course of action* (permission to go!). Requesting permission usually involves *a course of action*, and "impressing someone" can involve the goals of *attention*, *affection*, or *praise*. If Johnny gives an excuse to his mother for his behavior, his communication goal might be *understanding* or *sympathy*. Why do we make people laugh? Probably, to gain their *attention* or *affection*.

Although it is virtually impossible to ask children what their goal of communication is, it is both reasonable and important to ask them what they hoped to accomplish in talking to someone—their "mission" or task. If a child seems to have trouble reporting her difficult or easy tasks, then ask her to think of a particularly easy or difficult "talking situation" that happened recently and to describe it in detail. Often, this approach will draw an appropriate statement of the communication task. (Such a request is made in question 8 in *The Communication Guide.*)

As we discussed in Chapter 12, the effectiveness of the child's communication in any given situation must be measured from a co-orientational standpoint. If a boy's goal in communication is to impress his friend with his collection of marbles, and if he is able to achieve this goal without compromising his friend's needs and goals at the time, then the child's communication has been successful. On the other hand, if his goal is to obtain permission from his mother to go to a friend's home, and if he fails to obtain that permission, but for solid reasons ("Some other time—we have prior family plans"), then the child's communication has not been less effective because he didn't get his way. In fact, from a co-orientational point of view both the child and the parent are compelled to seek a joint goal, a goal quite different from the initial goal brought to the situation by the child. In return, the child receives an appropriate reason for the need to shift his original goal. Both the child and his parent gear their communication to account for the lack of fit between the child's original goal and the realistic needs of the here and now. By talking about the critical communication situations they encounter, children can begin to understand something about what it means to *change goals* in the course of communication, a predicament most children do not like to find themselves in.

Communication strategies. Each child is asked to talk about a critical communication situation ("tough task") with each special person. The child is encouraged to provide a blow-by-blow account of this situation so that communication strategies—the successful and the unsuccessful ones—can be recorded. Leading questions help to elicit the mention of strategies:

1. "When you did that (said that), did it seem to work? Did (name) think you had a good idea?"
2. "How could you tell that (name) thought it was a good idea (bad idea)?"

Although it is not necessary that the teacher directly record strategies, per se, it is essential that "what the child says and does" be carefully recorded. After the interview is completed, the children's account can be converted into statements of communication strategies. Since communication strategies are the actual verbal and nonverbal choices made by the child in a situation, the child's "message" in that situation must be studied in terms of the communication channels that were employed. The following are sample categories of strategies we have discovered in our use of *The Communication Guide:*

1. *Verbal strategies*
   repetition of a statement
   plea: an appeal to emotional and social well-being
   conventions: a statement of current practices
   reasons: based on age, experiences, ability, information, and other factors
   related information (often called an "excuse"): positive information in some
      area related to the subject
   direct questions
   statement of fact
   command
   suggestions

2. *Nonverbal strategies*
   raising the voice
   showing a sad (happy) face
   shaking my fist
   moving close
   whispered voice
   a smile
   fussing, bothering

A teacher will add and delete categories as appropriate for the grade level. Examples of other categories can be gathered from textbooks on persuasion. The next major section of this chapter presents ideas on how a teacher can record children's strategies.

The child's communication "wish." How often do we give children the chance to express a wish? Probably once a year—before they blow out the candles on their birthday cake. Even then we usually suggest that the wish be made silently; otherwise, it might not come true. Children's wishes often reveal something about them that we should know but don't. If we gave them more opportunities to express their wishes, we might learn about the most important ways we can help them develop.

In many instances, what a child considers to be out of the realm of the possible (and thus a wish) is not really impossible at all. A young girl may wish that someone was her best friend; with a few helpful hints from someone who cares about her that wish may come true. A young boy may wish that he was nicer looking but may consider that wish an impossible one. But appearances are often the outcome of personal relations and conversations. They're perceptions, not realities. A child who is respected by a friend—looked up to for advice and companionship—is usually considered attractive, physically. A child's wish that he were better at convincing a girl to like him may seem totally impossible from the child's point of view. With careful attention to the strategies he uses in trying to convince the girl to like him, he might realize that he was taking the worst possible approach. With some new ideas and a healthy discussion of how he appears to others, the boy's dream may come true.

If an instructional program is carefully geared to children's critical communication situations, then the most important effect should be seen with the child's wishes. Actually, a "communication wish" is the concept closest to a communication goal. Since the fulfillment of a wish (achieving a goal) is the product of successful strategies, instruction that centers on communication strategies should be most beneficial to the children as they try to make their wishes come true.

recording communication strategies: some examples

How can you discover the communication strategies that children use? An excellent method for becoming acquainted with the nature of communication strategies is by reading some examples found in an interview with Karen, a fifth grader. Karen talked with us about three important persons: her mother, her teacher, and a friend. Karen's comments are summarized for easier reading.

Mother: "tough task." Karen said that the most difficult job she has in talking to her mother is convincing her that she (Karen) should be allowed to choose her own clothes to wear to school. It seems that Karen is *the only* person in the fifth-grade class whose mother buys and selects clothes for her daughter "without even asking." As a result, Karen is the "worst dressed girl in the class." When Karen was asked what she said or did to try to change the situation, Karen said she told her mother 500 times that all the other girls in the class make fun of her clothes and that they all were allowed to select their clothes. Further, Karen said she always screamed to her mother that she wasn't a baby anymore but was always treated like one. Her mother's usual response was that Karen should stop acting like a baby.

Karen's "tough" situation with her mother could be characterized like this:

Topic: clothes selection (or Karen's maturity)
Task: being allowed to choose her own clothes
Setting: in Karen's bedroom, before she goes to school
Participants: Karen and her mother
Communication strategies:

Verbal	*Nonverbal*
repetition (asking again and again—500 times!)	screaming (raising her voice)
plea ("Others are making fun of me.")	
conventions ("Everyone else does!")	
reason based on age ("I'm not a baby anymore.")	

Teacher: "tough task." Karen has a lot of trouble informing her teacher that the reason she does so badly in math is because she isn't good at math, not because she doesn't study enough. The other day, when Karen received a poor grade on her math assignment, she knew she had to talk to the teacher about it. She approached the teacher at an appropriate time and whispered her "excuse." With her "sincere" smile she began to explain the predicament to her teacher. She said she could spend all day doing math problems and she still wouldn't do well; therefore, it's silly to spend much time doing math when she loves reading history. The teacher has told Karen's mother that the child would do significantly better on her math assignments if she would only spend more time on them in the evening. Karen thinks her teacher simply doesn't understand her. In fact, this misunderstanding is probably based on the fact that her teacher just doesn't like her—because of her clothes! (Karen snickered when she made this statement, but the interviewer thought she might have been pretty serious.)

Topic: mathematical inadequacies
Task: making excuses for poor performance
Setting: in the classroom, when assignments are returned to students
Participants: Karen and her teacher
Communication strategies:

Verbal	*Nonverbal*
reason based on ability ("I'm incapable!)	"sincere" smile
reason based on experience ("More time wouldn't help.")	whispered voice
related information ("I'm better in history.")	
plea ("You just don't understand me.")	

Friend: "tough task." Karen has trouble persuading Eric that he should be her boyfriend. Eric doesn't really like girls very much, but even if he did, he probably wouldn't like Karen (her own analysis). Eric even refuses to come over to her house after school. She asks him in a "polite" voice but it doesn't work. To show Eric that he isn't being nice, Karen calls his house and hangs up when he answers the telephone. (We were told that this was "confidential information," not for release to Karen's mother or Eric's mother.) Karen also has her girlfriends call Eric and hang up. As you might have guessed, Karen blames her lack of success on her terrible clothes (See, she was serious!) and on the fact that Eric is "too dumb" to listen to "reason." Karen asked the interviewer for her opinion as to the best method for capturing Eric as a boyfriend. The interviewer, wise in the ways of fifth-grade boys, suggested that perhaps Karen should find a new boyfriend and, at the least, stop calling Eric.

Topic: someone you'd like as a friend
Task: getting a person to "notice" you and like you
Setting: a variety of places—homes, school, neighborhood;
          times: during school, after school, at night—any time!

Participants: Karen and Eric; Karen's friends
Communication strategies:

Verbal	Nonverbal
direction question (the invitation	use of a "polite" voice
	fussing and bothering (all the telephone calls)

In spite of the light tone in our descriptions of Karen's problems, these problems are real situations in which Karen feels herself *powerless to act.* These are critical communication situations for Karen. She claims to have tried everything she could think of, without much success. Her communication strategies—strategies that she thinks are reasonable—lack that certain something, in most cases. Other children may excel in similar situations but have difficulties in others. Maybe Karen could learn something from her classmates if activities were constructed on the basis of the factors in the critical communication situations Karen has described.

Each of Karen's strategies can be related to more general techniques of persuasion, which have been studied for centuries in adult courses in persuasive speaking. There is no reason why instruction on "how to be convincing" should wait until we are members of the adult community. Children must deal with critical communication situations just as adults must deal with them. The child must be aware of the options she has in talking about anything that affects her life.

THE REPERTOIRE
OF COMMUNICATION STRATEGIES

As we discussed in Chapter 12, children often have little to say about what they do. At home, children are told when they must eat, what they should eat, and how to eat. They are told when to sleep, when to wake up, and how to act in a variety of situations. Often, reasons do not accompany such orders. If there is too much protest, punishment may await them. In the classroom, children are subjected to numerous rules of behavior. They are told when to be quiet, when to play, when to "feel like reading," and, perhaps most important, how to stand in a straight line to march to the bathroom. Moreover, children are too often viewed as empty containers, crying to be filled with information. Teachers often ignore those very human emotions of being bored, tired, hungry, or unhappy as justifiable reasons for "improper" behavior. Children who dare to express themselves are often labeled behavior problems through the school year. From this standpoint, children are the least powerful creatures on this earth.

For the children to have power in their interpersonal relationships, they must be able to increase their repertoire of communication strategies for dealing with important situations. Instruction at the elementary-school level can provide the children with opportunities to experiment with strategies they have not tried and talk about those they have found to be either successful or unsuccessful in certain situations. More important, instruction based on these goals cannot help but increase children's understanding of themselves, their communication, and hopefully, their relationships with others.

An important product of the interview with the children is the creation of a class profile of critical communication situations. Each situation is accompanied by a series of communication strategies organized according to their verbal or nonverbal nature. Further, the strategies can be ranked according to frequency of usage by the children in the class. A strategy-profile characterizes the range of communication strategies for any number of important communication situations cited by the children.

Question 8 in *The Communication Guide* serves as the basis for compiling the class profile. The children are asked to talk about difficult (task) situations for each of the three special persons they talk to. The total number of critical communication situations presented by the children should be three times the number of children. Fortunately, duplication of situations occurs, and so the total number of different situations will be more manageable. It is important that the similarities among situations be noted and that the number of times each critical communication situation is mentioned should be recorded on the profile. For example, if there are twenty-five children in a class and each talks about three difficult communication situations, then the seventy-five examples must be analyzed for similarities. Chances are that many children will mention similar situations, so that the master list *may* contain not more than a dozen situations (mentioned by a number of children) and their associated communication strategies.

Communication strategies are the verbal and nonverbal choices employed for a communication task. The *verbal* strategies are the most obvious in a child's account of a difficult communication situation. Often, the verbal strategies are identified by the child as "my reason," "an argument," or "a good point." At other times, the verbal strategies are labeled in a more subtle fashion by the child: "I just said. . . ." "I kept telling her. . . ," or "I tried to make him realize. . . ."

The nonverbal strategies are not mentioned with such frequency and are probably more difficult to "locate." Children may give only hints about their physical behavior or tone of voice. Their reports of nonverbal strategies will be weaker, mainly because in the minds of children words are the primary channel of communication. They fail to understand that nonverbal channels of communication are often more powerful than verbal means in performing a communication task. Simply note the nonverbal cues that are mentioned by the children.

To illustrate how the profile is prepared, let's explore some examples. Let's assume that we have discovered a similarity of description among four critical communication situations given by the children. We have reasoned that all four situations are similar enough to merit being called *Critical communication situation A:*

> *Critical communication situation A: child tells sibling he (she) wants privacy in the home, while playing with a friend after school, or during the weekend; child meets with a certain degree of resistance from sibling.*

The following are brief summaries of the children's descriptions:

1. Ann doesn't like to play with her little sister when her friend Sally comes over to play, but her mother likes her to keep an eye on the little child. Ann tries to tell her sister to go play by herself but she won't. She screams at her but this doesn't seem to work. The only way she can be alone with her friend is to tell her mother to take her sister away.

2. Frank likes to talk with his friend privately in his room when he comes over, but his sister always tries to "barge into" his room. He thinks she's a pest, but she "takes her time" leaving. He tells her the room is *his*, not hers, but that doesn't seem to impress her. Finally, after repeatedly ordering her out of his room and giving her a push, she leaves.

3. Beth often has a friend over for lunch on the weekend. She likes to have lunch with her friend—without all her brothers around. They pester the two of them constantly. Beth tells them they should be alone, but her brothers don't move. Finally, if she starts to cry, they go away.

4. When Gary and his friend Bob are playing with Gary's trucks and cars, his brother wants to play with them. He tells his brother to play by himself, but that doesn't seem to work. He makes suggestions about what he can do, but the suggestions don't interest the boy. The only thing that works is getting his mother or father to intervene and settle the problem.

By analyzing each of the descriptions, we might arrive at a list of strategies that looks like this:

verbal strategies	*nonverbal strategies*
plea for parental assistance*	screaming (raising the voice)
command to sibling to go*	pushing sibling away
repetition of command	crying
reason based on ownership	
suggestion to sibling of what to do	

*offered more than once in children's response

With more than four children, frequency of occurrence for strategies can be noted more specifically.

According to the children's accounts, some of the strategies were apparently successful and others were not. The apparent utility of each strategy can be noted. What were your reactions to the children's strategies? As you read the accounts, did you want to offer them suggestions? Did you wish you could have told the child about this idea or that idea? Maybe you hoped to offer more "reasonable" or "effective" means of achieving privacy. If children were more aware of the different communication strategies available to them in achieving their communication goals, then their selection of the most appropriate strategies for the situation would result in consequences more favorable to their wishes. Our purpose is to encourage children to ask "strategy questions" in difficult communication situations.

The final two chapters of this text outline the direction of classroom activities based on critical communication situations. Chapter 14 is based on an analysis approach: talking about communication situations. Chapter 15 is based on a synthesis approach: participation in communication situations. Both chapters provide suggestions for accomplishing the goals of communication instruction.

SUMMARY

The primary goal of communication instruction is to increase the child's repertoire of communication strategies in critical communication situations. The secondary goal is this: children will participate in a greater variety of communication situations if they feel confident that they can communicate appropriately. The instructional model contains two components. The major component reflects the parameters of communication in critical situations. Situations are defined by the four parameters of participants, setting, topic, and task. The second component includes the range of communication strategies employed by children in these communication situations. Communication strategies include the use of both verbal and nonverbal choices.

The starting point for communication instruction is gathering information from the children about the critical communication situations they encounter. A *Communication Guide* called "People I Talk To" is proposed and explained. Its purpose is to elicit from children valuable information about both easy and difficult factors of communication situations. The overall purpose of the questionnaire is the creation of a list of critical communication situations relevant to the children in the class. Each situation is accompanied by a list of verbal and nonverbal strategies that children employ.

CHAPTER

14

communication analysis:
a child's approach

When children are given an opportunity to say what they think about
something, almost anything can happen. *Life* magazine gave children
the opportunity to say what they thought about their own
communication, their parents, weekly allowances, their school, and a
number of other very important topics. Children were encouraged to
complete a questionnaire and mail it to the editors of *Life*.[1] The
polling firm of Don Bowdren Associates tabulated the responses of
over 250,000 children and presented the results to the editors. A
follow-up article was based on the children's responses.[2] Over 5,000
children attached letters to their questionnaires that explained their
opinions and feelings in greater detail. Most of the children's
responses indicated a strong awareness of a lack of effective
communication between children and adults.

Children took advantage of such a rare invitation to communicate their opinions and ideas. Comments made by children illustrated
their desire to be heard and to play a more powerful role in everyday
communication situations:

[1] "For Children Only," *Life*, October 17, 1972, 66.
[2] Tom Flaherty, "250,000 Children Have Their Say: 'We Don't Want to
Rebel, Just Be Heard,' " *Life*, December 29, 1972, 87-88D.

"Just because we're short doesn't mean that we can't say something worth listening to."

"My family has what they call a family meeting. Everytime I make a suggestion I am told to be quiet."

"My parents really don't listen to me. [They] think of me as a little child, and why should they listen to a child's opinion, right?"

"My parents only listen when they're mad at me."

"Did you know that parents and teachers can scream at you, but you cannot scream at them? We have feelings too."

In fact, one child suggested that the situation was serious enough to deserve sociopolitical action:

"I think there should be a Children's Lib."

An important implication of the article is that children want to talk about their rights and responsibilities, whether the setting is weekly allowances or communication with their family. The instructional focus of this chapter is based on this concern: children enjoy talking about communication situations and can profit from the analysis of such events.

The *communication analysis* approach has a distinct advantage for children of all ages and from all ethnic backgrounds: it is adaptable to the needs and concerns of the children in the class. Communication situations that are the focus of the analysis sessions can be selected with the children's needs and interests in mind. The situation-based approach is not biased toward children of a particular age from a certain background who speak a special form of the English language. Because the analysis sessions center on the entire event—the communication act—and not on speech conventions, per se, instruction cuts across age, geographic, and ethnic boundaries. The approach takes into account the fact that children have special needs, based on the communication rules generated by family and culture. The situational approach avoids the prescription of speech patterns typical of only a segment of our society. The goal of instruction in communication analysis is to build the children's repertoire of communication strategies with which they can deal with critical communication situations in their families and in their culture—in their own special world.

We proposed three methods of analysis instruction for meeting this goal:

1. "Who? What? When? Where? Why?": Children analyze critical communication situations according to the parameters of the event.
2. "How Could You Tell?": Children analyze a communication event in terms of how the various channels convey affective meaning.

3. "Do You Have a Few Words to Say?": Children use recording aids to tape interviews with other children; situations are then analyzed according to the communication parameters.

The three methods involve communication activities. These activities offer examples of communication situations to be discussed and analyzed by the students in the class. The analysis sessions focus on parameters of the event and the channels of communication. The instructional objective of the activities is this: children will gain strategies for effective communication in a particular situation by observing and analyzing models of that situation.

"WHO? WHAT? WHEN? WHERE? WHY?"

This activity presents children's terms for the four parameters of the communication event outlined in Chapters 12 and 13. In essence, the linkage is this:

participants = who?
topic = what?
setting = when and where?
task = why?

Based on the class profile of critical communication situations, the teacher can begin searching for examples of the situations. Examples can take the following forms:

1. *The filmed event:* a communication situation portrayed in a movie or a segment of a film.
2. *The televised event:* a communication situation presented in a television program.
3. *The picture event:* a communication situation pictured in a magazine article, photograph, or cartooned drawing, coupled with a prepared dialogue to be read to the class.
4. *The witnessed event:* a communication situation that all children in the class witnessed as it happened.

The presentation of the communication event can assume any one of these four forms; the children thus experience the event in a firsthand manner.

The sample situations should be relevant to the children's needs and experiences. This is another way of saying that the activity is based on critical communication situations. The teacher is responsible for translating the parameters of the children's situations into sample situations that the children can observe and analyze. The process of translation is based on the parameters of communication previously discussed: topic, task, participants, and setting. Children answer the "who," "what," "when," "where," and "why" questions for each event. Five questions can be employed in the analysis of communication events:

1. *Who* are the people in this conversation? Tell me about them. (participants)
2. *What* were <u>(name of participants)</u> talking about? What was the subject of their conversation? (topic)
3. *When* did their conversation take place? Tell me about the time. (setting: time)
4. *Where* did their conversation happen? Tell me about the place. (setting: place)
5. *Why* do you think they had a conversation? Did each person have a different mission or purpose? (task)

participant question

The "who" question asks the children to identify the persons involved in the communication situations. It is important that all communicators be identified, not simply those who talk the most or say something aloud. Children, as well as adults, tend to identify only the "speaking" individuals, eliminating those who send their messages by means of body language or spacing patterns. If this happens in an analysis session, take the opportunity to outline the many ways we send our message—with our words, our voice, our bodies, and the space "we make" around us. Explain that people don't have to speak words to communicate.

The following model situation may help clarify this point. Children in a fifth-grade class watched a scene from a television program in which a girl was asking to be forgiven for a misdeed. She was doing most of the talking, but her father was asking questions throughout the emotion-filled conversation. The mother was probably more upset than the father, but since she simply sat on the couch, watching and listening but not talking, the fifth graders identified the participants as *child* and *father*. When the teacher asked if the mother was "in the conversation," the children said, "No—she didn't say anything." "But is she saying something?" asked the teacher. "Do you know how she feels? How do you know?" Because the children couldn't forget the mother's sobs and sad face, they admitted her "message" was clear—she was very upset about the whole situation and she was definitely communicating this non-verbally. Following this exchange the fifth graders agreed to include the mother as a participant.

topic question

Children should be encouraged to name the topic of communication in *specific terms*. A relatively easy way to encourage this is by suggesting that they use the wording of the participants whenever the topic is stated too generally. In fact, the selection of topic language is an excellent focus for discussion. The following questions are based on a magazine picture that portrays a boy talking to his father, who is repairing the engine of the family car. The teacher created a dialogue between the father and boy that demonstrated the boy's awareness of the names of parts of the car. After the presentation of the picture and dialogue, the teacher asked these questions:

1. When you talk about cars, do you use words like this boy used (words such as "carburetor," "plugs," and "points")?
2. Were there other things the boy could have said about the car?
3. If you talked like this boy did about cars, do you think other people would understand what you're saying?

By asking children to think about the way they talk about a certain topic, we can expand their repertoire of communication strategies that are related to that topic. If the sample situations are relevant to the children's experiences, they will provide an excellent opportunity for the children to explore new words (morphology) and patterns of words (semantics, syntax) that can be used in critical communication situations.

setting questions

The analysis of communication setting often produces the liveliest segment of the discussion. Following the identification of the time and place of the communication event, the children are asked to talk about the relation of the setting to the outcome of the event. The following questions are helpful in directing children's attention toward this relationship:

1. If this had happened (name another place), would it have happened in the same way?
2. If this had happened (name another time), do you think it would have turned out the same way?

Since most communication events are strongly tied to the communication setting and since "what happens" might be a product of the setting, children should consider the setting-outcome relationship.

To illustrate, let's consider a communication situation involving a *witnessed event* that all the children experienced. In the middle of the lunch period in the school cafeteria, a boy at the next table was acting inappropriately—yelling and pushing food around. A teacher approached the boy and scolded him for his behavior. Everyone in the lunchroom heard and saw what happened; all talking stopped and all eyes were on the teacher and boy. In response, the boy dropped his head, said nothing, and didn't look up for quite some time. In this example, the setting had a strong effect on the participants' feelings and behavior. If the boy had been scolded in a different setting, not in the lunchroom where everyone could watch, the situation might have been very different. From the boy's point of view, the setting was very embarrassing.

The task of selecting the most appropriate setting for communication is often the child's downfall. Requesting permission to go to a friend's home may produce unpleasant results if a child approaches her mother in the privacy of her bedroom (place) when she's engaged in an important telephone conversation (time). Asking Father for that new baseball as soon as he arrives at the front door (place) after a difficult day at work (time) can be disastrous from the child's point of view.

task question

Understanding the communication task(s) in a conversation requires careful attention to how the participants interact with each other. The question "Why do you think they had the conversation?" urges children to think about the communication task(s). The term "mission" can help in focusing attention on the goal of a participant's message. To determine a person's "mission," children should be encouraged to pay close attention not only to what a person says, but also to how he says it. Is his face telling us something that his words are not? Is his voice showing one "mission" while his words seem to be saying something else?

If the participants do not share a compatible goal of communication, then the analysis of *task* can be difficult. Let's assume that children have viewed a cartoon drawing of a mother asking her little girl to clean up her room. The mother's mission is to make her child understand that she *must* clean up her room. The child's mission, on the other hand, is not compatible with the mother's: she wants to do something else. If the picture and dialogue portray the conflict of missions, then the children must be able to talk about the apparent conflict. The possible results of communication can be presented to the class:

1. The child cleans her room, (or)
2. The child is allowed to go elsewhere—she does not have to clean her room, (or)
3. A "bargain" is made—for example, she will clean her room when she returns.

"What will probably happen in this situation?" At this point, children are asked to propose which outcome seems to be the most likely one, based on the picture and dialogue. Did the child do a pretty good job convincing her mother that she "can't do it now"? Was the mother so strict in her face, body, and words that she wouldn't budge? Discussion of communication tasks eventually turns to the consideration of communication strategies, and children should be encouraged to talk about appropriate strategies for each situation.

"HOW CAN YOU TELL?"

The "How Can You Tell?" activity is based on critical communication situations that are role-played by children who volunteer. The situations must be planned in detail so that the children who role-play them will know exactly what they are to say and do. The purpose of the activity is to make the children more aware of the messages people communicate with their words, patterns of words, voices, bodies, and the space around them.

Critical communication situations (scenes) must be selected, and instructions for the children (how to "act the scenes out") must be provided. After the scene has been presented by the volunteers, the children in the class are asked two series of questions:

1a. How did (person A) feel about (topic)?
2a. How could you tell?

1b. How did (person B) feel about (topic)?
2b. How could you tell?

Questions 2a and 2b are designed to focus children's attention on how the channels of communication help explain a person's feeling toward the topic of conversation.

To assist children in answering the "How Could You Tell?" questions, a framework for their answers can be provided. In fact, options can be listed on the blackboard to stimulate the analysis session. For older children (say, grades 4-6) the teacher may wish to list the channel options in this manner:

1. The *words* he (she) used were the best clues.

2. The *voice* of the person was the best clue.
3. His (her) *body*—face, arms legs—gave the best clue.
4. The *distance* between the persons talking was the best clue.

For younger children the options can be presented visually. Figure 14.1 suggests a visual manner of presenting the channels of communication. The chart can be demonstrated vocally and visually for the children as it is recorded on the blackboard. For example, the teacher should be prepared to present the "glad voice," the "sad voice," and the "mad voice" aloud.

The following are examples of critical communication situations that could be employed in "How Could You Tell?" activities. The major purpose of the examples is to provide guidelines for the teacher in preparing the scenes. The descriptions must contain at least as much detail as is provided in the examples, so that the students who role-play the scenes know what they must accomplish.

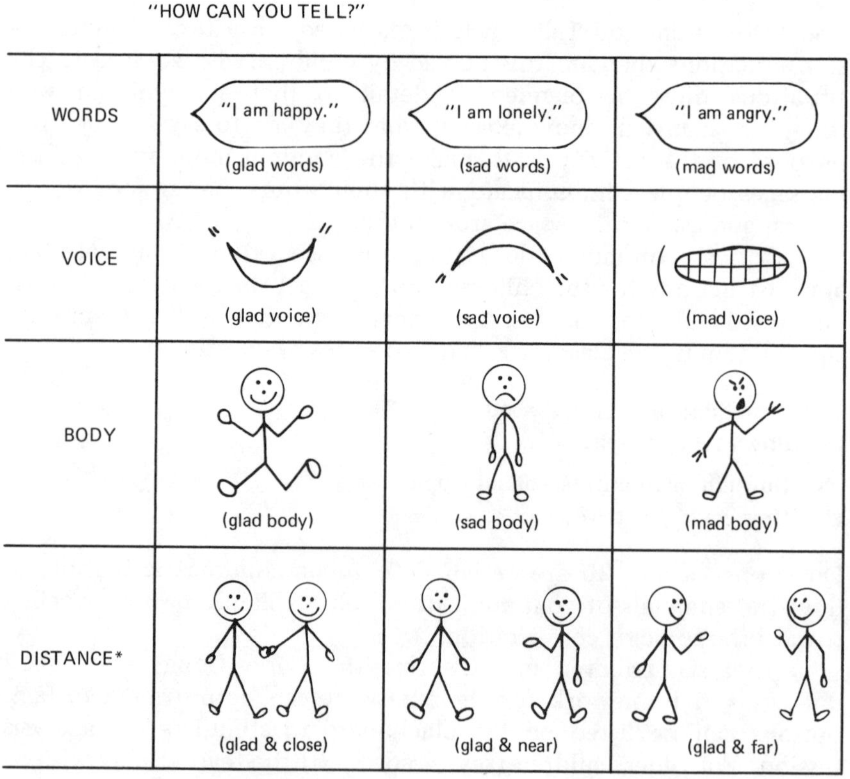

"HOW CAN YOU TELL?"

*Only one emotion (gladness) is pictured with the close, near and far distances. Others could be pictured at each of the three distances.

Figure 14.1. *Visual representation of the channels of communication.*

SCENE 1: "The Bad Report Card"

Topic: a student's bad grades on a report card

Task: The child (Richard) is embarrassed about the grades he received. When Richard shows his report card to his father, he tries to give excuses for why he did so poorly ("Everyone did lousy"; "My teacher's not very fair"; "There must be a mistake"). The father is very angry and upset with his son. He scolds him as they talk.

Setting: after dinner, in the home

Participants: father (person A) and Richard (person B)

SCENE 2: "The Secret Plan"

Topic: playing a trick on the teacher (for example, putting a frog or some other animal in her desk)

Task: Tommy explains his plan to play a trick on the teacher to his friend Billy. Tommy is very excited about his plan to put a frog in the teacher's desk after recess. He tries to enlist Billy's help. Billy is scared—he doesn't think they should do it. He tries to talk Tommy out of doing it, coming up with reasons why it would be bad ("We'd get caught, for sure"; "She would probably faint"; "I'm too scared— I don't dare!").

Setting: on the playground, during recess

Participants: Tommy (person A) and Billy (person B)

SCENE 3: "Dressing for School"

Topic: selection of clothes to wear to school

Task: Johnny tries to make his mother understand that he must be allowed to wear his old blue jeans and tie-dyed T-shirt to school that day. ("All my friends are wearing their grubbiest clothes today—I have to, too.") He sees that his mother doesn't agree with his idea, so he becomes very upset as the conversation continues. His mother thinks the clothes look terrible and tries to make him understand that children shouldn't dress like that. She is horror-stricken with his selection of clothing and suggests that he wear something else.

Setting: in the home, before breakfast (and school)

Participants: Johnny (person A) and his mother (person B)

The success of "How Can You Tell?" activities depends partly on the effectiveness of the role playing. To insure success, the teacher can give the children precise instructions as to what is to take place. If the children understand their roles, they will be able to create an interesting and often humorous scene. Their feelings will be communicated in many ways: through their words, their voices, their bodies and in the space they keep between themselves and the other participants. Consequently, the class should be able to identify more than one channel for the communication of feelings in each scene.

"DO YOU HAVE A FEW WORDS TO SAY?"

If the school has cassette tape recorders available for classroom use, this activity offers an excellent opportunity for introducing children to the use of audio-visual aids. Further, children can learn something about conducting interviews. With increased exposure to television interviews, whether of the news variety of *Sesame Street* interviews with Kermit D. Frog, children have some notion of how interviews are conducted. The recorded interviews provide the materials for communication analysis. If only one cassette recorder is available, the children can take turns using it.

The activity works best when children are encouraged to interview a friend or sibling, a relatively easy participant to talk to. The child should not be a member of the class, however. The interview format might look like this:

Interviewer: Hello. My name is __(name)__ , and I'm here today to interview my friend, __(friend's name)__ . I have a few questions to ask you about what makes you happy and what makes you sad. First, let's talk about *what makes you happy.* Do you have a few words to say?

Friend: (answers the question)

Interviewer: Very interesting. Now, tell us about what makes you sad. Do you have a few words to say?

Friend: (answers the question)

Interviewer: Good—very interesting. Can we quote you on that? (a semilegal tactic)

Friend: (says "yes," hopefully)

Interviewer: Thank you very much. This has been __(name)__ reporting to you from __(location)__.

Preparation for the interviews should include instruction on the following topics:

1. How to use a cassette recorder.
2. How to conduct a brief interview (using a format like the one above).
3. How to encourage someone to talk. (For instance, if the friend doesn't answer the question, ask it again, using other words.)

Each child in the class records an interview and plays it for the class at a scheduled time.

The happy and sad stories usually provide interesting materials and ideas for the discussion of communication events. Each situation can be discussed according to its communication parameters:

1. Who is———with when he is happy (sad)? (participants)
2. What are they talking about, if they are talking? (topic)
3. When did this take place? (setting—time)
4. Where did this take place? (setting—place)
5. What was———trying to do? (task)

Although the recorded interviews may not provide answers to all these questions, the student interviewer can make suggestions or guesses based on his knowledge of the friend or sibling.

The value of "Do You Have a Few Words to Say?" activities rests with the threefold opportunity for learning: (1) the use of audio-visual devices, (2) interview procedures, and (3) analysis of communication parameters.

TEACHER GUIDELINES: COMMUNICATION ANALYSIS

Communication analysis activities can result in exciting awareness sessions about communication. Generally, however, the degree of awareness will depend on certain factors within the teacher's control. Following these guidelines will help insure the effectiveness of this type of instruction.

1. The teacher must select appropriate communication situations for analysis. Careful planning before the class session is necessary. Selection should be based on the critical communication situations derived from the class profile.
2. The communication events to be analyzed by the children must be well executed. If they are presented by audio-visual devices, the playback levels should be adjusted appropriately so that all children in the class can hear (and see) the event with ease. If pictures or cartoons are employed, an overhead projector might be the best method of presentation. The volunteers for the role-played situations should be encouraged to study their roles carefully before beginning and to enact the situation so that everyone can see and hear what's taking place.
3. The analysis session must hinge on criteria (such as a list of communication channels) or specific questions (for instance, "Why do you think they had a conversation?"). A discussion without specific guideposts becomes rambling, whereas a discussion guided by a list of things to talk about helps steer learning in effective directions.

SUMMARY

To increase a child's repertoire of communication strategies for critical communication situations, the approach of communication analysis can be employed. This approach involves observation and discussion of communication situations that children encounter. Three methods of analysis are suggested:

1. Children analyze "live" communication situations or those presented on film, on television, or in a picture coupled with dialogue. The objective is to define the communication parameters ("Who? What? When? Where? and Why?").
2. Children analyze communication events in terms of how the channels of communication (words, voice, body, space) convey affective meaning. These are "How Can You Tell?" activities.
3. Using cassette recorders, children conduct interviews with their friends. The interviewer asks "What makes you happy?" and "What makes you sad?" The activity, "Do You Have a Few Words to Say?" offers instruction in audio-visual aids, interviewing, and communication analysis.

The communication analysis method aims to increase children's awareness of the situational factors operating in communication events.

CHAPTER
15

participation
in communication situations

The *participation approach* to communication instruction allows every child in the class the opportunity to take part in communication experiences. The major advantage of the participation approach is that children are given assistance in their *performance* in communication events; the children do not simply talk about such situations. An example of the participation approach to learning should be helpful in illustrating this advantage. A first-grade class was engaged in a unit on career education. The objective of the unit was to create an awareness in children of the various types of careers available to individuals. The teacher decided that the best way to foster an awareness of various occupations was to create role-playing situations centered on the job interview. Groups of two were formed, and the children were allowed to decide who would be the employer and who would be the person applying for the job. The children were free to select the job opening and the dialogue of the job interview.

The results were informative and amusing, from an adult viewpoint. A girl interviewing for a maid's position was asked if $500.00 per week would be an adequate starting salary. A boy applying for a teaching position (in their own elementary school) was told that the yearly starting salary was "a big $1,000.00." The descriptions of duties given by the "employers" were humorous: a business executive simply had to dress well, a bank teller merely had to be able to count to 100, and a worker in a garment factory had to have twenty-twenty vision. The role-played interviews provided the teacher with material for follow-up discussion on the nature of various careers and their prerequisite talents.

The value of the participation method, at least in this instance, was that the children were actively involved in presenting their own ideas about careers. The role-played interviews exposed their conceptions and misconceptions, indicating to the teacher what direction the discussion should take. The participation approach in communication learning follows this same rationale: children actively participate in critical communication situations, which are then discussed in class.

The following are three activities based on the participation approach:

1. Critical communication situations are role-played by the children in the class; the situations to be role-played are "real" ones.
2. The critical communication situations to be role-played by members of the class are "unreal" ones.
3. Children encounter critical communication situations through field experiences in communication.

Whereas the focus of the analysis approach (see Chapter 14) was on the parameters of communication, the focus of the participation approach is on communication strategies.

ROLE-PLAYING COMMUNICATION SITUATIONS

Among the various speech communication activities available for instruction, role playing is probably the activity the children enjoy most. Role playing is an active form of instruction. Participation involves all channels of communication: words and patterns of words, the voice, the body, and the use of space. The teacher should define the situations to be role-played in terms specific enough for the children to understand their roles.[1]

---

[1] The role-playing categories, "real" and "unreal," including methods for employing them in classroom instruction, are based on Diane Shore, "Teaching Territoriality To Children," *Illinois Speech and Theatre Journal*, XXV (1971), 29-32.

"real" situations

The "real" communication events are drawn from situations frequently mentioned by children in *The Communication Guide*. In other words, the situations to be role-played are based on communication events encountered by the children in the class. The teacher translates the critical communication situations into hypothetical examples, however; "real" names and exact places are not employed. The teacher's re-creation should approximate the children's experiences.

Selection of participants for role playing can be done on a volunteer basis, or the children can simply take turns. Each child is given his or her role in the event, including information in these areas:

1. Who am I? (participant) (Specific names should always be given.)
2. Where and when is the event taking place? (setting)
3. What is the subject of communication? (topic)
4. What is my mission? (task)

The purpose of the exercise is to give each child an opportunity to accomplish a mission in the best possible manner. The communication strategies (verbal and nonverbal) employed by each child in the role-played situation will be the highlight of the class discussion that follows.

"unreal" situations

A second approach to role playing—one that children seem to enjoy because of its uniqueness—involves an "unreal" situation—unreal because one of the channels of communication is *altered* in the description of the scene to make the event seem silly or unusual. By altering a channel of communication, such as *communication space* (for example, having a child express affection for a friend in the public distance zone), the event takes on a certain value: in their attempt to perform normally in the communication situation, the children will see the importance of the altered channel more vividly than if all channels operated normally.

The following are examples of unreal role-playing situations with one channel ("the hitch") altered.

1. Participants: girl and boy (Jane and David)
   Setting: on the playground, during recess
   Topic: What to do after school

Task: the girl tries to convince the boy to come over to her house; she has a new puppy that she wants him to see; the boy pretends he doesn't want to come over, but the puppy interests him.

The hitch: the girl is very excited, but she isn't allowed to move her face, her arms—her entire body—when she tries to convince the boy. She has to remain "frozen." (body language channel)

2. **Participants:** teacher and boy (Mrs. Jones and Bob)
   Setting: before school starts, at the teacher's desk
   Topic: assignments not completed by the boy
   Task: the teacher scolds the boy for failing to turn in his assignments—three drawings of flowers and trees they studied; the boy tries to make excuses about why he doesn't have them done.
   The hitch: the boy isn't allowed to look directly at the teacher. He has to look somewhere else and can never look into her face or eyes. (space channel)

3. **Participants:** a boy (Jim), his boyfriend (Ralph), and Jim's sister (Beth)
   Setting: Saturday morning in Jim and Beth's livingroom, in front of their television set
   Topic: who should be allowed to be in the room to watch cartoons
   Task: Jim tries to make Beth leave the room so that he and Ralph can have privacy. Beth really wants to watch television, too. Jim gets very angry with his sister. Ralph says he doesn't want Beth there either.
   The hitch: Jim is not allowed to change his voice at all—his voice cannot be an angry voice (but he's definitely angry). (voice channel)

4. **Participants:** a girl (Leslie) and her mother (Mrs. Parker)
   Setting: in Leslie's room, before breakfast
   Topic: what Leslie should wear to school
   Task: Mrs. Parker had selected a dress for school, but Leslie doesn't want to wear the dress. She wants to be able to choose her own clothes, but her mother doesn't think she's old enough. They argue about this.
   The hitch: Leslie tries to convince her mother she should be able to choose her own clothes, but she can't give *age* ("I'm old enough!") or *friends* ("All my friends can!") as reasons. (word channel)

Of course, any of these unreal situations could serve as a real situation for role playing if the "hitch" is removed. The rationale for role-playing unreal situations is that this activity emphasizes the importance of the various communication *channels* in verbal and nonverbal strategies. The activity helps children realize that accomplishing a communication goal is a product of their words and how they say something, the messages sent by their voices and bodies, and the communication space that they employ. The unreal situations help children see how much they take the nonverbal channels of communication for granted. The "hitch" may seem unrealistic, but its role is to help children understand that communication strategies are both verbal and nonverbal.

talking about the role-played situations

A crucial portion of the role-playing activity is the classroom discussion of the events after they are performed. For the real situations, the teacher should encourage discussion of the communication strategies employed by the children (the participants) by asking direct questions about word choices, ways of saying things, tone of voice, facial expressions, and so on. If situations 1-4 were used without the "hitch," discussion questions might be the following:

1. What different things could Jane have said to convince her friend David to come over to her house after school? (situation 1)
2. What else could Bob have said or done in order for his teacher to better understand his position? (situation 2)
3. How could Jim get his sister to leave the room without creating hard feelings? Could they make some kind of a deal? (situation 3)
4. What other reasons could Leslie have given her mother for being allowed to select her own clothes to wear to school? (situation 4)

Questions such as these ask the children to consider alternate strategies of communication—strategies not employed in the role-played event. They are encouraged to think of the many ways that a communication goal can be accomplished. The teacher can encourage children to give suggestions based on their own experiences. Some of the suggestions will relate to strategies that were successful and others that were not so successful. Consideration of the *appropriateness* and *effectiveness* of these strategies should be discussed.

The discussion period following the unreal role-playing situations can begin with the approach just outlined, but can be expanded to include a discussion of what effect the "hitch" had on the outcome of the conversation. Questions such as the following can be employed to initiate discussion about the importance of a communication channel to communication strategies.

1. Why did it seem silly that Jane couldn't move when she tried to convince her friend Bob to come over to her house? What could she have done with her face or arms, for example, to convince him to come to her house? (situation 1)
2. Why was it silly for Bob to give his excuses without looking at the teacher? If he looked right at her, would their conversation have been different? How would it have changed? (situation 2)

3. Why did Jim's voice sound funny when he was angry with his sister for bothering him and his friend? When we get angry, what happens to our voice? (situation 3)
4. Leslie couldn't say "I'm old enough!" or "My friends can!" in trying to convince her mother she should choose her own clothes. Do you think these reasons are good? Do they work in your house? Did Leslie really need these two reasons? (situation 4)

Questions such as these draw attention to one of the channels of communication to illustrate its importance in performing a "mission."

THE FIELD STUDY

The field study method of participation gives children a chance to take part in more natural communication contexts. The children are guided to experience certain parameters of communication "in the field." Field experiences are suggested by the teacher and are based on student needs. The situations are presented in terms of the parameters of the event: participant, topic, setting, and task. Field experiences are best arranged to occur after school. Following the experience, children describe to the class what happened.

This method is appropriate if certain restrictions are observed. For example, it would not be advisable to ask all children to go home to their parents and try to convince them they should receive a bigger allowance each week (or even an allowance, per se). This kind of field experience may cause school-home conflict, particularly if all children report to their parents, "Our teacher made everyone go home and do this, so you have to listen to me!" Activities should be used for the study of critical communication situations that have no relationship to politics, money, or sex.

The field study approach is effective for children at all grade levels. The activities selected should be appropriate to the interests and needs of the particular class. Let's examine three possible categories of field experiences involving critical communication situations; the categories are distinguished by the other participant in the situation: (1) a sibling (brother or sister), (2) an "important person," and (3) a new friend. We'll illustrate each category with examples.

the sibling field experience

The teacher might want to suggest that each child in the class approach a brother or sister (or friend, if the child has no siblings) with a plan of action. The field experience can be called *Mission: Impossible*. The children should plan their mission just as carefully as the staff of *Mission: Impossible* does. The topic and the task of the mission are given to the children, but they are allowed to select the communication setting. On the following day, the children report to the class a blow-by-blow account of what happened in their mission. Here are some examples of missions:

1. Making a bargain with a sister or brother: the child is encouraged to draw up a bargain (for instance, on exchange of chores or household obligations with a sibling).
2. Borrowing a favorite possession: the child attempts to borrow a sister's or brother's favorite possession to take to school the next day.
3. Trading a toy or possession: the child tries to initiate a trade of important toys or possessions with a sister or brother.
4. Asking a favor: the child asks his sister or brother a very important favor (such as finding a lost object, constructing something, or helping with an activity).
5. Seeking advice: the child is encouraged to ask the advice of a sibling on an important matter related to the child's future plans (for the evening or on the weekend, for example).

The children should be encouraged to make up a detailed *plan of action*. In fact, the children might be warned that even the best plans of the *Mission: Impossible* experts often do not work. Each child reports to the class on the outcome—even if the carefully planned mission was a failure.

Each report is followed by a discussion of the mission. The children should talk about why their plans were or were not effective. They should be encouraged to present reasons explaining why some missions failed and others were successful. Reasons can be based on three points:

1. The setting was not right. Because each child was allowed to select a setting for communication, the first issue discussed might be the relation of the setting to the outcome of the mission.
2. The strategies were not effective. Every *Mission: Impossible* expert employs strategies, and the children should understand an analogy between *MI* strategies (gadgets, tape recorders, weapons) and their own communication strategies (reasons, arguments, kindness, persuasiveness). Discussion should focus on the potential effectiveness of the child's strategies.
3. The mission *was*, for all practical purposes, "impossible." Select this reason for explaining the outcome only if the other two reasons don't help to explain the ineffectiveness of the mission.

the important-person field experience

A difficult communication situation for many children, as well as for adults, is meeting and talking with a person of relatively high authority. A school official, an employer, or a local politician may represent demands on the communication situation that stem from our perception of their status or authority. Experience in meeting "important persons" can begin during elementary-school years.

To begin this field experience, children in the class create a list of important persons in their neighborhood or community. The list might include doctors, nurses, firemen, policemen, store clerks, and drivers of public transportation. After the list is created, the teacher should lead a discussion about why it might be difficult to talk to important persons. Since most reasons will probably relate to not knowing what to talk about, the topic and task of communication in the field experience are given:

Topic: *danger* faced by people who do important work

Task: finding out what aspects of an important person's job are dangerous to that person and to others (*question*)

Danger can take a number of forms, and the purpose of the task question is to discover what these forms of danger are. The children are given this sample question: "What do you think is the most dangerous part of your job? Let's talk about it." From the standpoint of communication, children are given a *task strategy*—a question—for handling this kind of communication experience.

The value of the important-person field experience is that children are guided in meeting persons of high authority whom they would like to talk to. Because a task strategy is given to the children (a question about the dangers of a job), the communication situation can be more comfortable for children. The goal of the activity is to instill confidence in children for future encounters with important persons. The confidence stems from knowing what to talk about with the person—the discovery of task strategies.

In preparation for the field experience, children should be given instructions on introducing themselves to persons they do not know and asking questions to begin a conversation. The children might benefit from practice in both techniques. Role playing in the classroom might be an excellent way for the children to ready themselves for the field experience. The teacher can stress the importance of establishing a common ground with a listener (for example, by saying, "We live in the same neighborhood") before asking a question. The follow-up discussion can focus on two points:

(1) the various forms of danger in the different jobs; and (2) how it feels to talk to an important person, from the child's perspective.

the new-friend field experience

There are often times when children would like to meet someone—a new child in the neighborhood, an older sister of a friend, or a child in another classroom—but they aren't quite certain how to go about it. A field experience in meeting a new friend is helpful for children of all ages. The instruction consists of three parts:

1. Classroom instruction and discussion about what happens when we meet someone: how we introduce ourselves, what we talk about, how we feel when we meet someone new.
2. The actual field experience: getting to know a new person.
3. Reports and discussion in the classroom: what happened when the child tried to meet someone new.

The activity asks each child to think of another child they would like to have as a new friend. The task is meeting a new friend and talking to that person for a short period of time. Possible topics of conversation should be discussed in class.

The bond that usually ties children together in friendship is common interests. The real purpose of a first meeting with a new friend is to find out what these shared interests are. The teacher can tell the children some basic steps in meeting a new friend. For example:

1. Begin by saying hello and giving your name.
2. Tell the other child that you'd like to meet her; ask her what her name is.
3. Mention where you first saw him or when you first heard about him—to get the conversation going.
4. Ask her what her favorite interests are *or* ask her if she is interested in something you are interested in.

Life magazine reported information that might be very useful in this activity.[2] *Life* was interested in determining the interests and concerns of the often-neglected "middle-aged" child—the child between six and twelve years of age. The editors published a questionnaire—which was answered by over 250,000 children—that included the question, "What two or three things interest you the most?" Most of the children who responded to the survey said that

---

[2] "250,000 Children Have Their Say," *Life*, December 29, 1972, 88.

pets, sports, and music were among their favorite interests. These favorites held steady from six to twelve years of age. School was a favorite subject of the younger children, but older children did not mention this topic. The "world problem" that bothered children the most was pollution (mentioned by 71 percent of the children); killing wildlife (63 percent) and drugs (50 percent) were also mentioned often. The teacher can employ this information as background to the "new-friend" activity.

Favorite hobbies, pets, other friends, sports—any of a number of common topics—can help start the conversation. The children should be encouraged to ask questions, because questions are the best way to discover the interests that two persons may share. The class period set aside for follow-up discussion of the experiences can be organized according to two basic questions:

1. What interests do you and your new friend share?
2. How did you find out about your friend's interests?

The focus of the new-friend field experience is upon the topic strategies that are useful in getting to know someone.

further suggestions for field experiences

Field experiences in communication can be derived from classroom projects. For example, if the class is trying to collect money or clothing for a charity, the project can be organized around the communication involved in such a project. If parents are needed to help with some operation in the classroom or school, the request can provide the basis for a field experience for the children. Often, the success of field experiences related to class projects will be based on the adequacy of instructions and suggestions given prior to the field experience.

TEACHER GUIDELINES: PARTICIPATION APPROACH

There are two critical factors that the teacher must remember in participation instruction.

1. Children must be adequately *prepared* for the participation activity. Whether the activity is a role-played event or a field experience, children must be given helpful information on how to conduct themselves in the communication event. Classroom time must be devoted to getting the children ready for their communication experiences.

2. The follow-up discussion should focus on the communication strategies that were important in each experience. Whether the focus is on verbal and nonverbal strategies (as in the role-playing exercises) or on the setting, task, or topic strategies (as in the field experiences), the discussion must highlight the nature of these strategies in terms the children understand.

SUMMARY

The participation approach to communication instruction allows children to play an active role in communication situations. The children become participants in communication events. We outlined three participation activities; the goal of each is to build the child's repertoire of communication strategies for dealing with critical communication situations.

The first activity presents children with real communication situations that can be role-played. The situations are based on those often encountered by the children in the class. Each participant is given a specific role for the situation, including the communication topic, task, and setting. The follow-up discussion focuses on the verbal and nonverbal strategies employed by the participants.

A related activity involves an "unreal" communication situation, one in which the children are asked not to employ one of the communication channels in accomplishing their task. For example, a boy might be told that he has to convince a friend to play a certain game; but he must not use his body in any way to communicate his message. The follow-up discussion focuses on the importance of both verbal and nonverbal channels in communication strategies.

The field experience in communication guides the children in potentially difficult communication encounters. The sibling experience is called "Mission: Impossible." The children select a communication mission (such as trading toys) that involves a brother or sister and then attempt to accomplish that mission. The "important-person" experience guides children in meeting persons of high authority by offering them a task strategy: talking about the dangers faced by the person in his or her job. The third field experience is meeting a new friend. Instruction on how to introduce oneself, how to ask questions, and how to find common interests are at the center of the activity. The follow-up discussion in the field experience activity centers on communication strategies helpful in such situations as bargaining with a sister, meeting an important person, or meeting a new friend.

the communication guide

PEOPLE I TALK TO*

Name of child:_____
Age of child:_____
Sex of child:_____

Who do you live with? (Who lives in your house or apartment with
you?)
_____

Introduction (teacher): We're going to have an interview. That's a
time when two people get together and talk about something.
Usually somebody asks questions—important questions—and
somebody tries to answer the questions. We are going to have an

*The present author created the interview format, *People I Talk To,* which
has been employed in a project conducted by the Speech Communication
Association. The project, *The Development of Communication Competencies in
Children, Pre-K Through Twelve* (in preparation), is funded through a grant from
the Axe-Houghton Foundation. For further information, write to Ron Allen
(project director), Dept. of Communication Arts, University of Wisconsin,
Madison, Wisconsin, 53706.

313

interview about the people you talk to. I think you'll enjoy our interview, but remember one important thing—this interview is *private*. What you tell me about what you like to talk about and who you like to talk to is private information. I won't tell anybody about it, unless you really want me to. OK? Are you ready for our interview?

1. Think of all the people you talk to everyday—your friends, maybe sisters or brothers, your parents. I bet you talk to quite a few people, don't you? Well, we are going to talk about three special people that you talk to a lot. You can pick these special people. They could be your best friend, your father, your sister—anybody. Who will these special people be? Name them for me—three of them.

        1._____ (relationship to child:_____)
        2._____ (relationship to child:_____)
        3._____ (relationship to child:_____)

Questions 2-9 should be asked for each of the three persons mentioned in question 1. The children should talk about one participant at a time. For participants 2 and 3, questions may be paraphrased rather than repeated verbatim.

2. ("Easy" setting) When you talk to _(name)_ , you can probably talk at different times and in different places. Maybe you talk in the morning and after school or during recess. You may be in your house or on the playground. What's your favorite time and place to talk to _(name)_ ?

        1. easy time:_____
        2. easy place:_____

Why do you think this is your favorite?_____
_____

3. ("Tough" setting) I bet it's not so easy to talk to _(name)_ all of the time. What would be a time and place you talk to _(name)_ that is really tough?

        1. tough time:_____
        2. tough place:_____

Why do you think this situation was difficult?_____
_____

4. ("Easy" topic) When you talk to _(name)_ ,you probably talk about many things. Think of all the subjects you talk about with _(name)_ ,your favorite subjects. Pick the easiest one and tell me about it.

315

1. easy topic:_____

Why do you think this subject is easy to talk about with _(name)_ ?

_____

5. ("Tough" topic) Now let's talk about a subject that's not so easy to talk about with _(name)_ . Name a subject that's tough to talk about with _(name)_ .

1. tough subject:_____

Why do you think it's tough?_____

6. ("Easy" task) When we talk to people, we often have an idea in our mind—something we want to happen. Let's call this our "mission." Some missions are pretty easy to accomplish—maybe it's easy to get your friend to play a game with you. What's the easiest mission to accomplish when you talk to _(name)_ ?

1. easy task:_____

Why do you think this is pretty easy?_____

_____

7. ("Tough" task) Sometimes it's not so easy to convince somebody—accomplish your mission. You may try to say something and the other person doesn't agree with you. Let's call this a difficult mission. Try to name one thing it's hard to accomplish when you talk to _(name)_ .

1. tough task:_____

Why do you think this is hard to do?_____

_____

8. Let's talk about this situation a little further, the one you just mentioned. Try to make a story about what happens; tell me what you say and then what _(name)_ says. (encourage child to tell the story)

_____

_____

_____

(When appropriate, try to ask questions such as the following; they are related to the "success" of strategies.)

1. When you said (did) that, did it seem to work pretty well? Did _(name)_ think you had a good idea?

2. How could you tell that _(name)_ liked (did not like) what you said? (make notes below)

9. If you had one wish about talking—anything at all—what would that wish be? Now remember, it has to be about talking with somebody. (record notes here)

index